I0827917

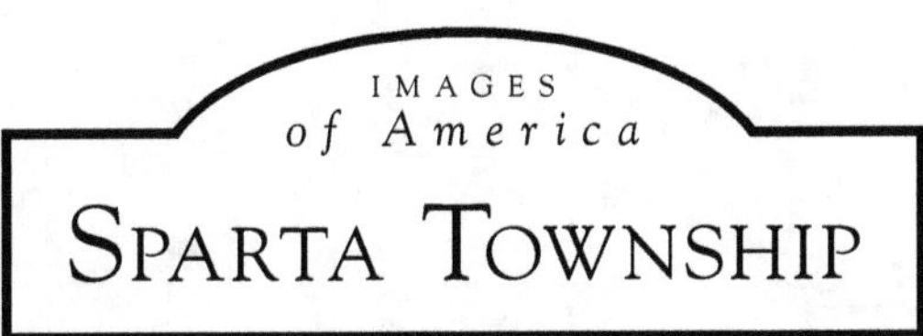
IMAGES
of America
SPARTA TOWNSHIP

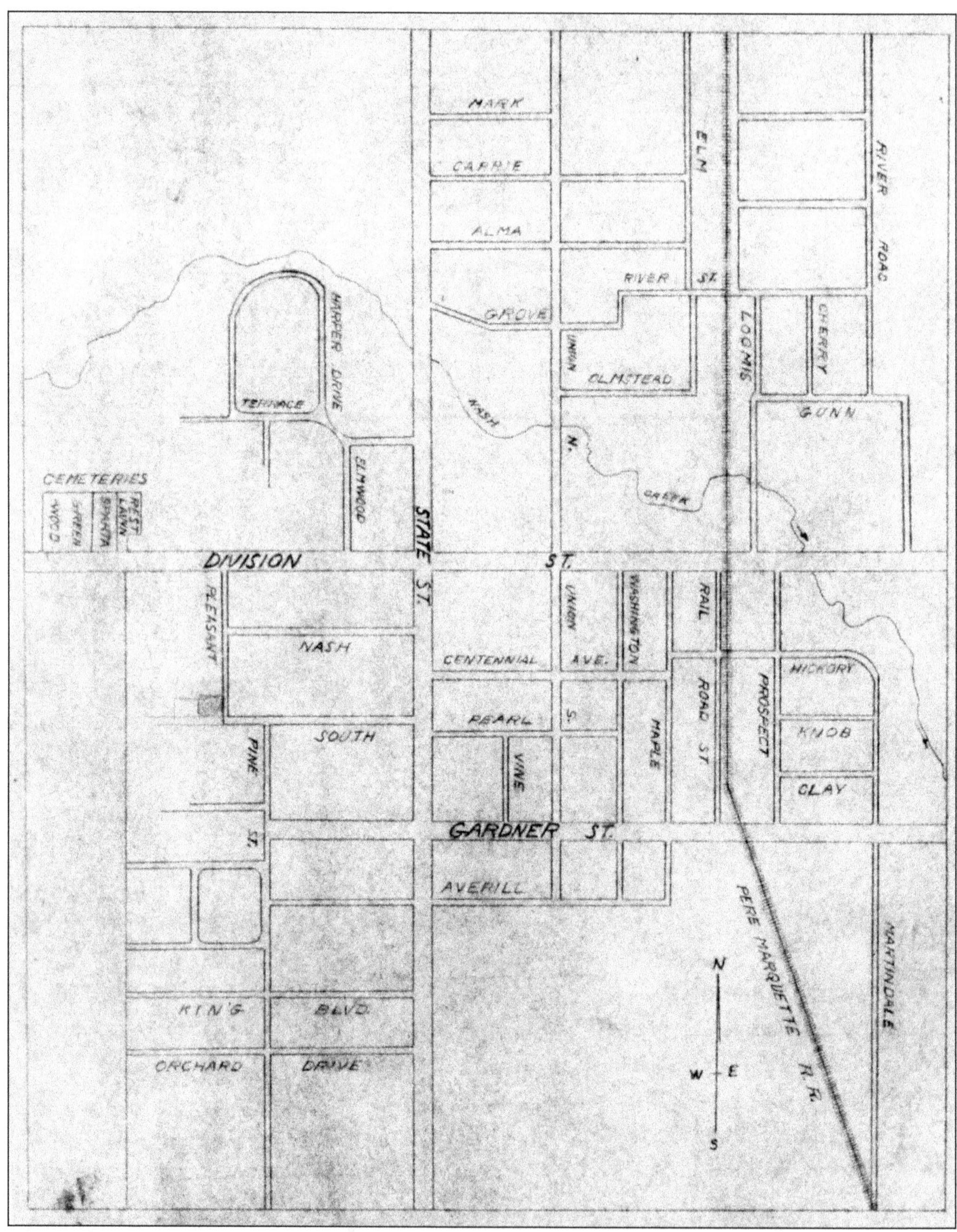

This early map of the village of Sparta may be helpful when referencing the locations of photographs mentioned in this book. Please note that Railroad Street later became Elm Street.

On the Cover: Celebrating a favorite summer treat, this group of children is taking part in a watermelon-eating contest at one of the parks in the township. These kids look to be enjoying this friendly competition in the 1950s or the early 1960s. (Sparta Township Historical Commission.)

IMAGES
of America

SPARTA TOWNSHIP

Kathryn Paasch and the
Sparta Township Historical Commission

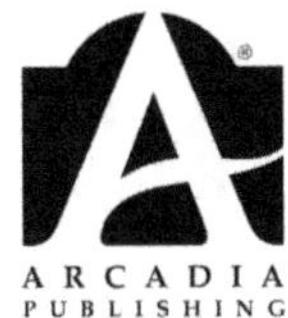

ISBN 9781531655396

Published by Arcadia Publishing
Charleston, South Carolina

Library of Congress Control Number: 2010931931

For all general information, please contact Arcadia Publishing:
Telephone 843-853-2070
Fax 843-853-0044
E-mail sales@arcadiapublishing.com
For customer service and orders:
Toll-Free 1-888-313-2665

Visit us on the Internet at www.arcadiapublishing.com

Contents

ACKNOWLEDGMENTS

Many volunteers have generously donated their time, expertise, and photographs for this project. These individuals, who are dedicated to the town they love, were essential to the presentation of the history of Sparta. I would like to thank Jayne Paasch, JoAnne VanderWerff, and Jeff and Jenifer VanSyckle for their many months of research and enthusiasm for local history. This book would not have been possible without the support of the Sparta Township Historical Commission. Unless otherwise noted, the Sparta Township Historical Commission provided all of the photographs and newspaper clippings that appear in this book. Additionally, photographs and first-hand information were provided by Joanne Lamoreaux Dake, Steve Warren, Harold Woolworth, Mary Waldherr Dunneback, Lowell and Gail Brooks Heath, Leonard Feerick, Vernon Cumings, Barb Erhart, Albert and Mary Hale, Marcia Anderson Fairchild, Tim and Steve May, Elizabeth Gorski Morse, Jamie Brooks, Don Bradford, Susie Weston, Mark VanderWerff, and Mary Jean Herwaldt. Also, I am grateful for my editor at Arcadia Publishing, Anna Wilson, for her encouragement and faith in this project. Finally, I would like to thank my family and, especially, my husband, Jon, for his love and support in all that I do.

INTRODUCTION

Sparta Township was settled as early people pushed their way across the Grand River Valley and north to establish their homes and raise their families. Explorers arrived on foot or by horseback, usually following the Chippewa Indian trails. Most of the early settlers came to log the area that was rich in maple, beech, basswood, ash, elm, white cedar, tamarack, and a variety of oak. The Rogue River, which skirted around the eastern edge of town, allowed for many mills for sawing and planing wood, as well as grinding flour. Although the township records were completely destroyed in a fire in 1876, the remaining settlers were able to recall the early history of the area.

In September 1844, Clark Brown scouted the area that would become the south end of Sparta, with plans to return with his family in the spring of the following year. However, he returned to find Lyman Smith, Norman and Edwin Cumings, Lewis Purdy, and Joseph English had already established homes in the area. Lyman Smith had been the first real resident of the township when he settled the area in 1844, on section 25, which was a mile south of the Myers School. He was a lumberjack and built a log hut for his family. Not long after that, brothers Norman and Edwin Cumings arrived from Byron, New York, and settled along the south line of Sparta. In the spring of 1845, Norman brought the rest of the family, which included his father, Philip; mother, Sally; brother, Nelson; and sister, Phoebe, to Sparta. Around the same time that Norman and Edwin first came in 1844, Lewis Purdy arrived and established the first log home in the township. It was located near Eleven Mile Road and Peach Ridge Avenue. His wife was the first white woman in the township.

In January 1845, Joseph English arrived from Grand Rapids with his wife, Diana, and their family. They settled 120 acres, which they bought for just $150, in the southwest corner of section 36. In search of timber, English had originally come to Grand Rapids from England in 1843. Once he arrived in Sparta, English cleared his land. Soon, however, he wanted more land and traded whatever he had, wagons or livestock, to secure more acreage on credit. Even though English was unable to read or write, he was successful in establishing a steam and water mill that would bring other settlers to the area.

The following June, John Symes, Elihu Rice, and Anthony Chapman met each other in Alpine Township while on their way to settle the land they had bought to the north. By comparing descriptions, the strangers realized that their properties were adjoined and decided that strength lay in numbers. They formed a plan for exploring the countryside. The next morning, Symes and Rice left the home of Joseph English and brushed out a road from Englishville to Ballards Corners. From there they turned north, between sections 34 and 35, along what is now Sparta Avenue. Meanwhile, Chapman returned to Mill Creek, which later became Comstock Park, to get the supplies that they would need in establishing their homesteads. Just as Symes and Rice were considering returning to the English home for the evening, Chapman arrived with their supplies. Despite the howls of wolves nearby, the men made camp and built a fire. There they spent the night before heading out the next morning to complete the road to their land in sections 26 and 27, near Twelve Mile Road and Sparta Avenue. Chapman's land was adjoined to Symes's land to the north. Along the line between the properties, there were three trees that would serve as the corner posts for a shanty. By adding a fourth post and some of the boards that Chapman brought from Mill Creek, they were able to build a simple temporary hut. The families of the three men were brought to the settlement the next day, and they would all live together until their individual homes were completed. Elihu Rice settled the land on Sparta Avenue, south of Sparta. The area became known as Rice's Hill. Symes's wife, Harriet, was the first schoolteacher in Sparta and she taught the children in their home. She also practiced obstetrics in the township, and when a new baby's arrival pulled her away from her teaching, Symes filled in as teacher.

Settlers continued to make their way to the area. In the northern area of the township arrived brothers Henry, Edward, and William Wylie, who had traveled all the way from Madison County, New York. In January 1846, the brothers purchased the 320 acres of land in sections 3 and 10 that Edward and William had previously explored and selected. While Edward cleared the land, William returned to New York to retrieve Henry and his family. Nearby, Myron Burd and Anthony Chapman also cleared land for their homes.

Others to arrive in the early years of 1845 and 1846 were Calet Amidon, Newel Barker, William Blackall, John Gillam, D. D. Hastings, Charles Hatch, C. C. and Z. M. Hinman, James Huff, David Martindale, Lyman Murray, Hiram Myers, John Pintler, William Rogers, two Simons brothers, Philip Slat, Garius Stebbins, and Nathan and Owen Whitney. In the summer of 1846, Myron Balcum arrived with his wife and settled south of Sparta. Balcum operated a hotel in Sparta, and his brother John Balcum came soon after to join him.

As the settlers established their homesteads, small communities were formed within Sparta Township. These early settlements included Ballards Corners, Englishville, Gooding, Nashville, Pintlers Corners, Sextonville, Shangles Tavern, and Summerville. Of these many smaller, contributing communities, only Englishville survived.

Lyman and Lusina Ballard moved from New York to Sparta in 1850, along with their three children and Lyman's two brothers. Generously, Joseph English provided them with an old shanty, which was where they stayed until they built their home at the intersection of Ten Mile Road and Sparta Avenue. Later that year, the Ballards hosted a meeting in their home, where it was decided that they would organize a school district. The plan was to build a schoolhouse the following summer on one of the three adjoining corners of land that they owned. After the school had been built, the Ballards then donated the land for the Ballards Church on the northwest corner. As the community expanded, the Ballards opened a general store, and the government established a post office. The intersection became known as Ballards Corners.

Englishville, at the corner of Alpine Avenue and Ten Mile Road, was formed when Joseph English established a steam mill and water mill on the north end of his farm. The mills brought many settlers looking for lumber work. As the men established homes, the community of Englishville was formed. The community once boasted a blacksmith shop, hotel, sawmill, post office, general store, Baptist church, school, and cemetery.

In 1840, Richard Gooding moved from New York State to Alpine Township. After living in Alpine Township for a number of years, he moved north to Thirteen Mile Road and Kenowa Avenue. The community he settled became known as Gooding, and it began growing when the Toledo-Saginaw and Muskegon Railroad (TS&M) came through the area in 1888. It once featured a hardware store, two grain elevators, a general store, a blacksmith shop, and an apple storehouse.

Pintlers Corners was named after settler John Pintler who arrived in 1846. He became the postmaster in 1848, and in 1859, when the post office was named Lisbon, the village also became known by the same name. By 1870, around 200 people called Lisbon home, and amenities included a hotel, flour mill, sawmill, steam-thresher works, a blacksmith shop, and a wagon shop. There were three churches, a grade school, and many stores that sold everything from hardware to farm implements and drugs to harnesses.

Sextonville was a small community located at Twelve Mile Road and Alpine Avenue. The settlement included Dr. Bliss Sexton's grocery store, which also sold drugs and books. Sextonville also had a hotel that loggers used as their timber floated down the nearby river. Shangles Tavern was a small stage-stop community on the west side of Camp Lake. Although not much is known about the community of Summerville, it is known that Garius Stebbins was the first postmaster for this settlement, and the post office had been located in his home, just 2 miles south of Sparta.

In 1846, Jonathan Nash came from Greenfield, Massachusetts, to settle the central area of Sparta, which later became the village business district. The tract of land had been donated to the state of Michigan by the federal government for aid to the schools. Nash named the settlement that was to become his farm Nashville, after himself. After initially selecting 120 acres, he later acquired an additional 80 acres to allow access to the creek, which he named Nash Creek. In 1848, Nash built a dam and a sawmill on the creek and began clearing the fine beech and maple that grew there. His first home was built on the southeast corner of East Division and State Streets, where he lived alone for several years until marrying Augusta Waite in 1855. In 1866, Nash built a new house that faced to the north in the area of Washington and East Division Streets. There the Nashes lived with their four children, Edward, Elvin, Warren, and Worthy, until Augusta died on January 17, 1872. Almost two years later, in December 1873, Nash married Lita Gardner, and they had three more children: Mary, Florence, and Caroline. Considered to be the founder and father of the town, as well as one of the prominent first settlers of the township, Nash served as postmaster from 1854 to 1864, township supervisor, and first village president, among many other duties that played a role in the early organization of Sparta Township. He was even nominated several times to serve in the state legislature. In 1886, Nash returned to Greenfield, Massachusetts, where he passed away at his home on May 25, 1912, at the age of 92. It has been said that Nash was generous to a fault, and though he was once quite wealthy, he died financially crippled because he could not turn down a friend in need.

Following Nash's settlement of the village, others continued to arrive in search of farmland. Among them was farmer Moses Bradford who arrived in 1852. He had farmed in Wayne County for 27 years and came after he bought 160 acres of land north of Sparta. The Bradford family would farm this same land for generations to come. As the forests were cleared, Sparta's agricultural industry began to blossom. In the late 1800s, wheat, corn, grain, potatoes, hay, wool, maple sugar, dairy products, and fruit were commonplace on the many farms that were cropping up on the fertile ground. "The Ridge" along the western edge of town was a prime location for the growing of fruit. This was possible due to the moisture-rich clay soils and its proximity to Lake Michigan, creating the ideal fruit-growing environment.

As the wilderness gave way to civilization and industry, a meeting was held on April 6, 1846, at the home of Clark Brown. Sparta, which had been an appended territory of Walker, was finally organized as a town itself. On March 25, 1846, Sparta Township was formed under authority granted by the Michigan State Legislature. Over the years, the settlement had undergone two name changes. Originally called "Nashville" after founder Jonathan Nash, the township board discussed new names for the settlement in 1847. Suggested names were "Aa" for its brevity and "Brookfield" for the many creeks and rivers that ran through the area. Brookfield was selected, but according to the state legislature, there was already a Brookfield, Michigan. So the state suggested a new name, "Sparta," which the township adopted. At this time, the township still included the area that later became Tyrone Township. The two were not separated until 1881. On May 16, 1883, the village was incorporated and approved by the Michigan Department of State.

The Pere Marquette Railroad arrived in 1872, connecting Grand Rapids to Newaygo by way of Sparta and many other stops along the way. The TS&M Railroad followed it in 1888. With the railroad came industrial development. Among the early industrial companies to establish themselves in Sparta were the Welch Folding Bed Company in 1884, the Sparta Condensed Milk Company in 1917, and Muskegon Piston Ring in 1921. With the growth came more people, and with more people came the need for many schools to support the rural areas, as well as a variety of local churches. The people of Sparta first enjoyed electricity around 1898, and the first phone exchange was opened in 1904. Although it was still a very young village, Sparta was well on its way to becoming a thriving, industrious, agricultural township where hardworking people would establish their roots and contribute to the community for generations.

One

Homes

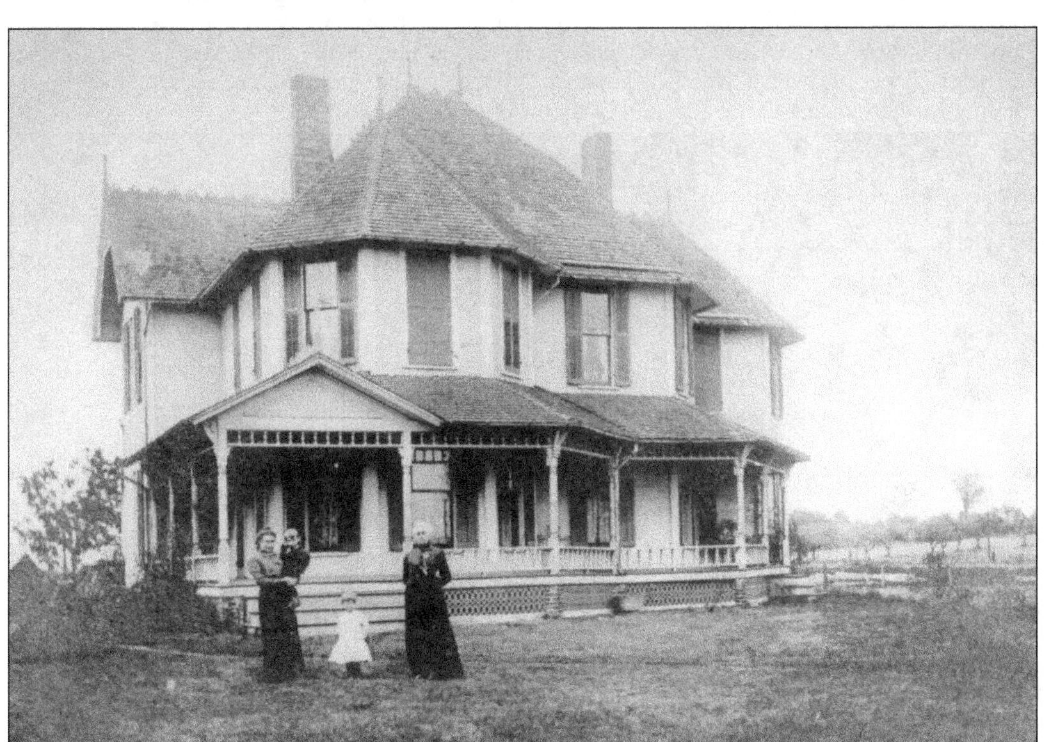

In December 1844, Joseph and Diana English purchased 120 acres in the township for $150. English built a large steam sawmill that brought people to the area. In the late 1870s, English's son Richard contracted Lorenzo Brown, a builder from Rockford, to build the home that stands on Ten Mile Road, east of Old Alpine Road. The family moved into the home in 1882. (Courtesy of Barb Erhart.)

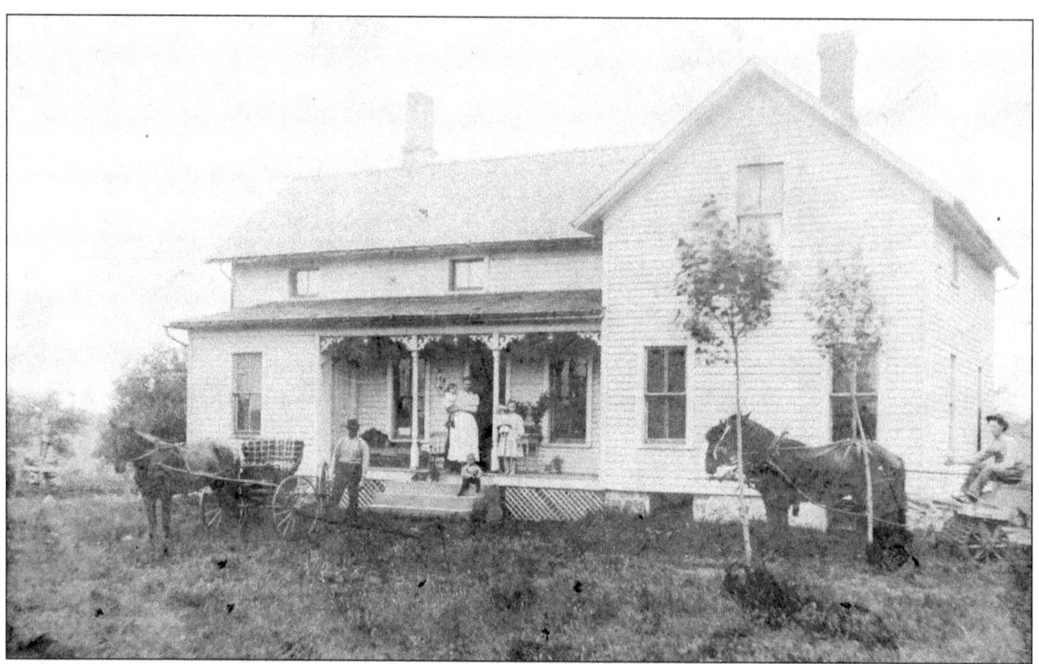

Posing in front of the Wilk homestead are, from left to right, Albert, Bertha, Lottie, Otis, Ethel, Tom, and Oxford Wilk. Oxford is seated on the roller. The Wilk farmhouse stands near the northeast corner of Twelve Mile Road and Fruit Ridge Avenue, among prized farmland that is commonly referred to as "The Ridge." (Courtesy of Jaime Brooks.)

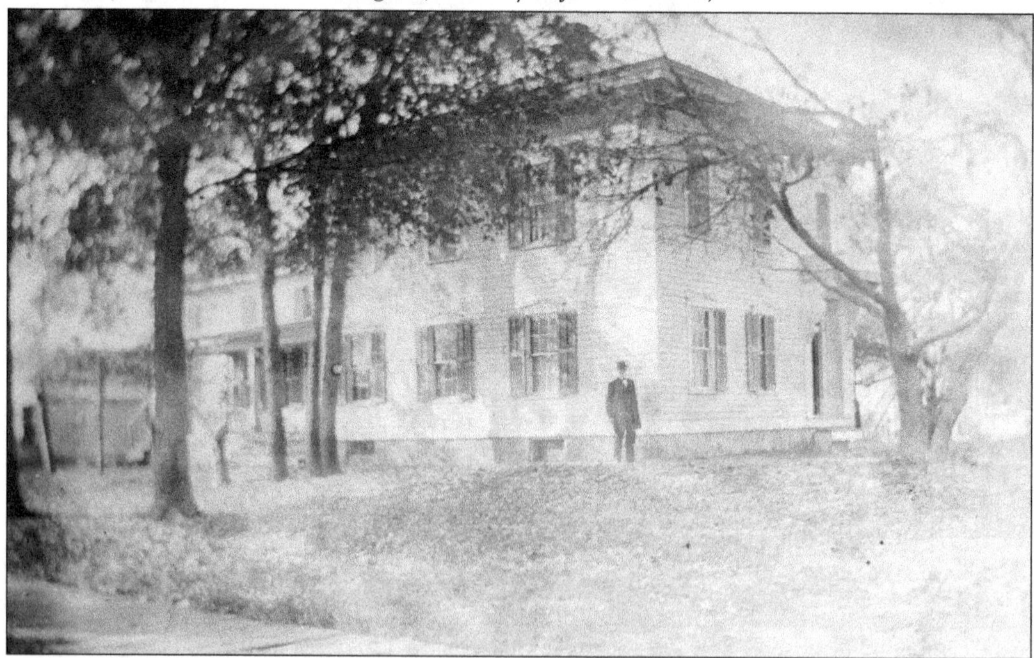

Believed to have been built by Jonathan Nash in 1866, the Nash home was originally located on Washington Street, just south of East Division Street. In 1988, this house and its carriage house were moved to Martindale Street, where they were restored to their original condition. Much of the original construction was done with hand-hewn boards and square-type nails.

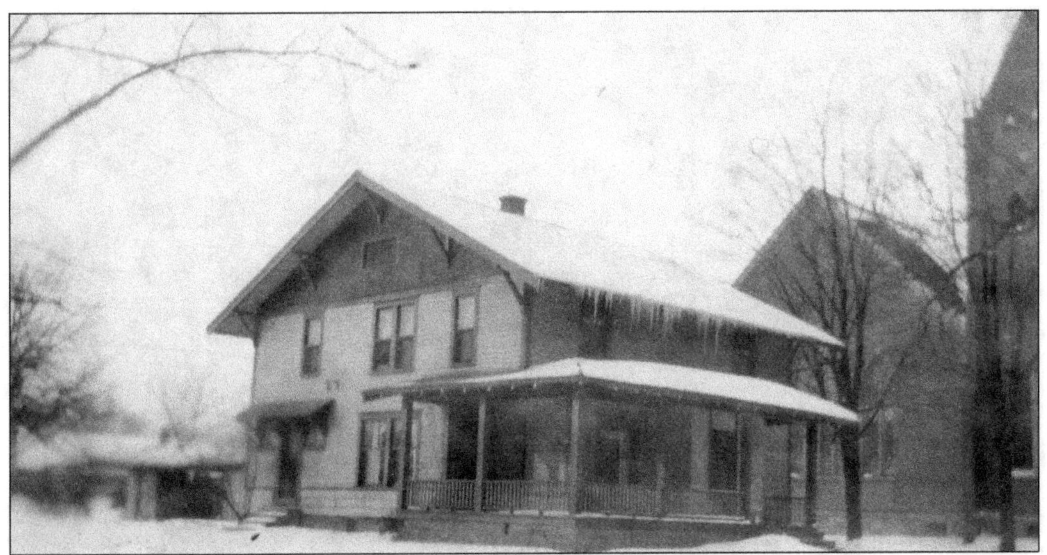

The Amherst Cheney house was originally located on West Division Street, where the Professional Building was later constructed. The house was moved to the adjacent lot to the south, which is where it still stands today. Cheney was a schoolteacher in both the Nash School and a private, select school that was held above Edwin Bradford's store, built in 1881, which was later destroyed by fire.

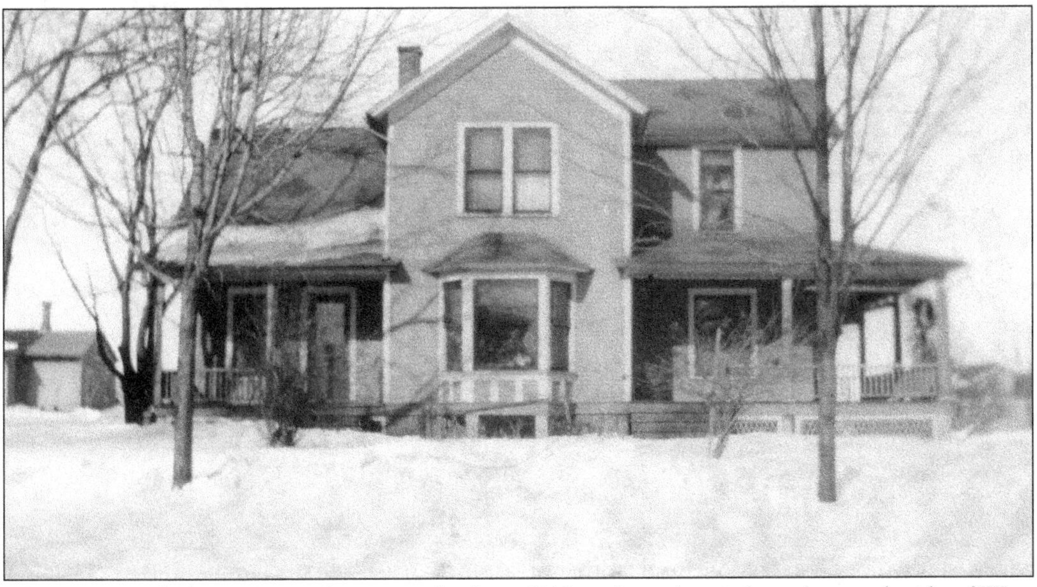

The James and Elenor Symes home was built in 1915 and was located on the north side of West Division Street, west of Elmwood Street. James was the son of John Symes, one of Sparta's first settlers. After James Symes's death in 1927, his daughter Lula continued to live in the home.

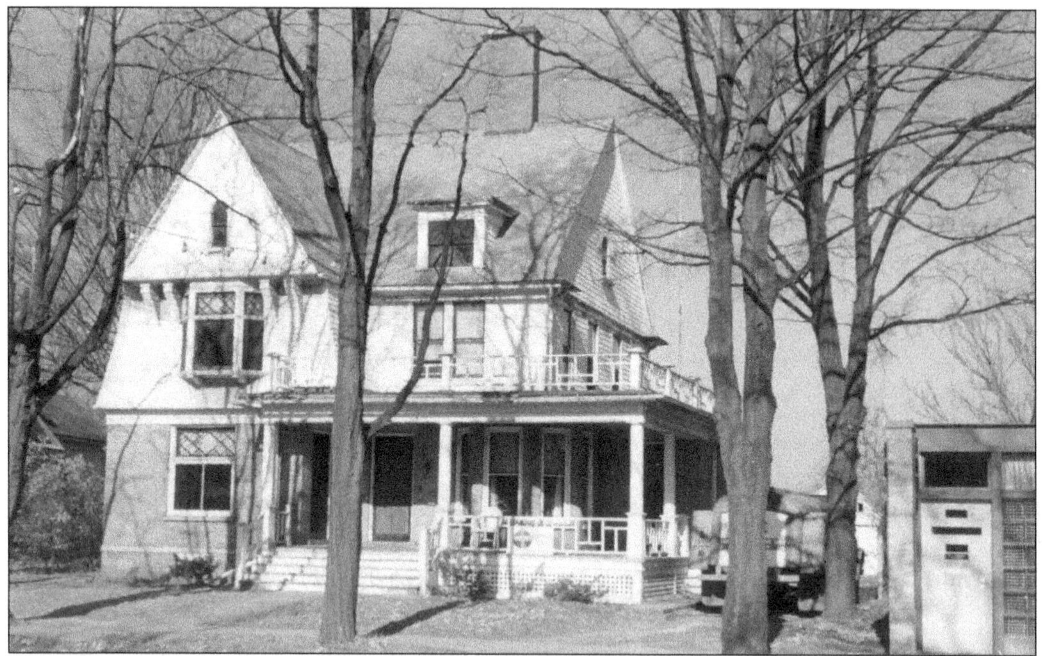

In 1856, Jason Bradford married Celina Hinman. In 1901, they moved from the family farm on Sparta Avenue to this house at 65 East Division Street. Bradford was the director of Sparta State Bank for several years. He died in 1912, and his wife lived in the house until her death on April 7, 1924. Bradford was the grandfather of Lynn Bradford.

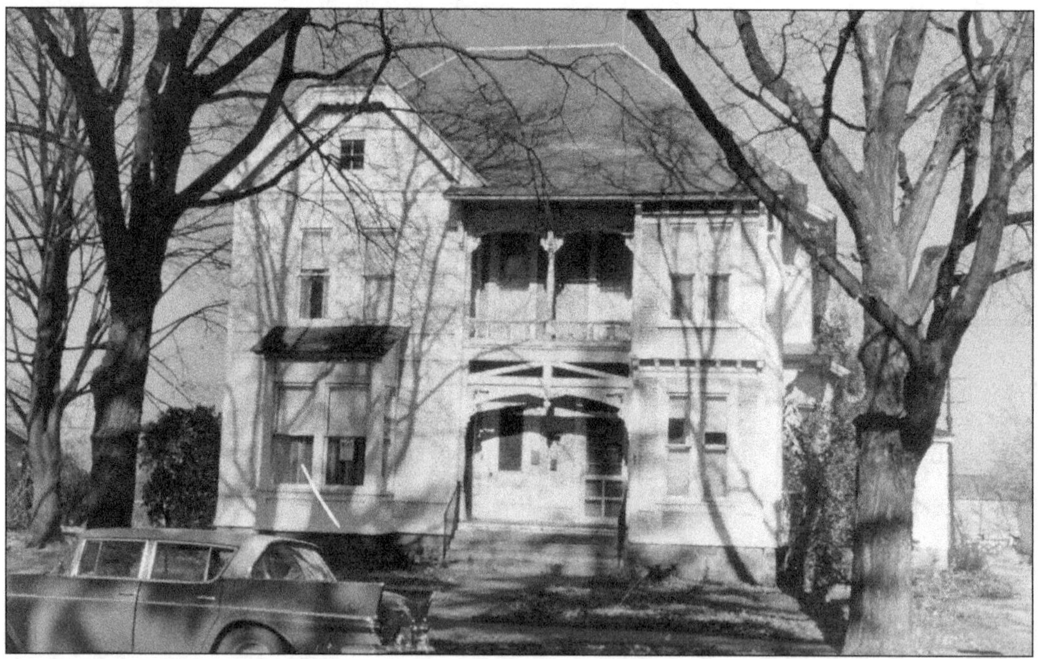

Edwin M. Bradford, son of Moses and brother of Jason, married Celestia Hinman, sister of Celina Hinman Bradford, in 1855. Their house at 87 East Division Street was built by Bradford in 1866. Maintaining his agricultural roots, Bradford was a grain dealer in Sparta. Celestia died in 1916, and Edwin died in 1918.

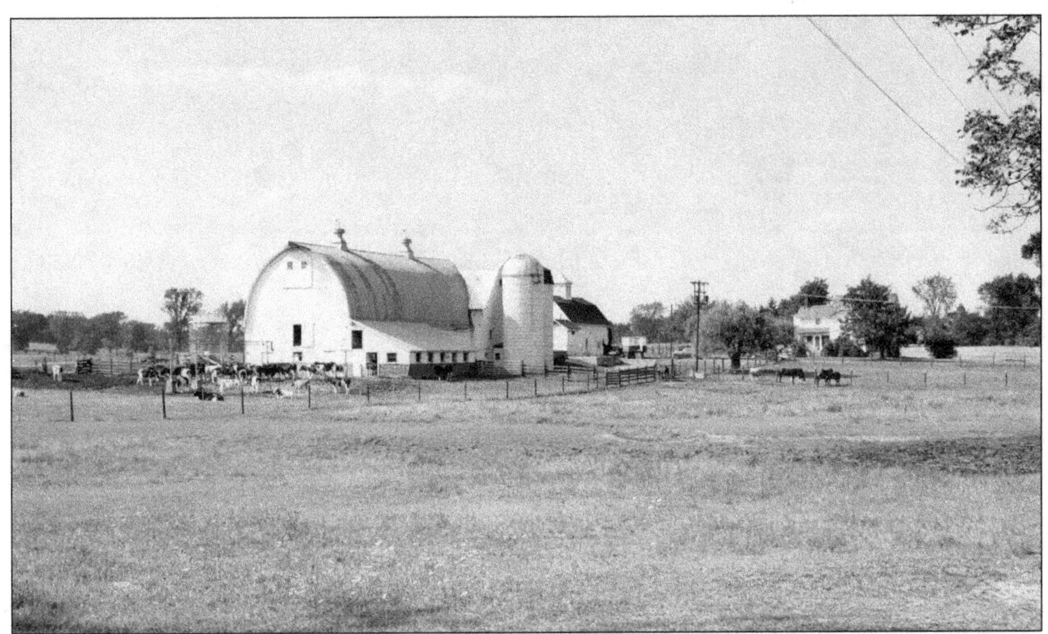

Generations of the Bradford family have established farms and have been community leaders in Sparta. Moses Bradford came to Sparta in 1852 and bought 160 acres of land north of the village. Moses's great-grandchild Lynn Bradford began farming this property in 1917. Located on Sparta Avenue, it is one of several properties owned by the Bradfords. The family has long been involved in dairy farming, business, education, and banking.

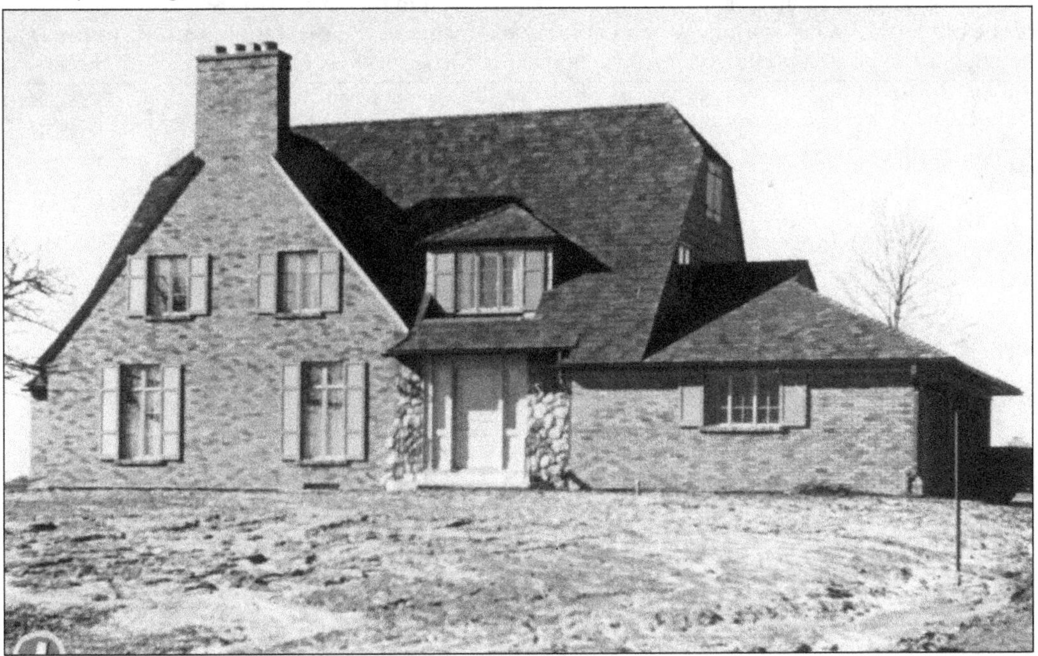

The Harold Vaughan farmhouse is located on Sparta Avenue, just north of town. Vaughan was, at one time, the president of the Muskegon Piston Ring Company. His dairy farm supplied milk for his local dairy store. Vaughan later sold his dairy farm, which went on to became B&T Dairy. He was able to continue to run his dairy farm and supply milk for B&T.

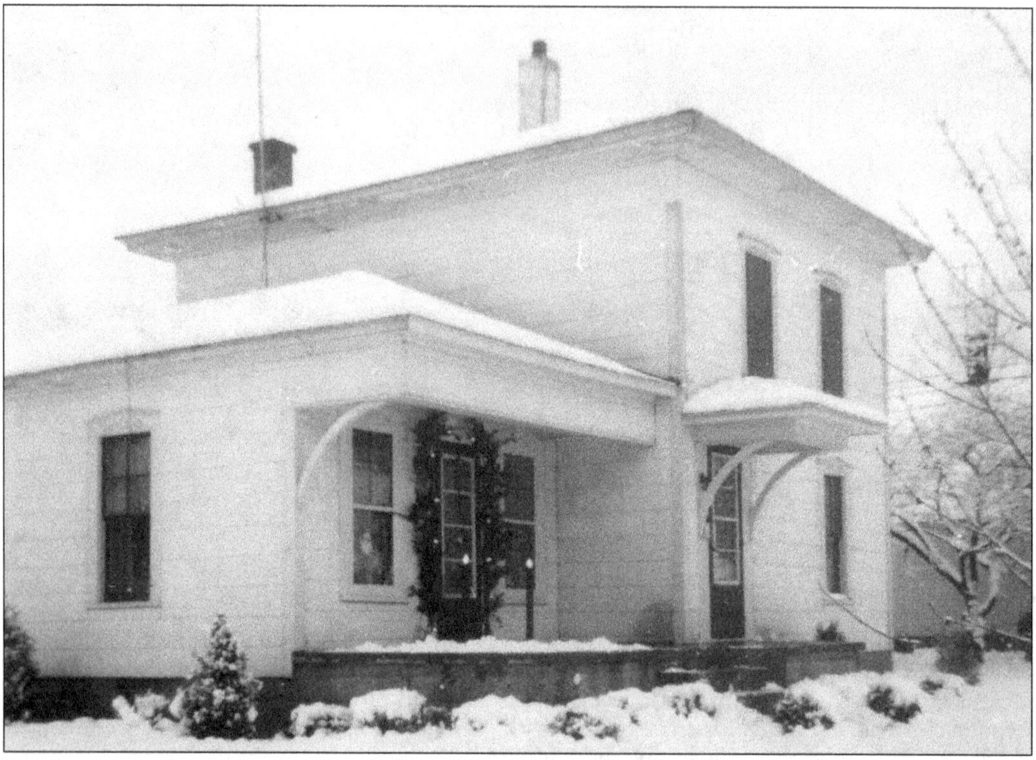

This house was first located on South State Street, across from the Sparta Baptist Church, just south of the old Sinclair Gas Station. When Leon Parker, owner of the gas station, wanted to expand, he bought the house and moved it to the northeast corner of West Gardner and Pine Streets.

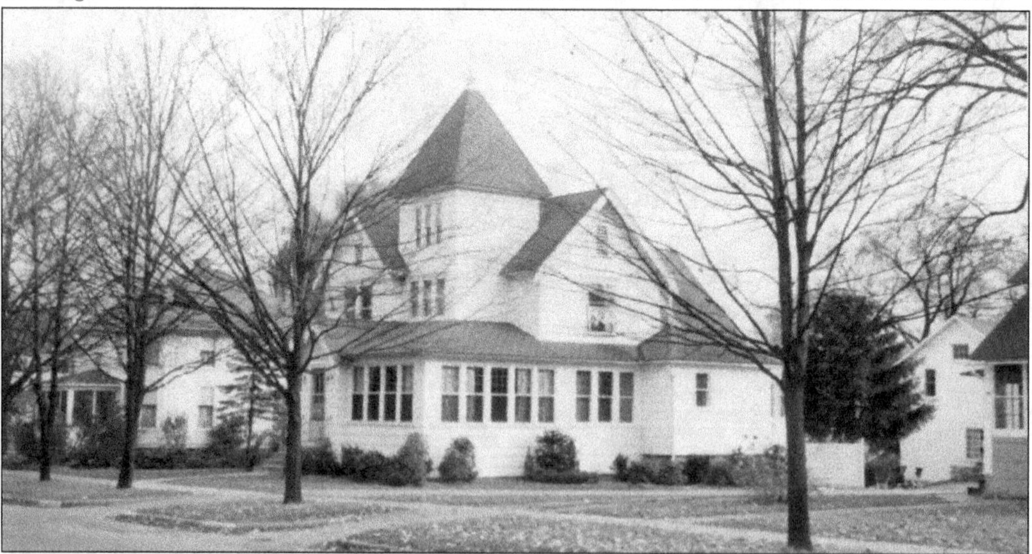

This photograph of Thurlow E. "Mack" McFall's home on West Division Street was taken around 1958. In 1951, Sparta honored McFall by naming him "Citizen of the Year" for his "contribution to the general welfare of the community." McFall served as president and CEO of Muskegon Piston Ring, president of Sparta State Bank, and president of Extensole Corporation. He was a supporter of veterans groups, Boy Scouts, and other organizations.

Two

Business and Industry

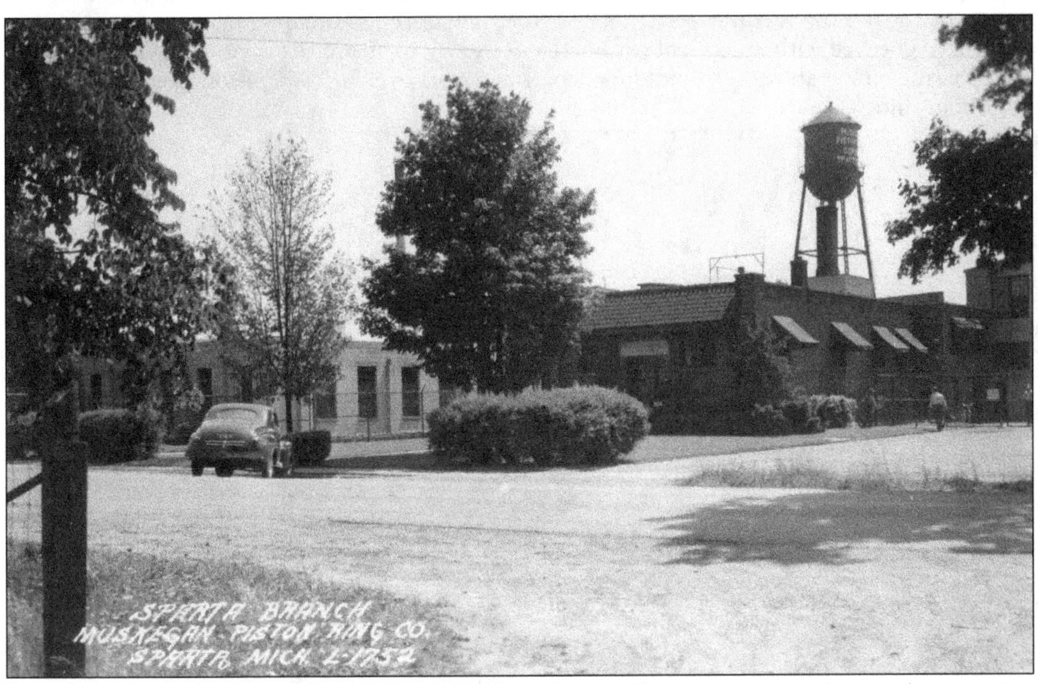

Founded in 1921 the Sparta Foundry was established to supply piston ring castings to the emerging auto industry. In 1936, the foundry merged with the Muskegon Piston Ring Company. The iron foundry was, for many years, one of the leading employers for the community and was considered the world's largest piston ring casting producer.

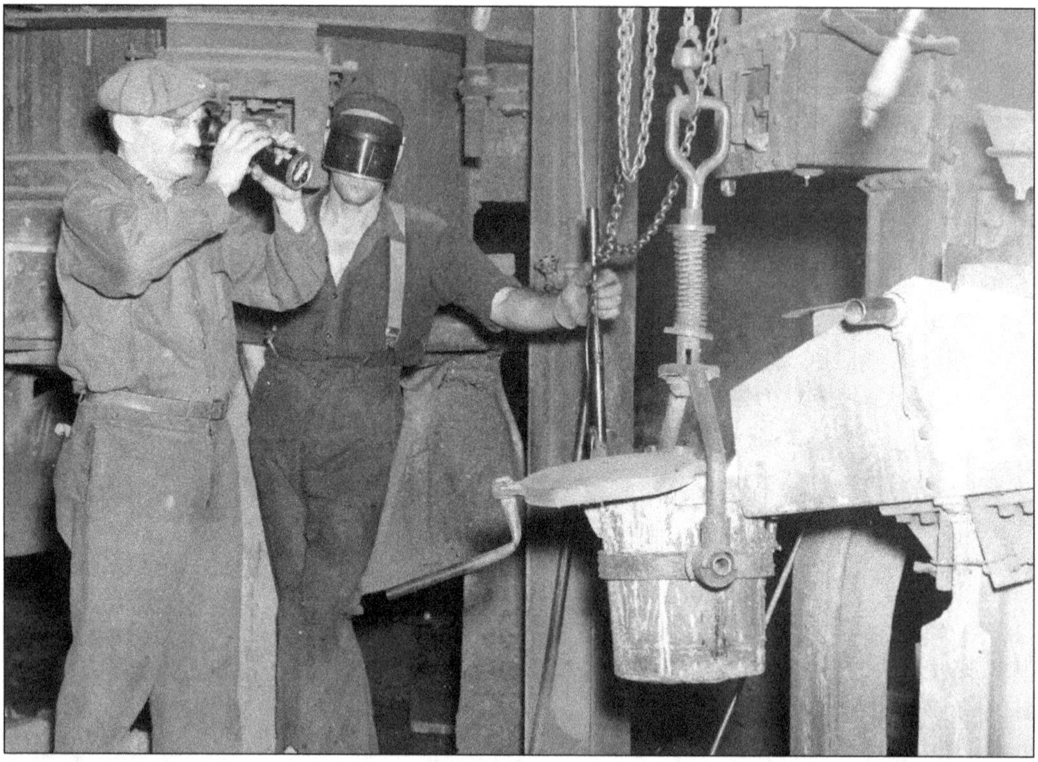

A heat of "Spartaloy" metal is being tapped from one of the four cupolas. The temperature of each tap is checked with an optical pyrometer, as shown, to assure the consistency of extremely high pouring temperatures. The molding department cast over 200,000 piston rings during each eight-hour shift.

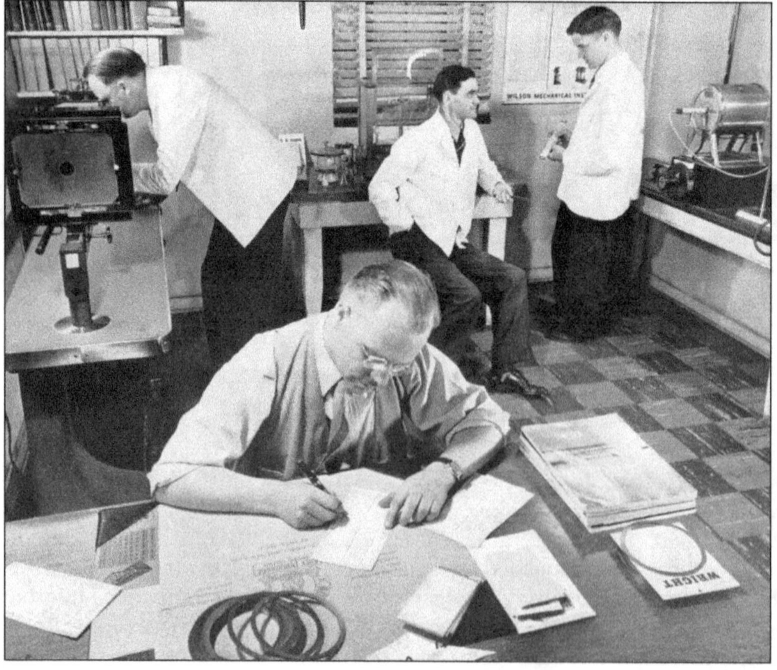

Sitting at the desk in the lab of Muskegon Piston Ring is Joseph Brooks, who was hired by Irvin McGowan, chief metallurgist, as his assistant. Later Brooks became chief metallurgist at Muskegon Piston Ring. Toward the back of the photograph, metallurgists Van Lundquist, Ken McCready, and Max Heppinstall are standing from left to right. McCready later replaced Brooks as chief metallurgist.

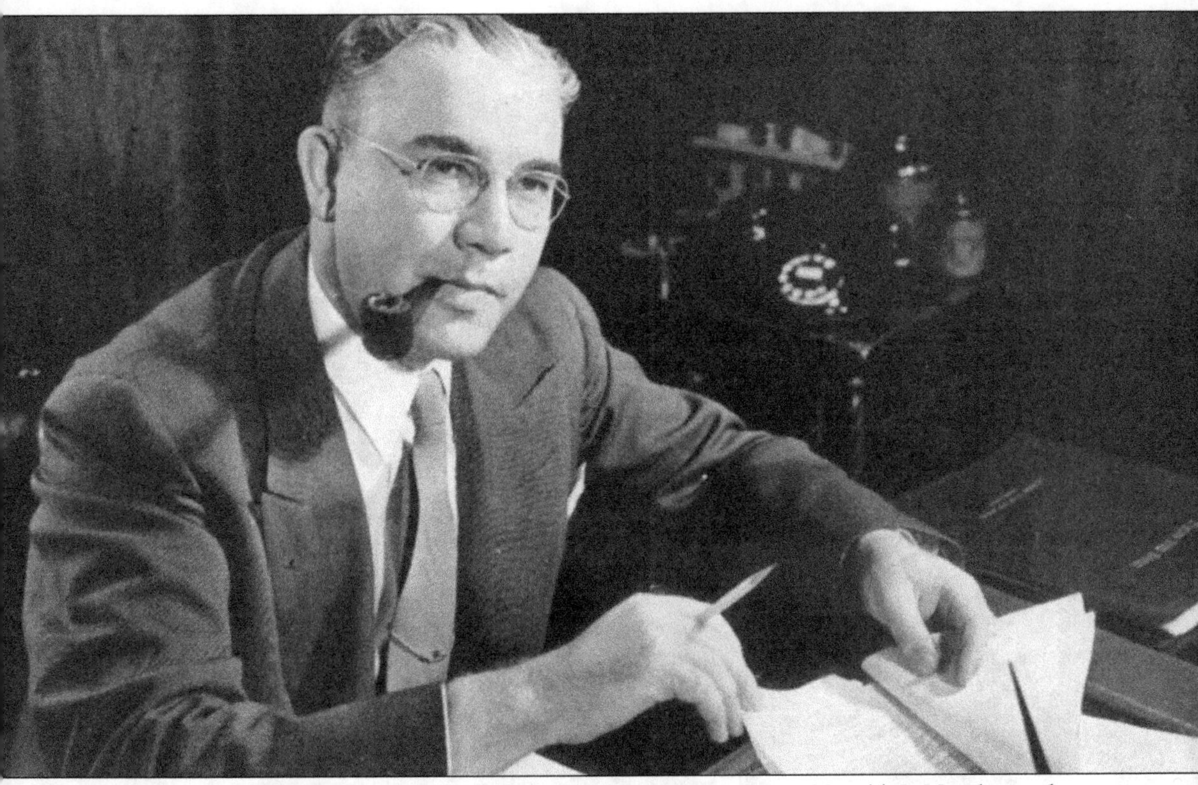

Among the founders of what would become Muskegon Piston Ring was Harold G. Vaughan, who was vice president in 1951, when this photograph was taken. Vaughan joined the company in 1926, at a time when the business was experiencing growth, and in 1927, the company actually paid a good stock dividend. In 1929, plans were made to expand again and to construct a new building. The structure was completed in 1930. It was around this time that Muskegon Piston Ring was feeling the Wall Street Crash of 1929, and work began to slow, but the company continued to show steady earnings and remained healthy throughout the Depression. Some of the foundry's early employees were Art Lockard, August Nelson, Cliff Lonnie, John Anderson, Shirley Fuller, Pete Campbell, Charles Krause, and Frank Hughs. Muskegon Piston Ring was the largest employer in Sparta at that time, creating hundreds of jobs and a need for housing that resulted in real growth for the community.

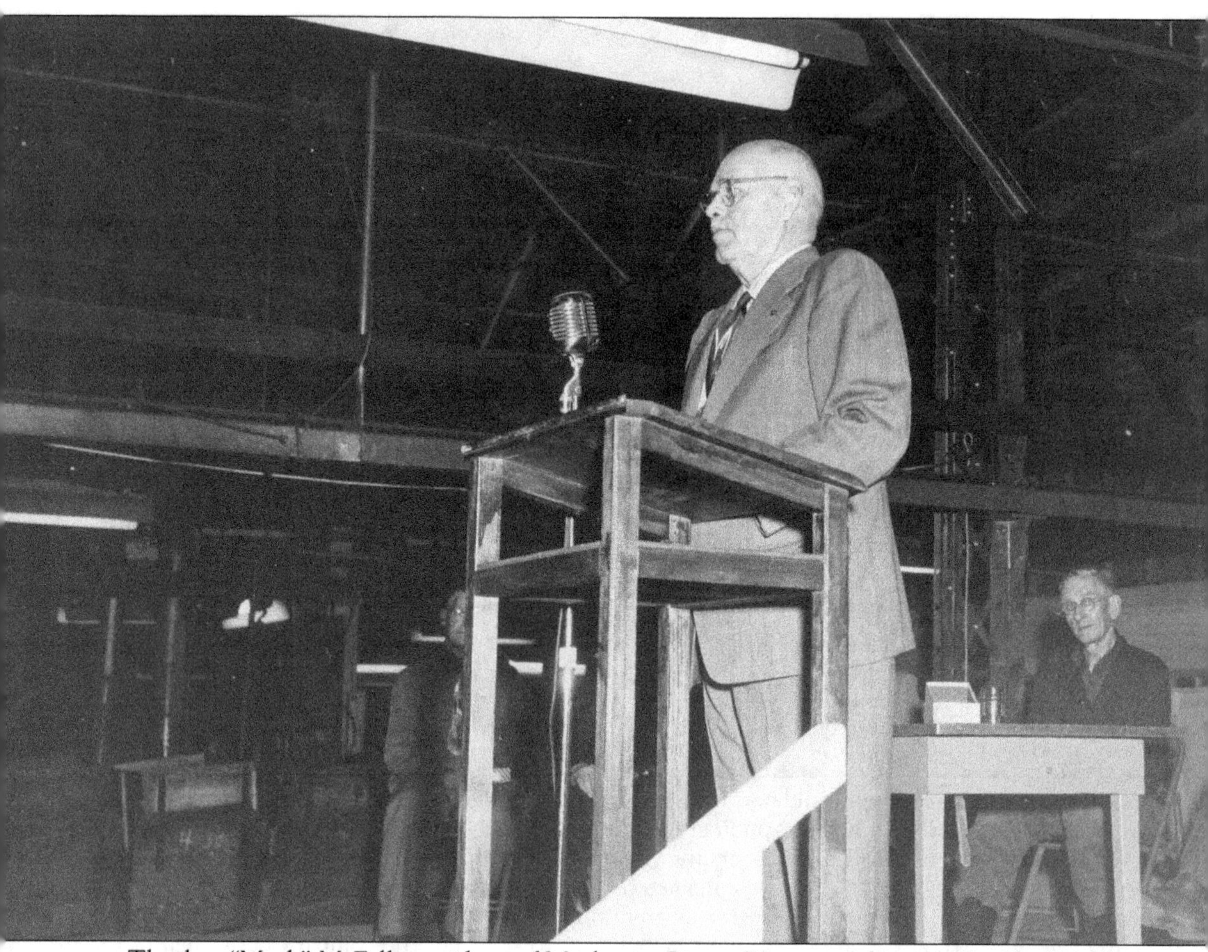

Thurlow "Mack" McFall, president of Muskegon Piston Ring, presides over Family Day Open House in December 1951. Addressing a group of men who had worked for the company for 20 to 25 years, McFall presented, on behalf of the company, gold watches to seven foundry employees who had completed 25 years of service. The seven men who received gold watches were Frank Hughs, Willis Davis, Don Lymburner, Charles Krause, Art Lockard, Lloyd Knowlton, and Frank Watkins. Over 40 employees also received an award button for 20 years of service. Before the ceremony honoring them, the employees, together with their families, enjoyed tours through the plant, the offices, and the laboratories. Other features of the ceremony included movies for the family to see and refreshments. Vice president Harold Vaughan spoke to the employees and their families of the great importance of the work of the foundry.

This photograph of a few of the Muskegon Piston Ring employees was taken in 1958. Those pictured are, from left to right, (first row) Bob Lee and unidentified; (second row) Allan Witbeck, Pete Nelson, and Charlie Warren; (third row) John Nieboer, Walt Blackmer, Jerry Goering, and Joe Stortz. The men were proud of their accomplishment of 200 consecutive days without a lost time accident.

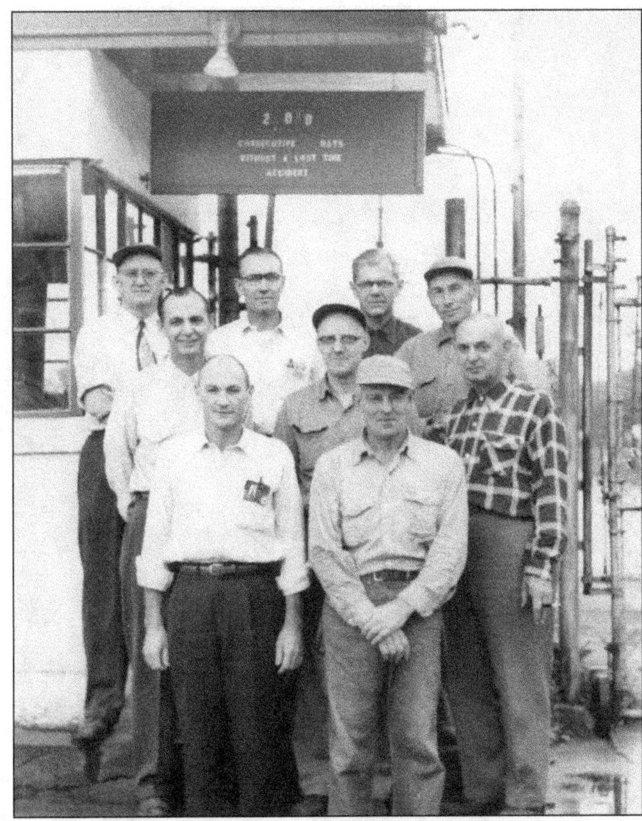

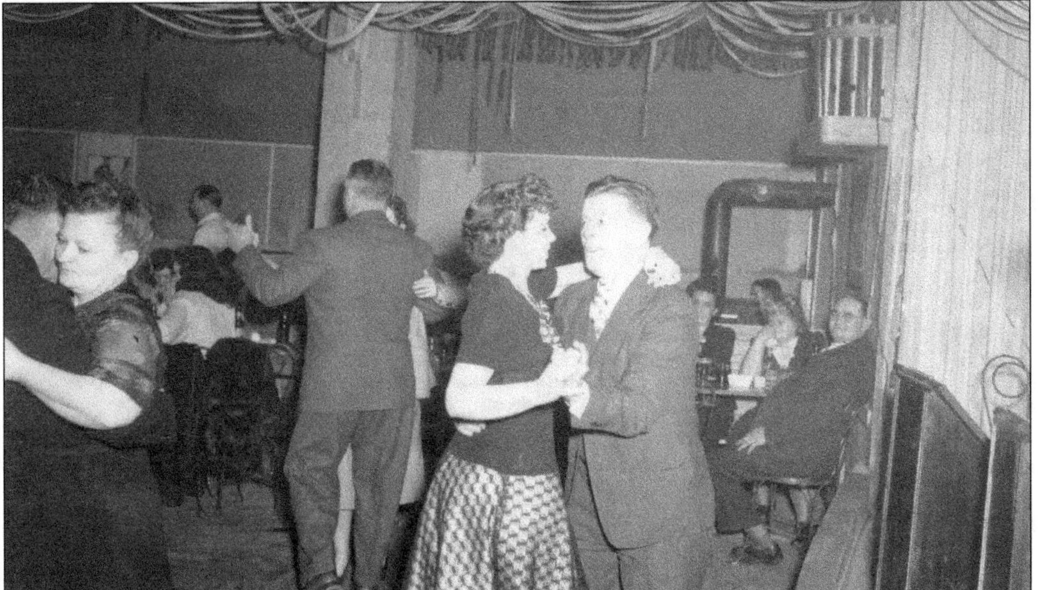

Company parties, like the one pictured above, were commonplace during the post-war years. The photograph above is thought to be a party for Sparta Foundry employees. Parties like this were often held at the American Legion Hall or the Sparta Township Hall. Dancing to the music are Ken and Edna Ferguson, who were both employees of the foundry.

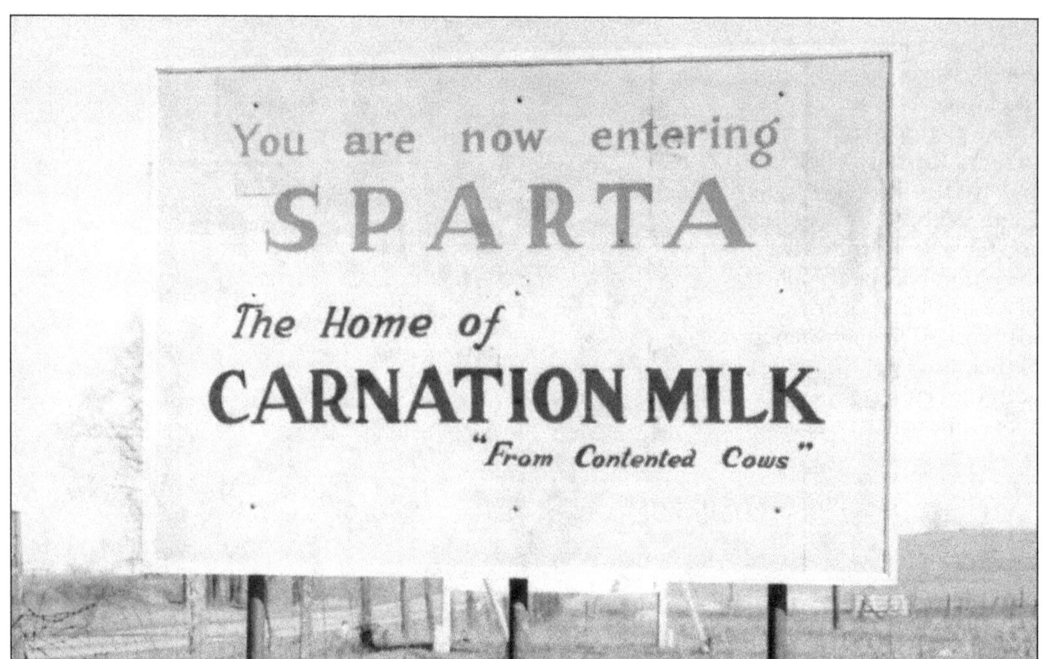

In 1917, the Carnation Milk Company built a plant in Sparta. Located on East Gardner and Prospect Streets, milk was hauled every day. The condenser purchased its milk from local dealers. Gradually, there were fewer milk producers in the Sparta area, which, by 1960, forced the Carnation Milk Company to close its doors.

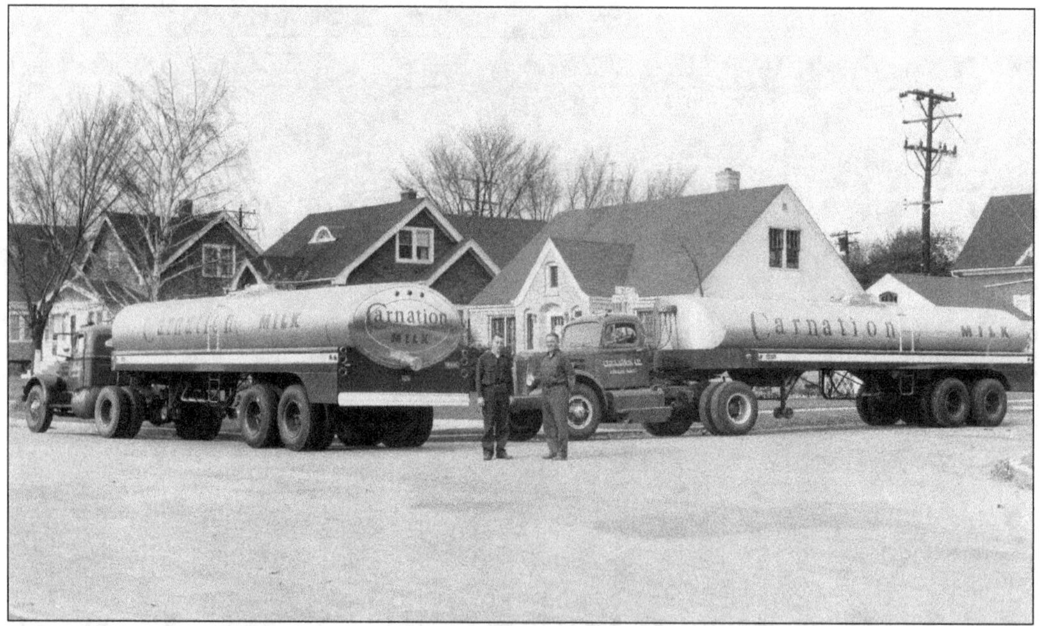

Pictured are Albert "Bub" Hale and Sid Schoolmaster in Heil, Wisconsin. They had driven to Wisconsin early one morning in two old Carnation Company trucks and returned that night with these two new tankers. When this photograph was taken, Bub had been with Carnation for about 11 years and Sid was with the company a little longer. Both worked for Carnation until it closed. (Courtesy of Albert and Mary Hale.)

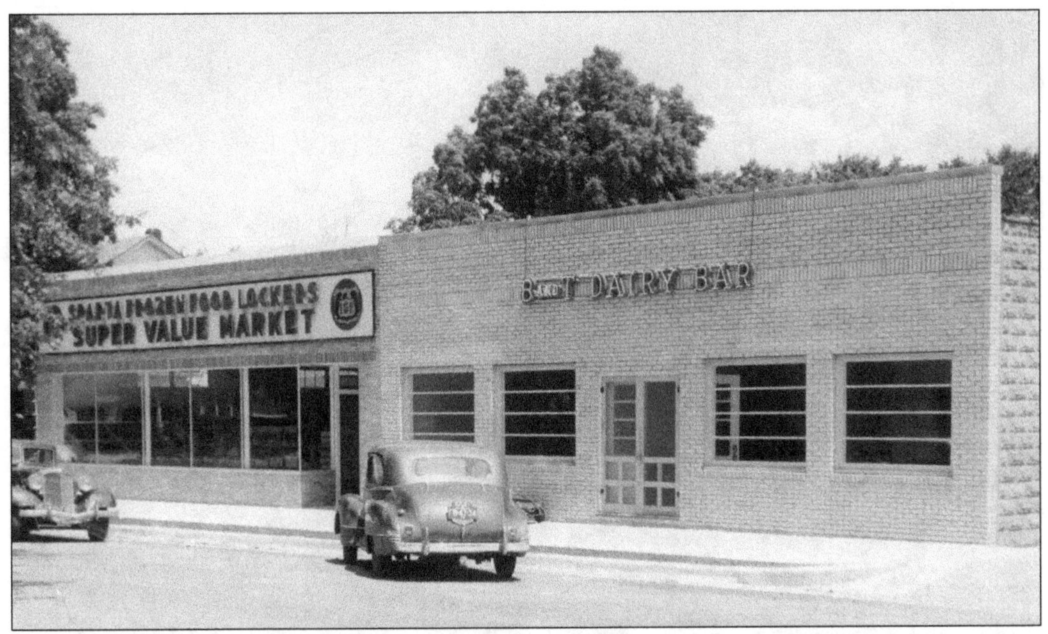

The south half of this building housed a dairy owned by Harold Vaughan in the late 1930s. Vaughan's son Leonard ran the dairy. In 1941, Vaughan sold the business to Floyd Buege and Lester Tanner, who added an ice cream parlor. The sale did not include the Vaughan dairy farms north of Sparta, and Vaughan continued to deliver milk to the new owners.

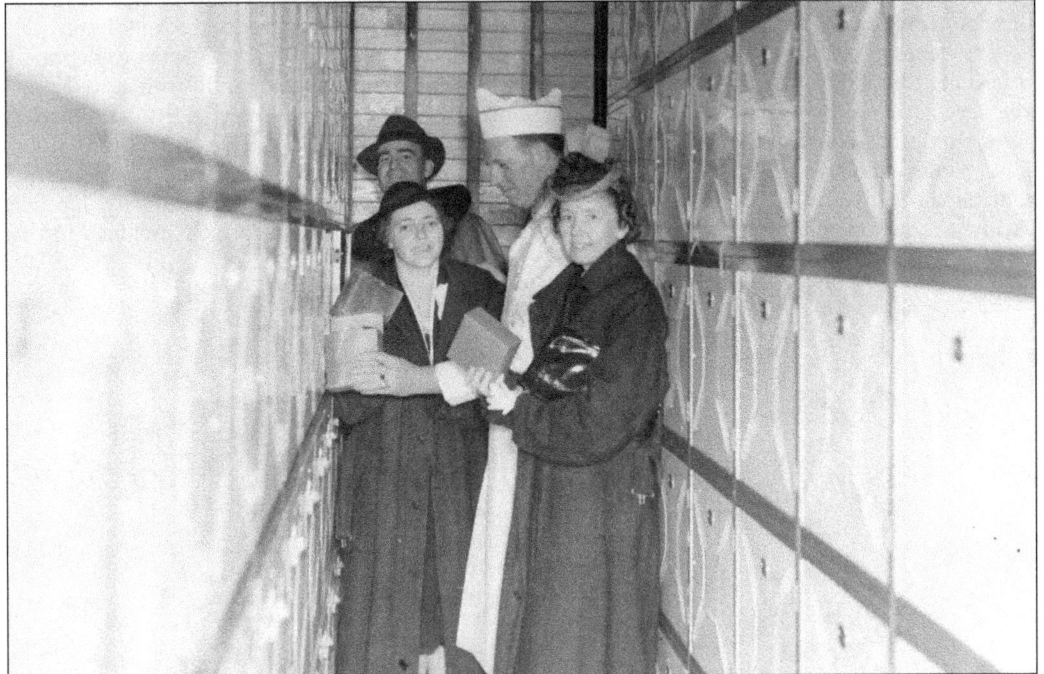

The Sparta Frozen Food Locker was a complete food-handling establishment where local people had fish, poultry, fruits, meat, and vegetables frozen and stored for future use. The retail division of the plant included a completely equipped meat market and grocery. Those pictured are, from front to back, Greta Bettes, unidentified, Kathleen Bull, and Dr. Frank Bull.

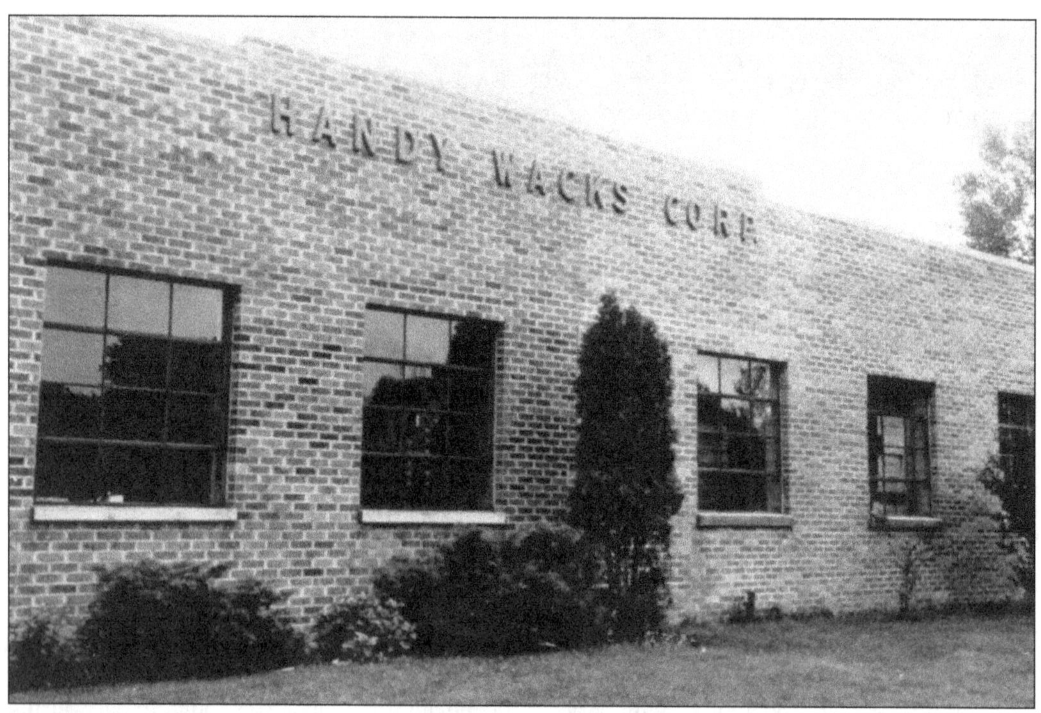

In 1938, Lou Atkinson Keller, became manager of the Handy Wacks Corporation. The company, whose original owner was Lou's father, Daniel Atkinson, continued to be a family-owned business. The company produces interfolded products using waxed paper, polyethylene film, and aluminum foil. Keller is remembered as one of Sparta's truly civic-minded people. In June 1962, Sparta celebrated Lou Keller Recognition Day, when she was honored as one of Sparta's outstanding citizens. Keller was very actively involved in the Methodist Church for many years. She was the secretary of the Community Foundation and a member of the Ladies Literary Club and the Sparta Garden Club. Keller's daughter Irene Keller Anderson and granddaughter Marcia Anderson Fairchild continued to run Handy Wacks after Keller's death in 1971. Pictured below on right is Clarence "Andy" Anderson, who was the son-in-law of Lou Keller. Andy was also actively involved in the community, as fire chief and postmaster.

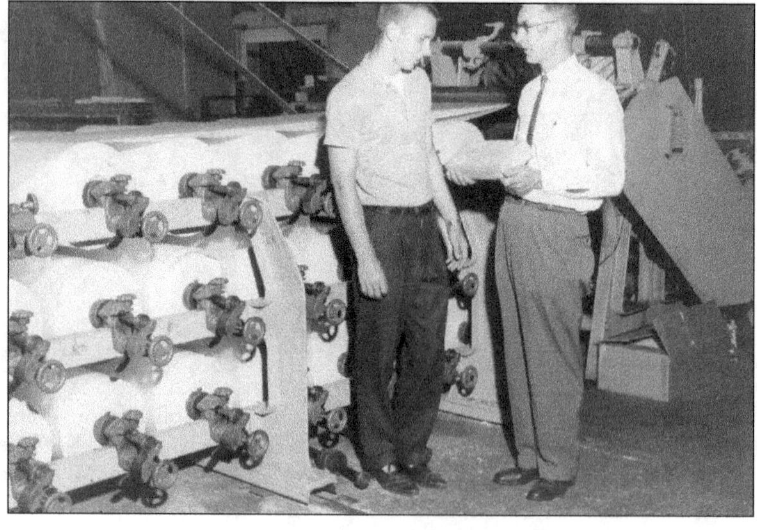

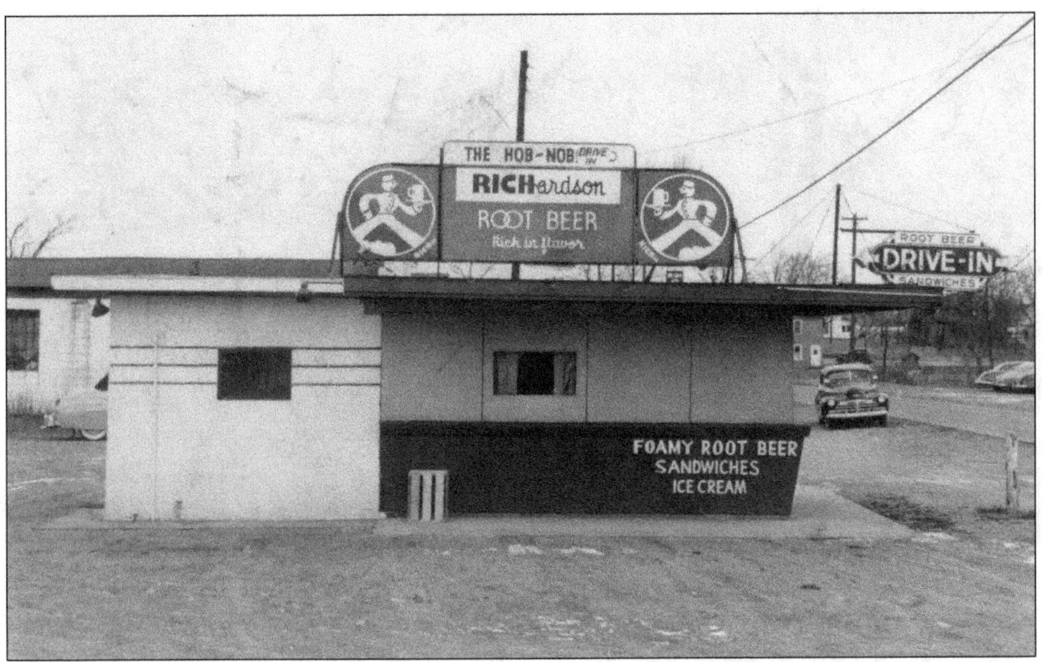

Located on North State Street, north of the bowling alley, the Hob Nob drive-in was a busy summer hangout for root beer, sandwiches, and ice cream in the 1940s, 1950s, and early 1960s. The Hob Nob was open seasonally and closed on Labor Day for the winter. Lester Erbes owned the bowling alley as well as the Hob Nob.

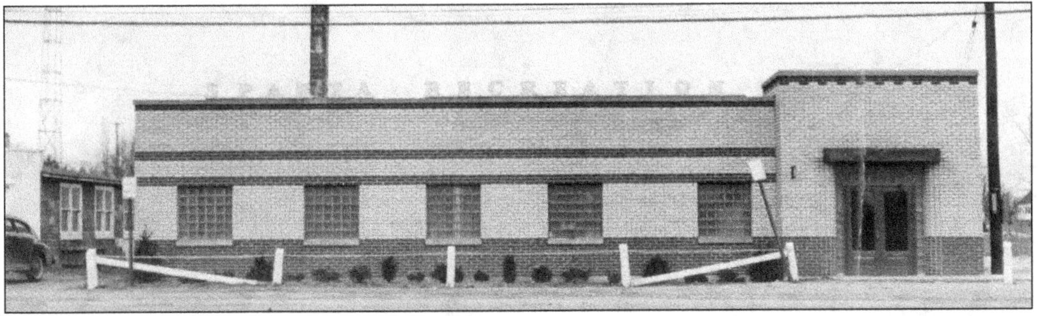

In November 1946, Lester Erbes opened the bowling alley, then known as Sparta Recreation. In those days, there were no automatic pin setters, so high school boys got jobs setting the pins manually. In the fall of 1946, William DeHart, superintendent of Sparta Area School District, allowed senior boys to go to the bowling alley during school hours and unload the trucks delivering equipment for the new business.

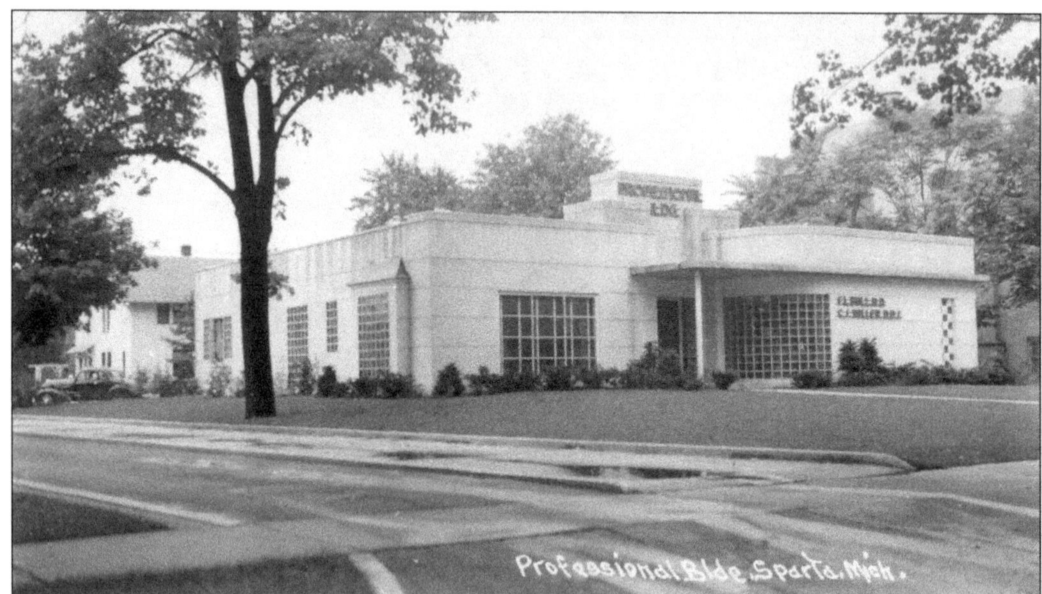

Built in 1941, this modern building was constructed by Dr. Charles S. Miller and Dr. Frank L. Bull. The Cheney residence originally stood at this site and was moved to the lot directly to the south of the building. In 1953, an addition was constructed, which later housed the Sparta Dental Lab. Eventually, Miller and Bull retired, selling the building and the practice to Drs. Edmond Eary, Thomas Fochtman, and Harold Miller.

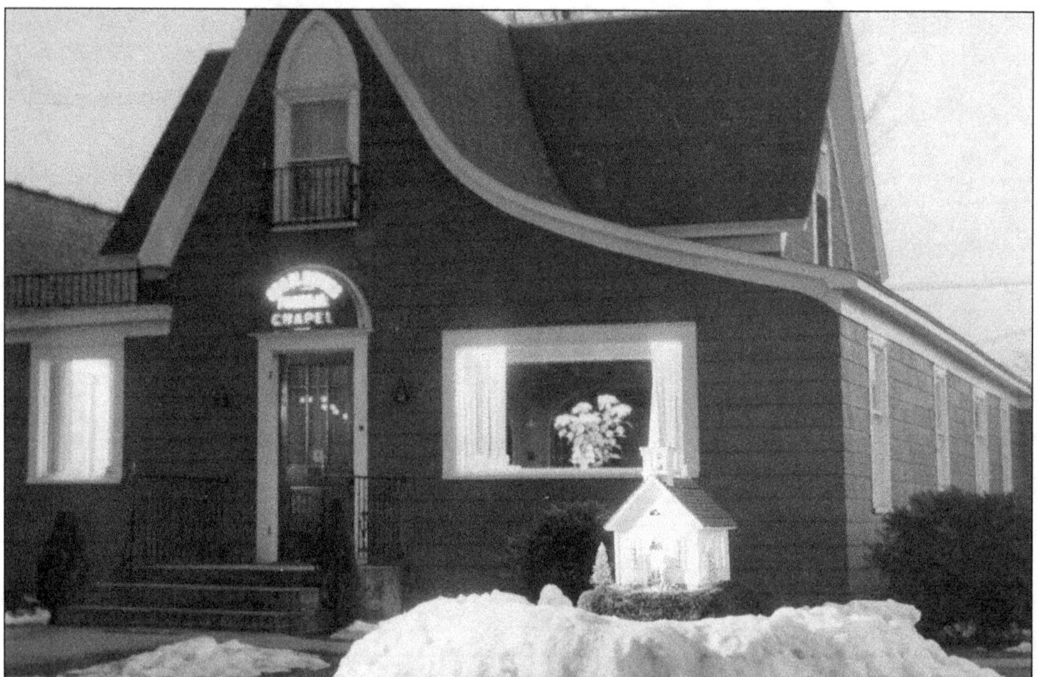

Built in 1907, the funeral home began as the two-story residence of J. C. Ballard, undertaker, who operated the funeral home until selling the business in 1922 to George Bettes. It was renamed the Bettes Funeral Parlor. In July 1947, Bettes sold the funeral home to Bernard R. Hessel of Muskegon. In 1964, Dan Cheslek joined Hessel, and it eventually became Hessel-Cheslek Funeral Home.

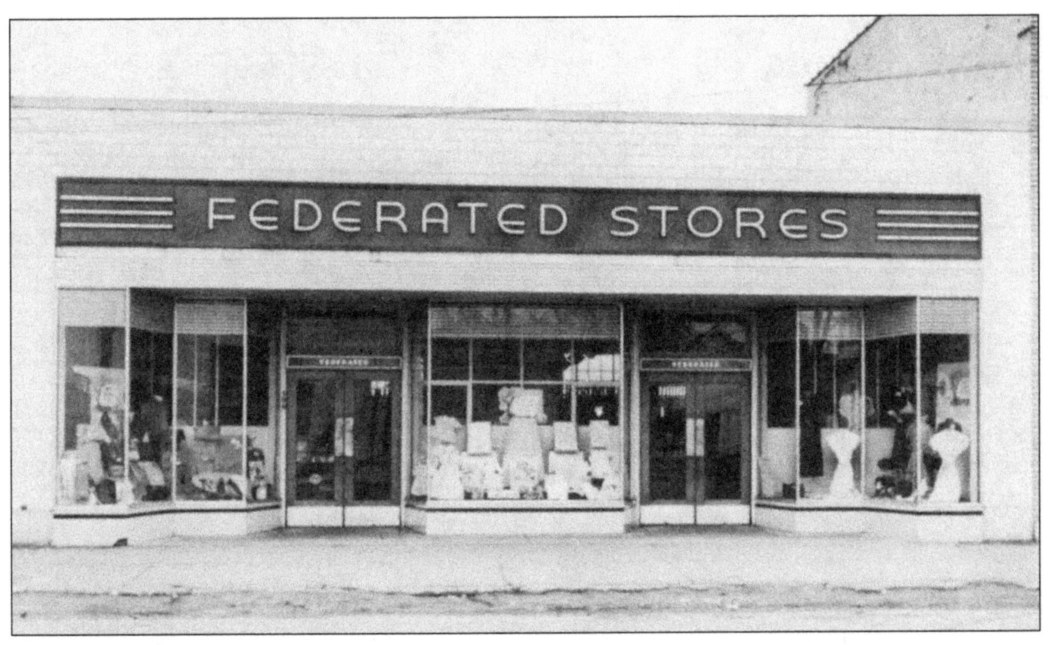

On March 19, 1941, a fire destroyed the Johnson-Smith department store, with a loss exceeding $100,000. The entire contents of the store were consumed. By July of that year, Christine Johnson decided to rebuild the store. The plans called for two store units, with one of the new units already having been leased to A. L. Brevitz of the Butler Company of Chicago. On Saturday, November 1, 1941, the new store, located in the east half of the Johnson-Smith Building, held its grand opening. The store was managed by Keith Brevitz, operating as the Ben Franklin store. Brevitz also announced that the west half had been leased to the Federated Store, another establishment of the Butler Company. The Federated Store held its grand opening on Saturday, November 29, 1941. The Federated Store later became the C. J. Walstrom Department Store.

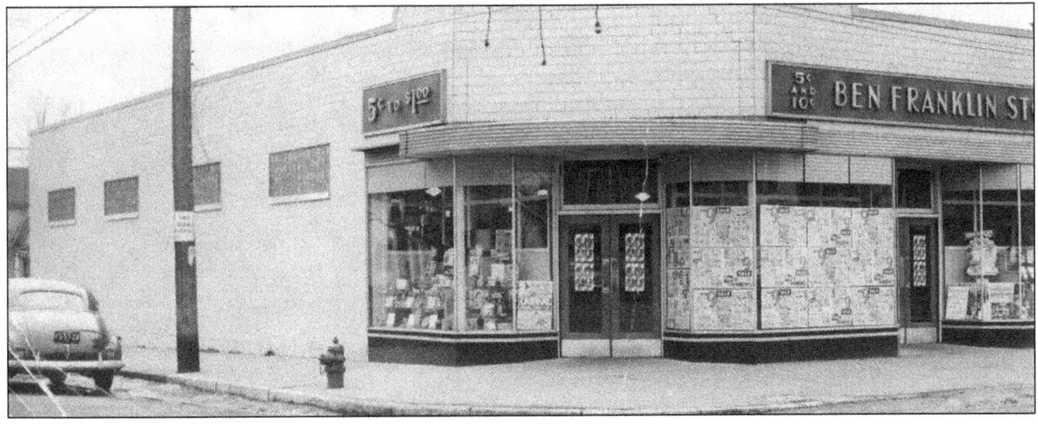

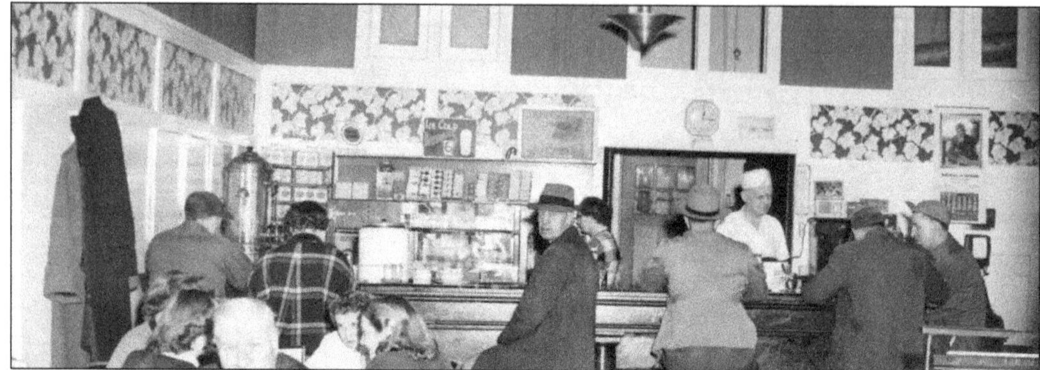

Sometimes called the "Crossroads of Sparta," Cnossen's Bakery was where townspeople gathered for a cup of coffee and to catch up on the happenings around town. Frank Cnossen (center right, dressed in white) owned the Sparta Bakery. Frank's nephew Jim went on to run the bakery, which also became a place for people to enjoy "fish night" on Fridays.

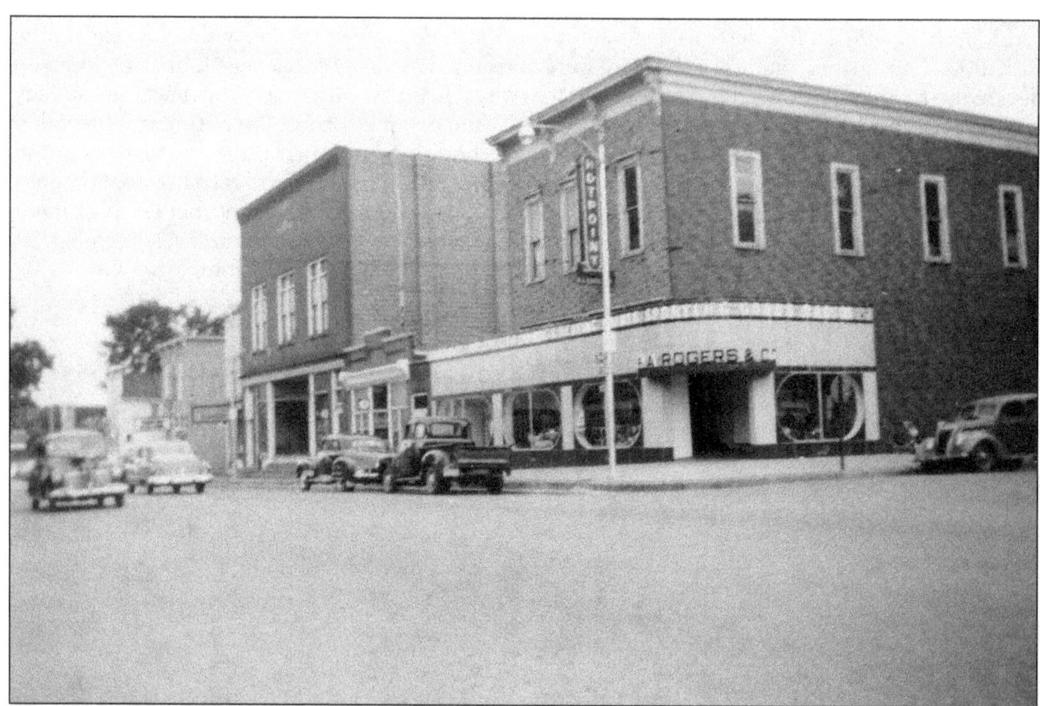

Rogers hardware store was originally located on the southeast corner of East Division Street and Washington Street. Founded by William A. Rogers and later operated by his son Melvin Rogers, this building was razed in 1970. The hardware was relocated to the north side of East Division Street and is still operated by William's grandson Alwin and great-grandson Paul.

Allen B. Way started this drugstore in 1881. In 1924, William J. Brack purchased the store. It was known as "Brack's" for 28 years. In 1946, Brack hired pharmacist Lester Momber, and in 1952, Momber purchased the store from Brack and changed the name to Momber's Pharmacy.

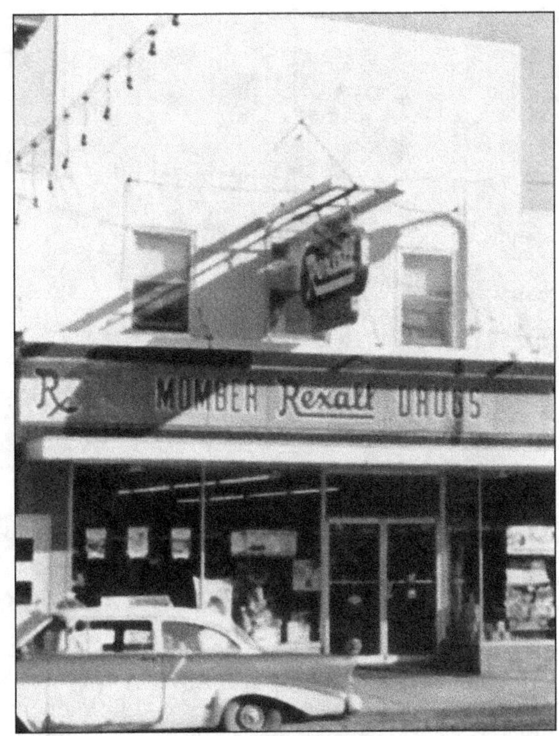

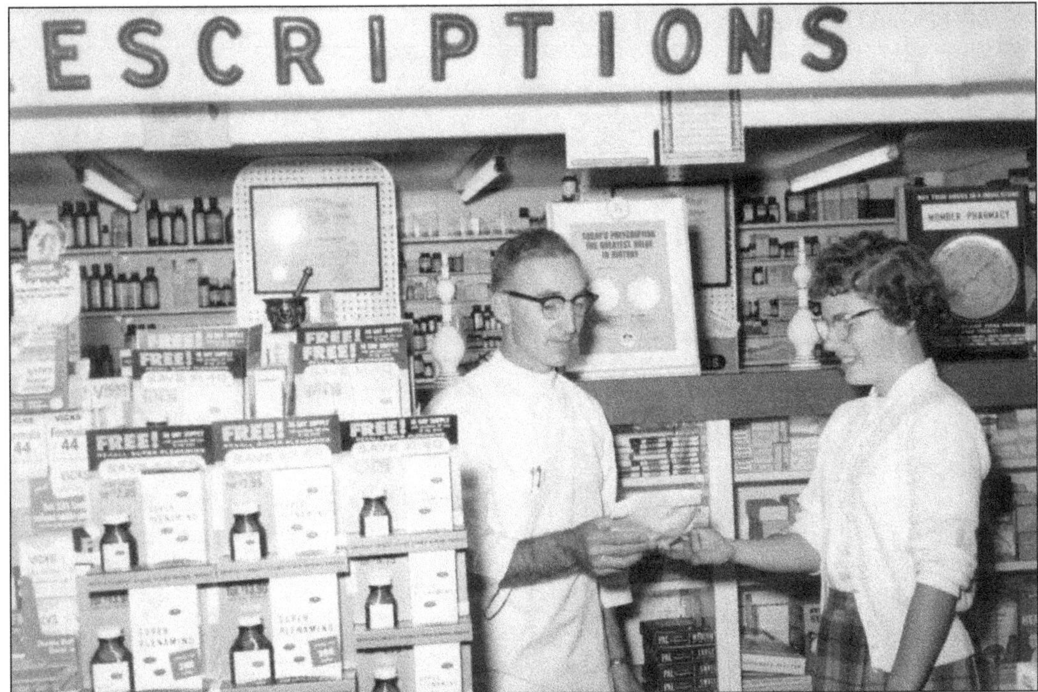

Lester Momber, owner of Momber's Pharmacy, waits on a customer in this photograph. Momber's was a full-service pharmacy, but a soda fountain was also located inside the store as well as plenty of other merchandise ranging from greeting cards to perfume. Many local teenagers looked forward to a day when they might work after school or on weekends at the drugstore.

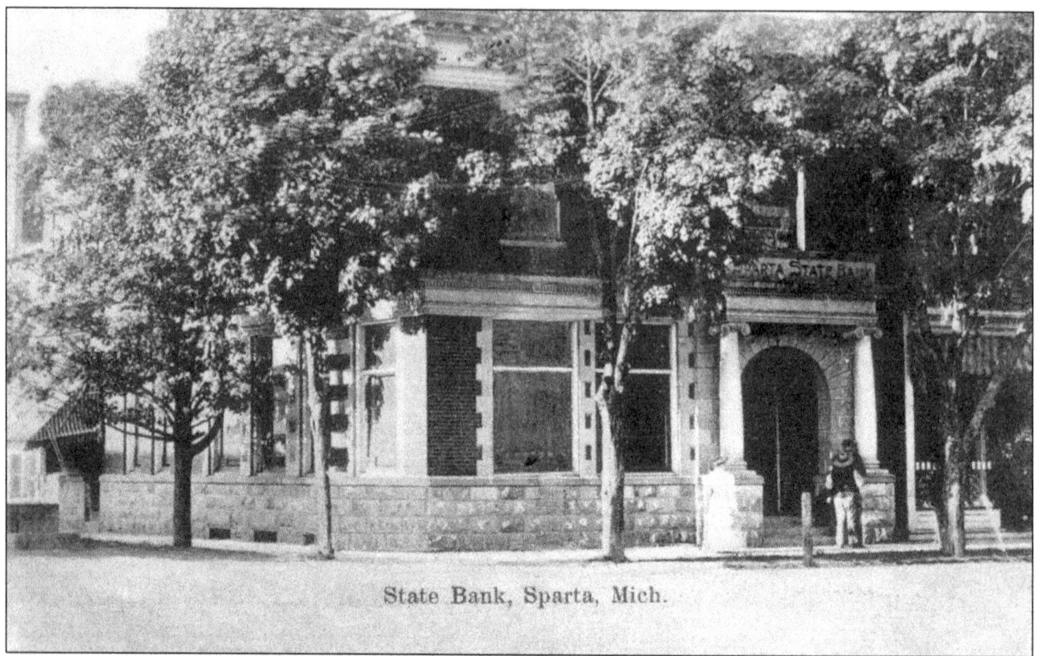

The Sparta State Bank was organized by Bruce N. Keister in 1901. In 1902, the lot for the bank was purchased at the northeast corner of Union and East Division Streets. Among the original directors were C. A. Bloomer, Jason Bradford, and John Manchester. Eventually, Jason Bradford's son Orson would become president of the bank.

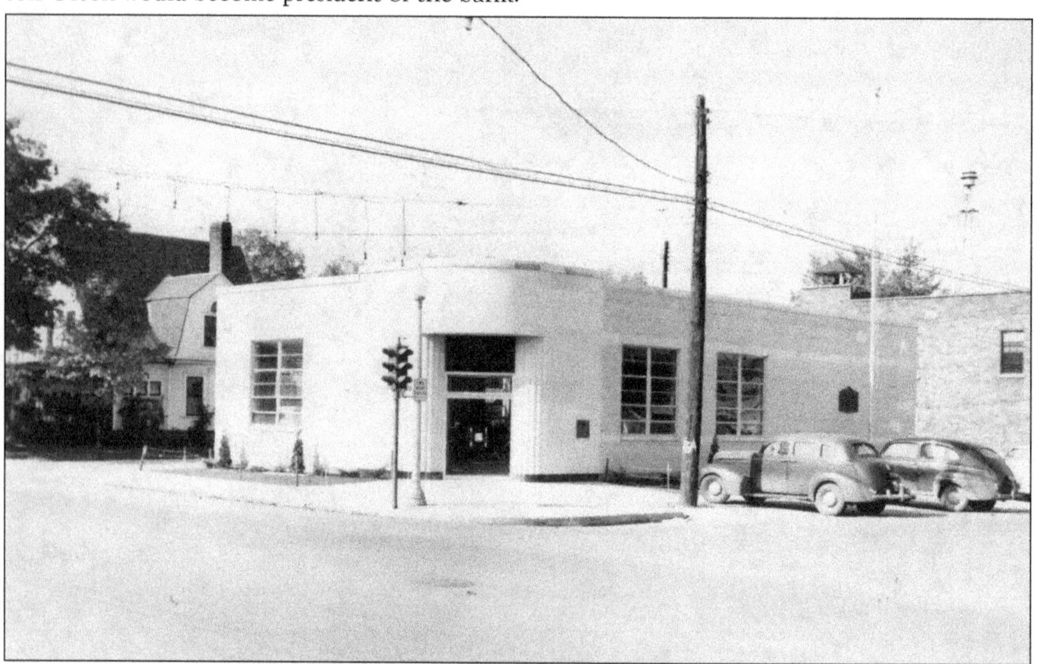

On Saturday, November 24, 1951, the new Sparta State Bank, located on the corner of East Division and Union Streets, held an open house. The public was invited to come and tour the bank building. As quoted in the *Sentinel Leader*, "Very few towns could boast of a bank building so modern and up to date."

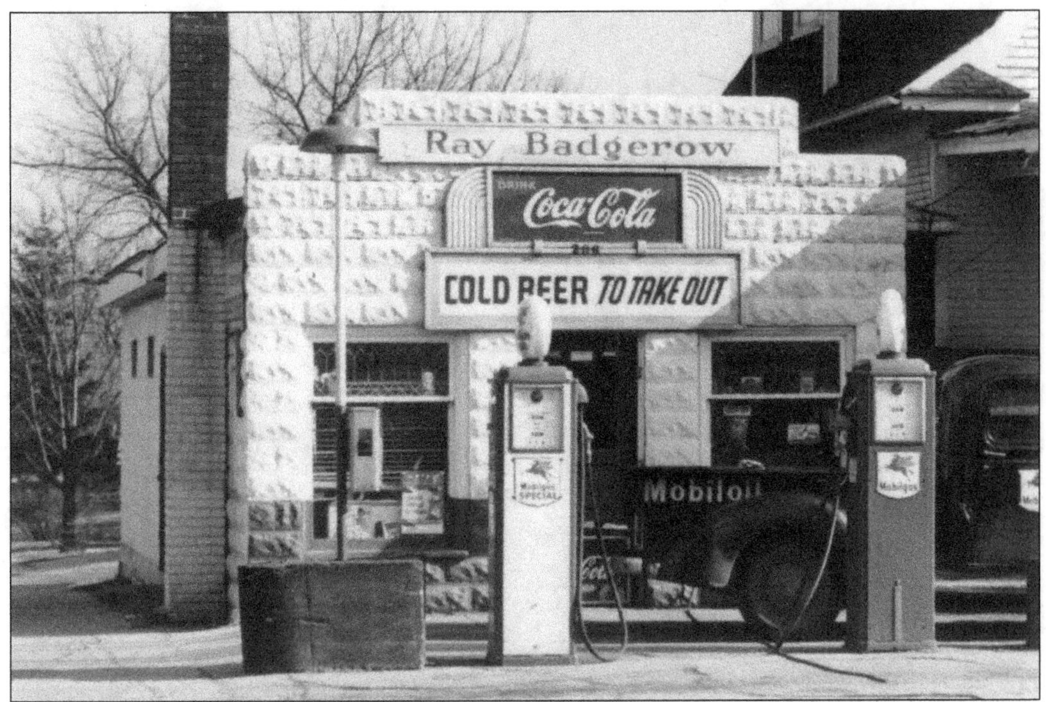

Badgerow's Store on the southeast corner of South State Street and East Gardner Street was a Sparta institution. Owned and operated by Charles Badgerow, and later by his son Raymond and grandson Carlton "Cart," the gas station was the place to go for groceries, deli meat, and treats for children. Badgerow's was a popular spot for neighborhood kids to get a Popsicle or a slice of summer sausage from Cart.

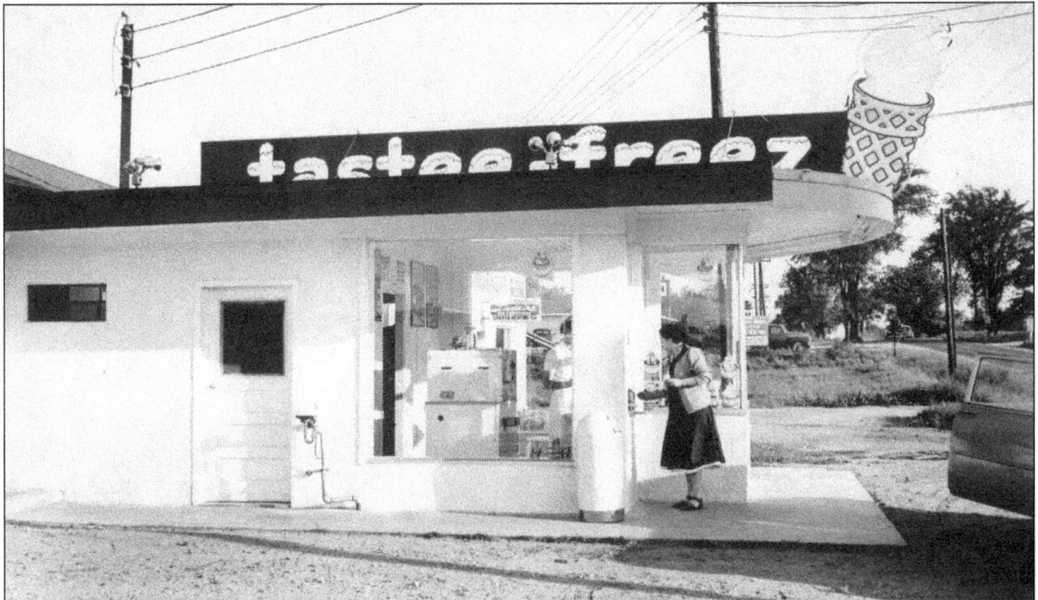

The Tastee Freez, located on South State Street, was a favorite stop for ice cream after little league games, Fourth of July picnics, swimming days at Camp Lake, and other favorite summertime activities. Later it became known as the Tasty Treat, which still continues as a small-town tradition.

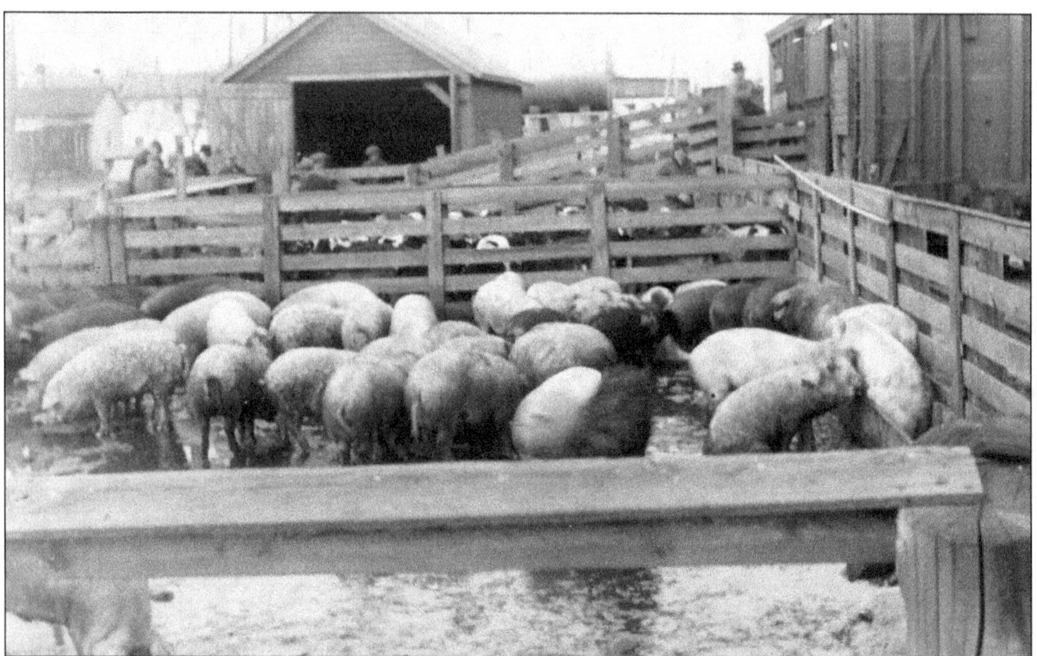

The Sparta stockyards, run by Jesse Bettes, were located on Railroad Street, later to become Elm Street, near the rail yards. Local farmers would haul their livestock to the yards, where they were loaded on the rail cars to be taken to the slaughterhouse. This photograph was taken in the 1930s.

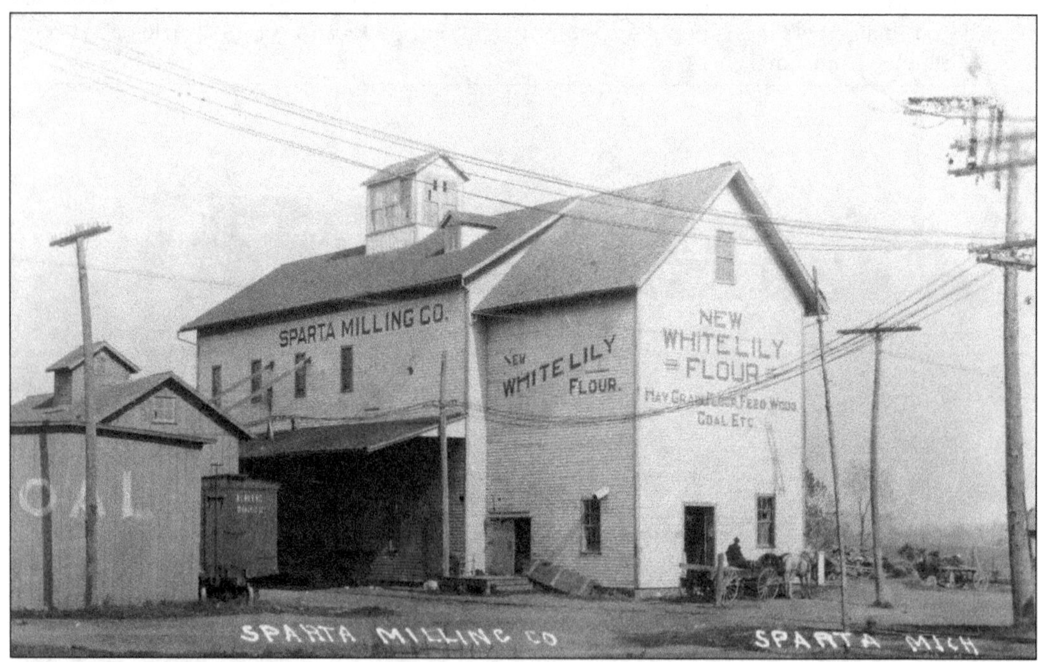

The Sparta Feed Store, built in the late 1800s, and originally known as the Jackson Feed and Grist Mill, later became known as the Sparta Milling Company. It is the oldest business on one site in Sparta. Porter Vinton bought the mill from Edwin Bradford. Many years later, it was sold to Clarence Emelander.

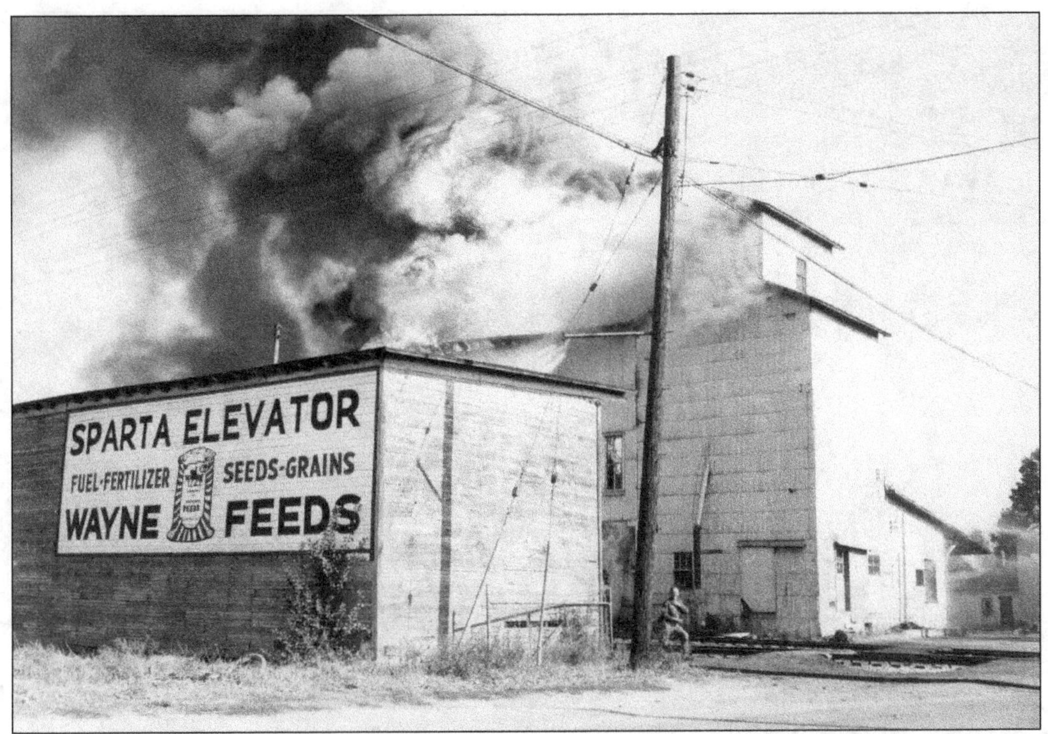

Then owner Charles Jackson installed a steam-powered electrical mill system. It supplied the village with power until the Sparta Milling Company burned in 1911. After it burned, the mill was rebuilt only to tragically burn again October 13, 1952. The dramatic blaze destroyed all but the coal sheds, making it necessary for owner Clarence Emelander to start the rebuild of the business nearly from scratch.

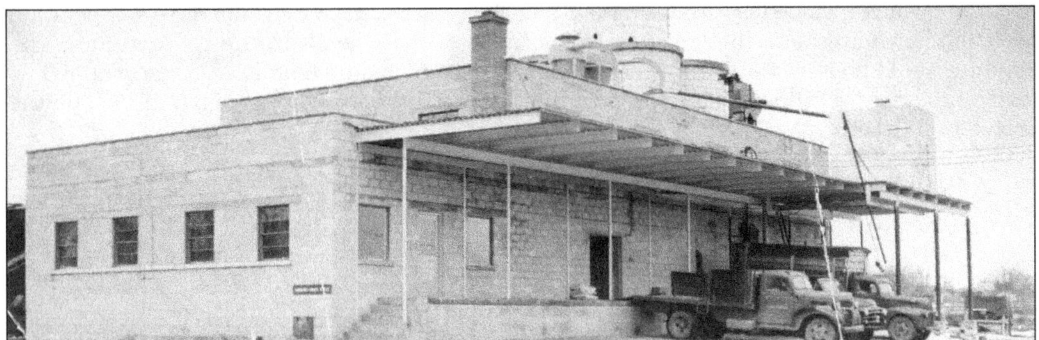
In 1947, Clarence Emelander purchased the local grain elevator. After a second fire in 1952, which destroyed all but the coal sheds, the elevator was once again rebuilt. Emelander continued to operate the mill as Sparta Elevator, and eventually, Emelander's daughter Lois managed the business. Sparta Elevator provided service to local farmers who would sell or store their harvested crops or purchase feed for farm animals.

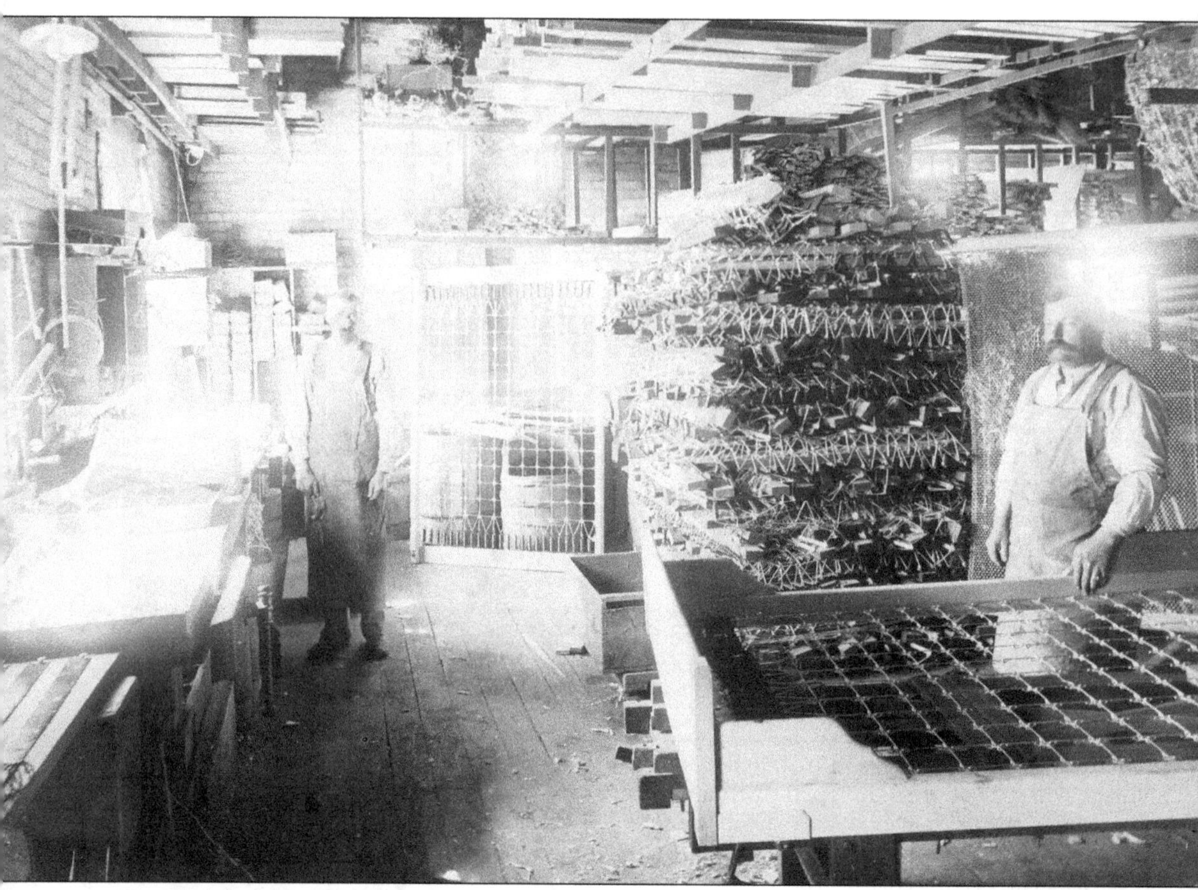

The Welch Folding Bed Company was established in 1884 by Lyman G. Welch. The company manufactured folding beds and sectional bookcases. As folding beds became more popular, Welch improved upon the original design and created a distinguished product that was recognized around the world. As demand increased over the years, the facility was expanded several times. Eventually, the manufacturer combined with another, and it became known as the Welch-Wilmarth Corporation. In 1908, they discontinued making folding beds and started a new line of retail furniture, which included clothing cabinets and showcases. The Welch-Wilmarth Corporation became known as one of the largest manufacturers of these goods in the country. Later the building would house a variety of other manufacturers, including Extensole Corporation. The man on the right is William "Plug Hat" Smith who ran for governor of Michigan in 1902 on the Prohibition ticket.

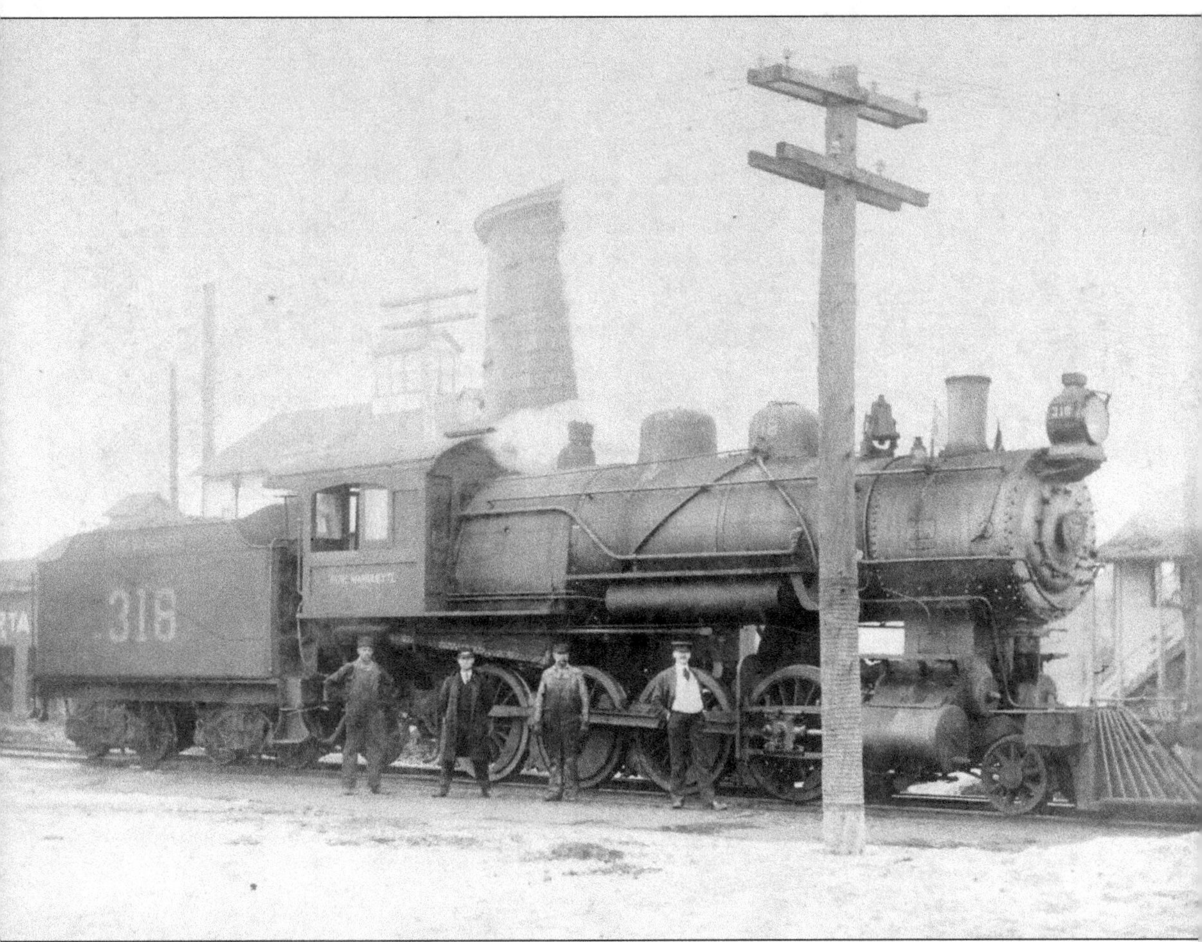

The first rail line to Sparta was completed on May 9, 1872, from Grand Rapids and, later, extended to White Cloud in 1875. After several mergers, it became part of the Pere Marquette Railroad in 1899. The railroad was considered to be one of the key factors in the development of the Sparta community. The line brought passersby through the community as it connected Grand Rapids with the tourist destinations of Northern Michigan. This photograph was taken in approximately 1906, and the water tower used by the trains can be seen in the background. The passenger depot was located on Railroad Street, later to become Elm Street, to the west of the tracks. A freight dock was located to the south of the depot to load wagons with the goods brought to town on the train. Passenger service was permanently suspended in October 1966.

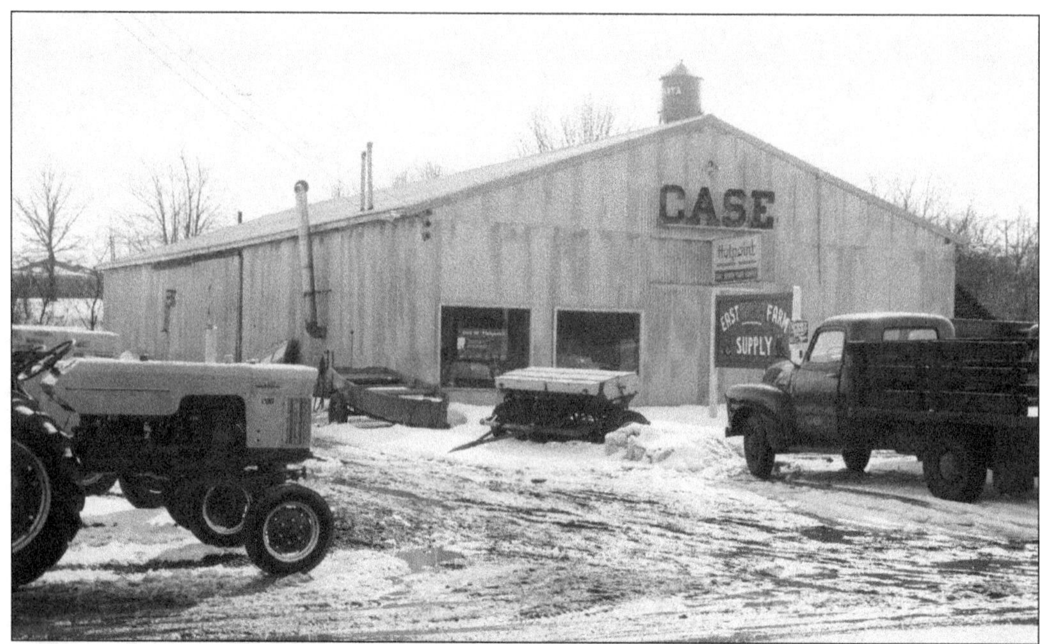

For many farmers in the Sparta area, one did not have to travel far to purchase new farm equipment, parts, or have service done on their implements. Allen Cumings opened this Case dealership in 1958. On January 23, 1960, an open house was held to showcase a new addition. East Sparta Farm Supply was located on East Division Street and River Road, just past the Sparta Feed Mill.

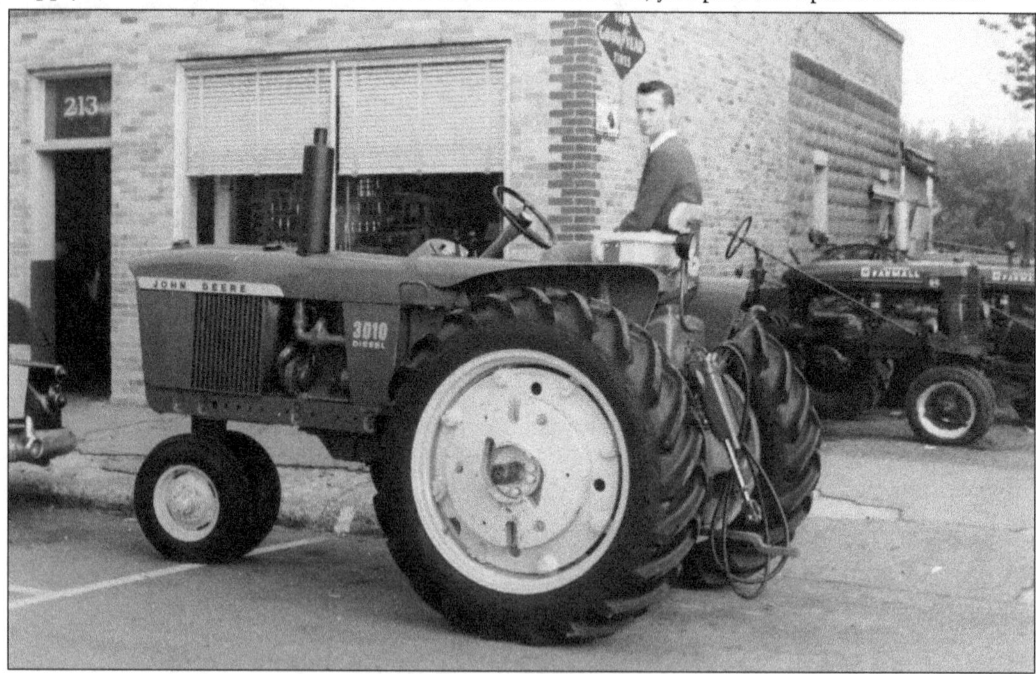

Sitting on a new John Deere tractor, in front of William A. Rogers Implement Dealership, is a young man posing for a *Sparta High School Yearbook* photograph advertisement. Over the years, the local John Deere dealership hosted yearly programs of special interest to area farms featuring guest speakers and film series.

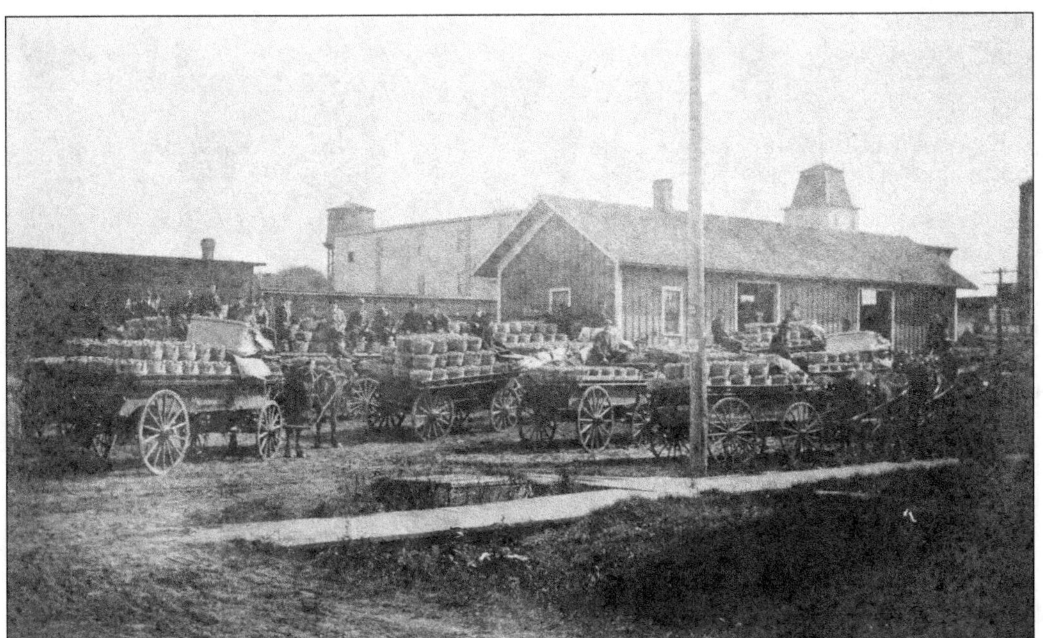

"The Ridge" along the western edge of town was a prime location for the growing of fruit, due to the moisture-rich clay soils and its proximity to Lake Michigan. Sometime just after 1900, these peaches are being loaded by Fisher, Darling, and Meeker to be transported by horse-drawn wagons to be sold at the Grand Rapids Market, which was 18 miles away.

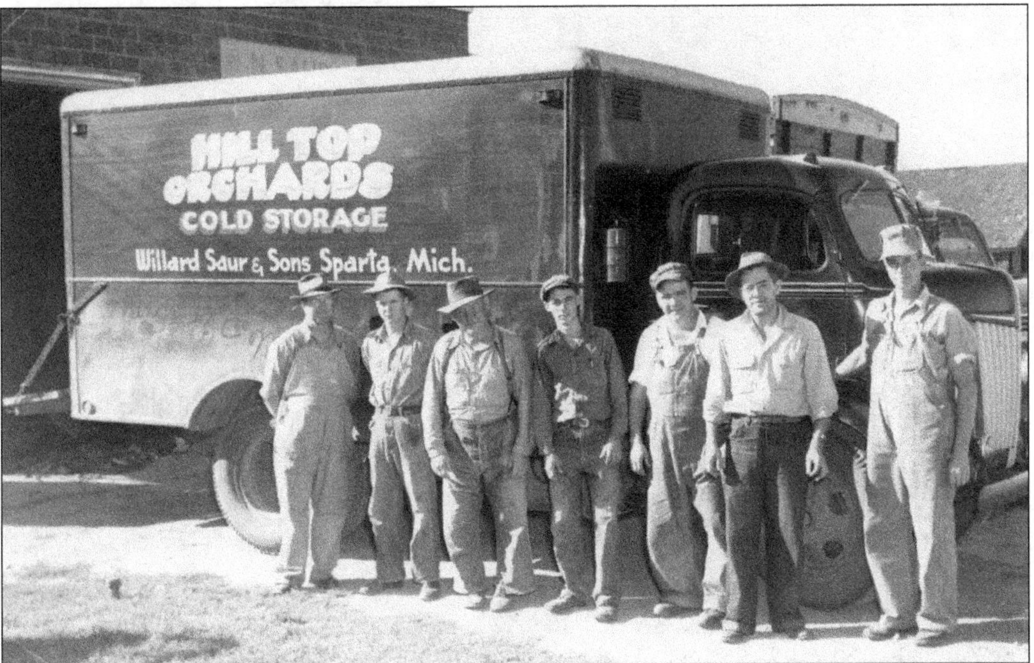

On November 3, 1949, these boys were loading peaches in the Hill Top Orchards Cold Storage truck to be taken to the Detroit Market. Those pictured are, from left to right, Willard Saur, Charles Saur, Elmer Coon, Lowell Coster, Lester Wilk, Walt Oberg, and Earl Baehre. The truck had a 300-bushel capacity.

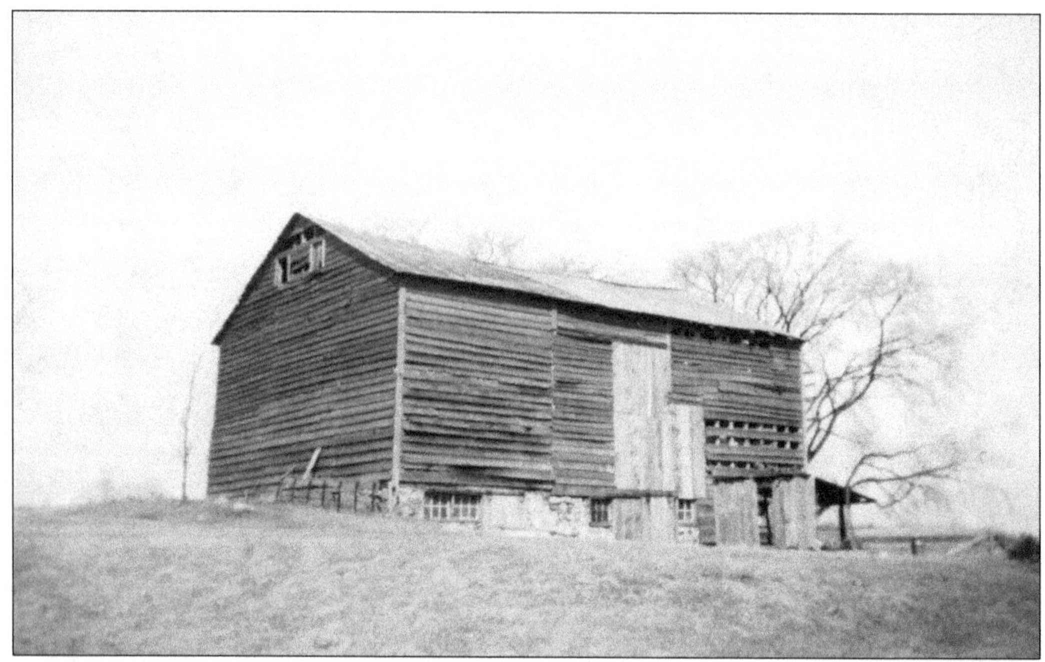

John Symes arrived in Sparta in June 1845 and, along with Elihu Rice and Anthony Chapman, he helped settle the area near Sparta Avenue and Twelve Mile Road. The three men built a temporary shanty for their families to share until their permanent homes could be constructed. Built in 1849 on Cherry Hill Farm by Symes, the barn was later part of the Clarence Johnson farm.

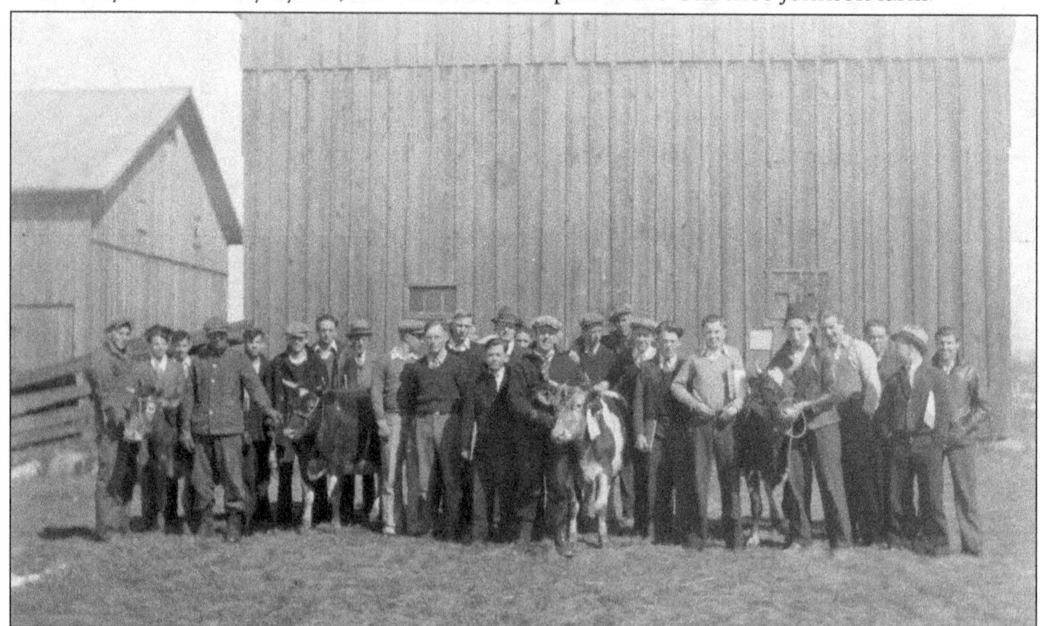

The Animal Husbandry class of 1933 consisted of, from left to right, Norman Olson, Orman Hippenstall, George Norton, Frank Olson, Vond Swett, two unidentified, Fred Humeston, unidentified, Lloyd Johnson, Richard Christenson, Bruce House, Wilbur Ostman, unidentified, Merlin Andrews, unidentified, Richard Nequist, Richard Johnson, Manson Vander Meer, Roger Bloom, unidentified, Donald Olson, Paul Larson, Wayne Helsel, unidentified, and Orval Westen.

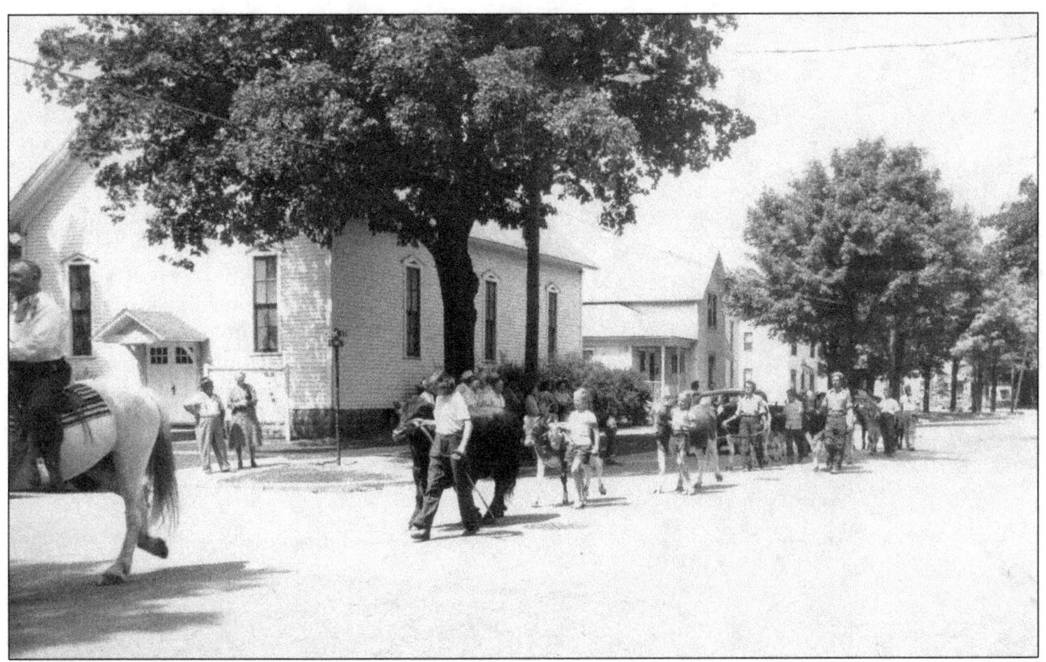

Looking north on Union Street, these young 4-H members are bringing their livestock into town. They were likely part of the parade that would begin at the school just up the street. In the background is the Sparta Free Methodist Church. Arzie Pinckney leads the group on the gray horse.

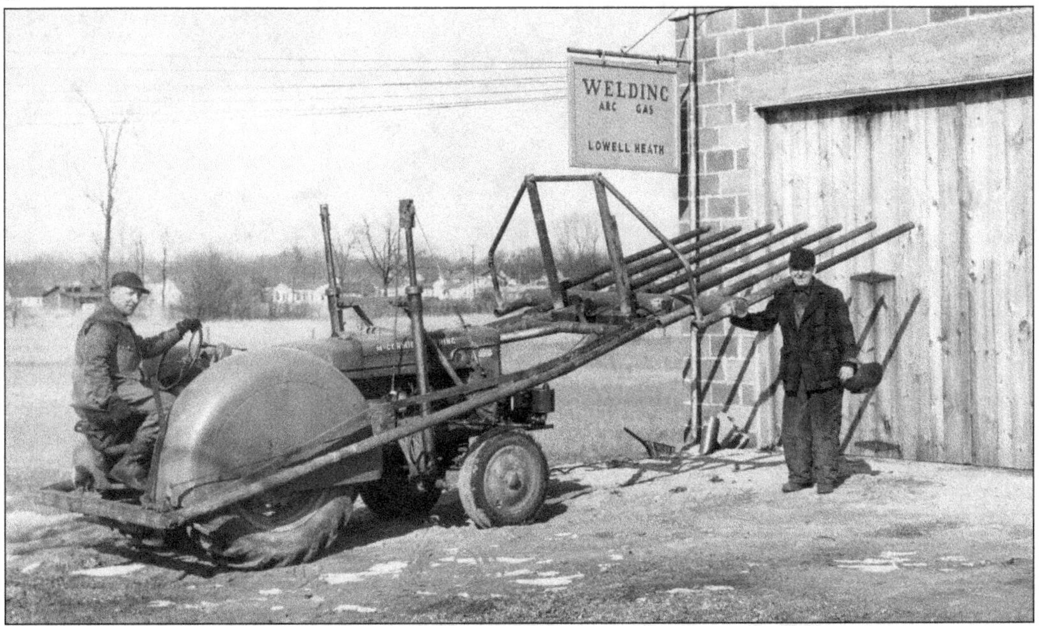

This buck rake was designed by Fred Blush and Lowell G. Heath. "The new rake is all steel permitting the placement of brush directly on the fire. The rake, manure loader, snow plow, or bulldozer can be attached by simply using two bolts," Heath said. The positive action of the trip and ease of operation were improvements for orchard operations. Those pictured on September 15, 1949, are Blush (left) and Heath.

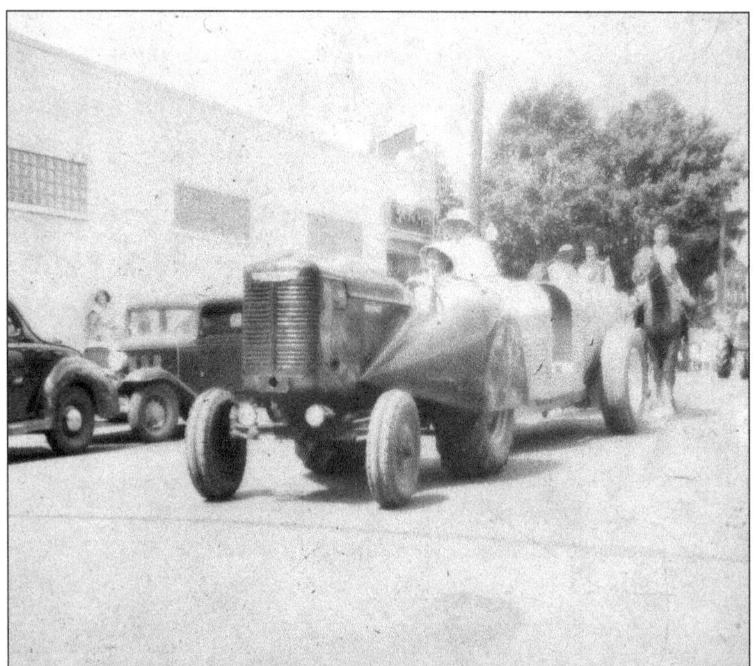

This Farmall tractor, equipped with orchard fenders, participated in the 1947 Farm Days Parade. Here it is pictured in front of Ben Franklin, traveling south on Union Street, just past East Division Street. The grill guard on the front of the tractor was there to keep brush in the orchards from puncturing the radiator.

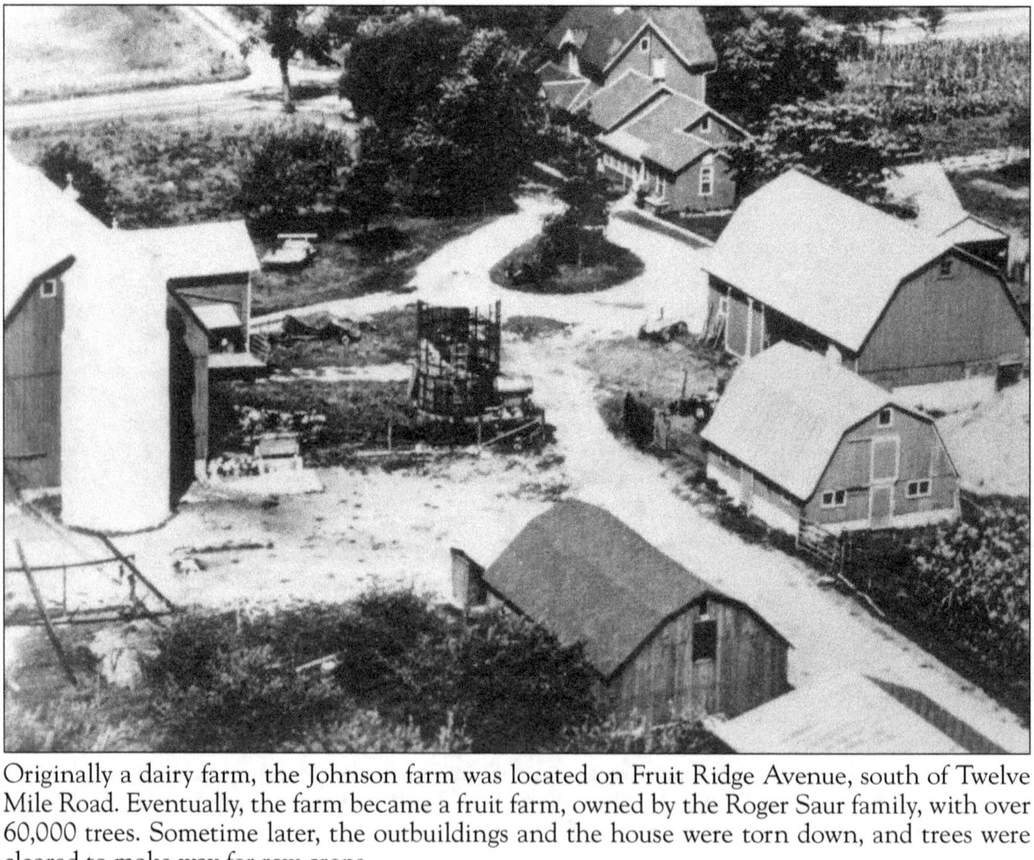

Originally a dairy farm, the Johnson farm was located on Fruit Ridge Avenue, south of Twelve Mile Road. Eventually, the farm became a fruit farm, owned by the Roger Saur family, with over 60,000 trees. Sometime later, the outbuildings and the house were torn down, and trees were cleared to make way for row crops.

Three

MILITARY

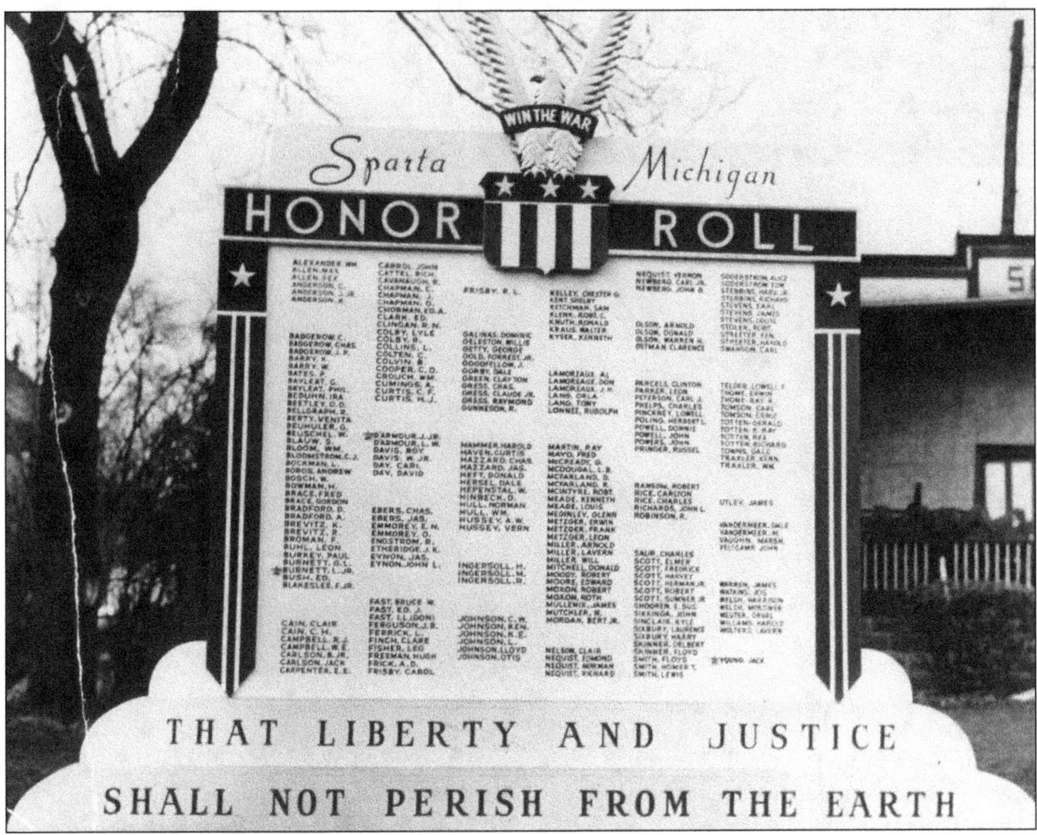

This image speaks to the all too many families whose sons made the supreme sacrifice for the community and the nation and acknowledges their loss. It seems especially cruel that so much treasure was spent in one small town. Their willingness to fight helped to secure the blessings of liberty and posterity, and their sacrifices are greatly appreciated by all.

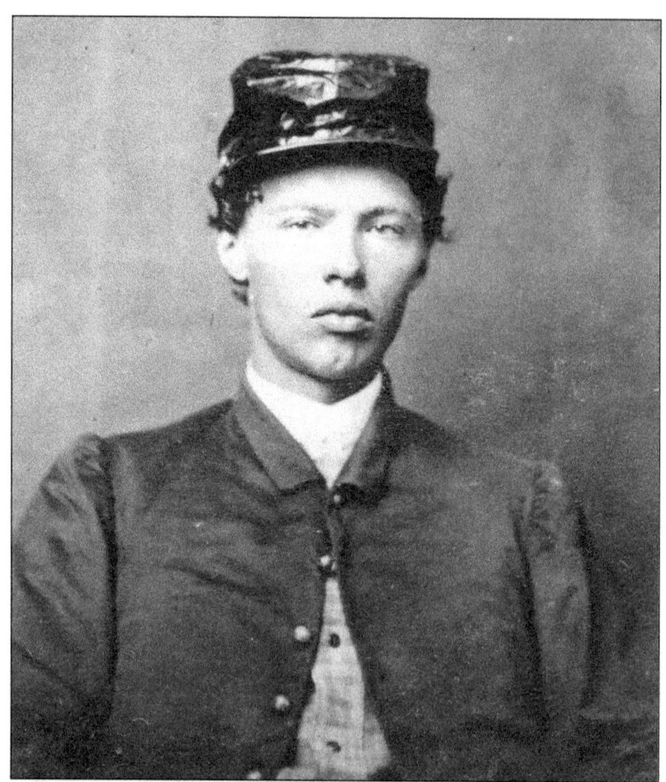

Amherst B. Cheney, resident of Sparta, enlisted as a private in Company B, 21st Regiment for the Union army in the fall of 1862. Cheney was wounded at the Battle of Bentonville on March 19, 1865. He returned to Sparta after the war to teach school. Cheney also established a bank and was elected state representative from the Third District in 1876. He was reelected in 1878, beating Jonathan Nash, the Democrat candidate.

Camp 21st Mich. Inft
Detroit June 19/65

Tina

I expect to go home Tomorrow. Any Orders, instructions, communications, or letters which you may wish to send to Sparta will be executed, or carried by me with pleasure.

Anything you may be pleased to send will reach me if directed to the Mich Exchange Hotel.

I have obtained those books.

Attended Elder Freeland's Church last evening and

This letter was written by Amherst B. Cheney while he was in Detroit waiting to come home from the Civil War. Cheney corresponded with Clementine "Tina" Heath throughout the war. When he returned home, he eventually married Genie Hinman, and they made their home in Sparta. Ironically, Heath later married Cheney's brother Zarrah.

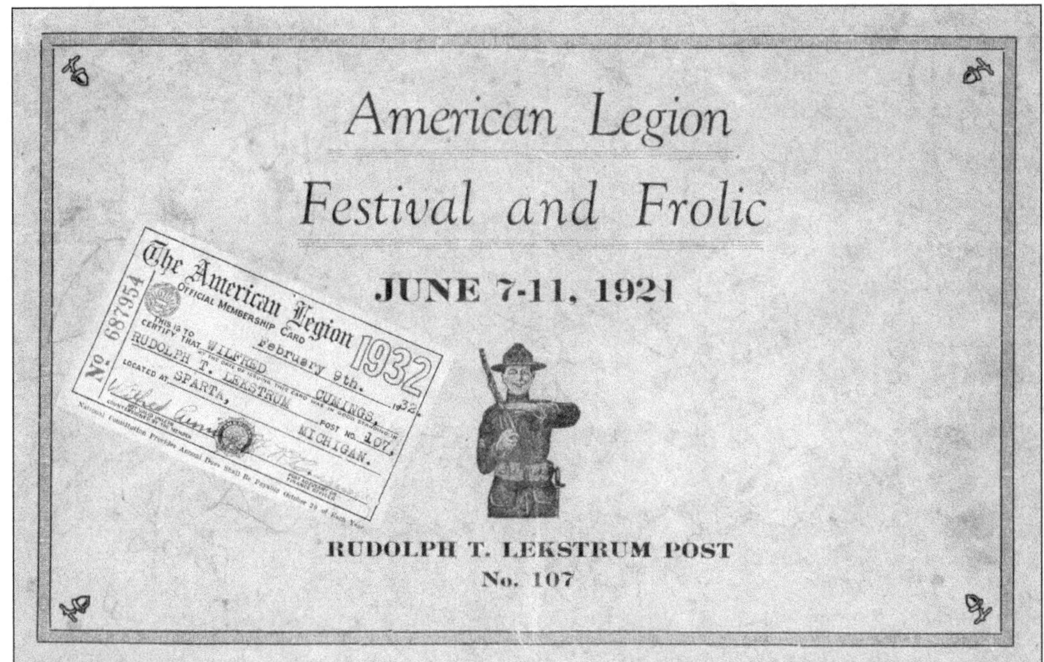

American Legion Post 107 was chartered in August 1919. The post was named for Rudolph T. Lekstrum who was killed in World War I. In 1935, the building, which had been the office for the Sparta Foundry, was moved to its South State Street location. The name was changed in 1946 to Lekstrum-Burnett to honor Louis Burnett Jr. who died in World War II. After World War II, the legion unveiled a new honor roll, located on the east side of the Sparta State Bank. Shown above is a program for the American Legion "Festival and Frolic" held June 7–11, 1921, and the American Legion membership card of Wilfred Cumings.

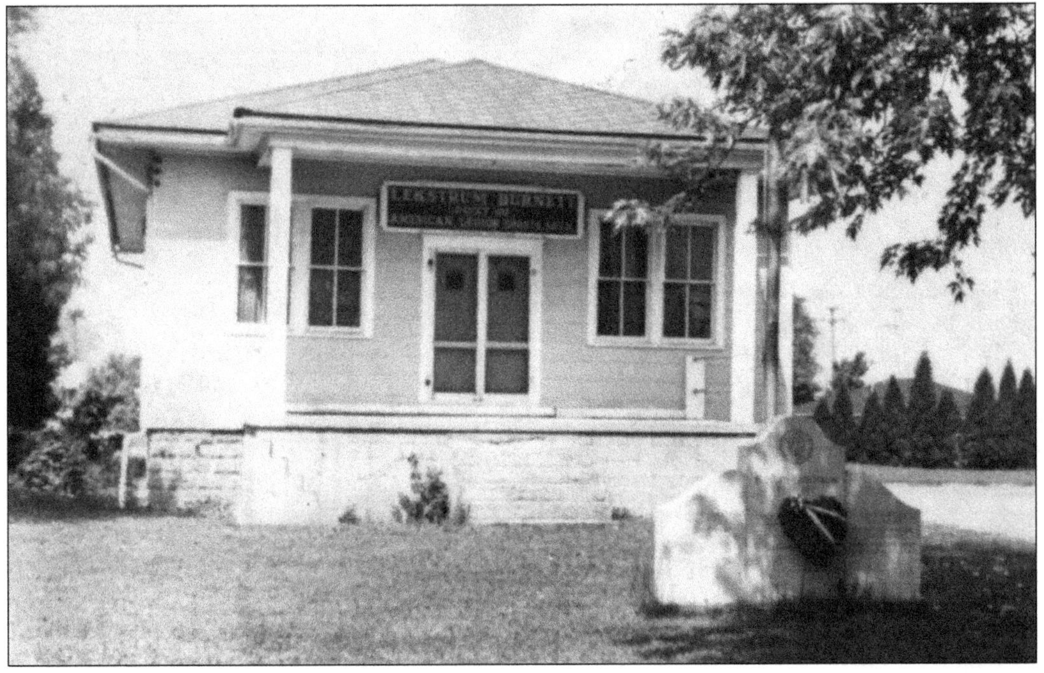

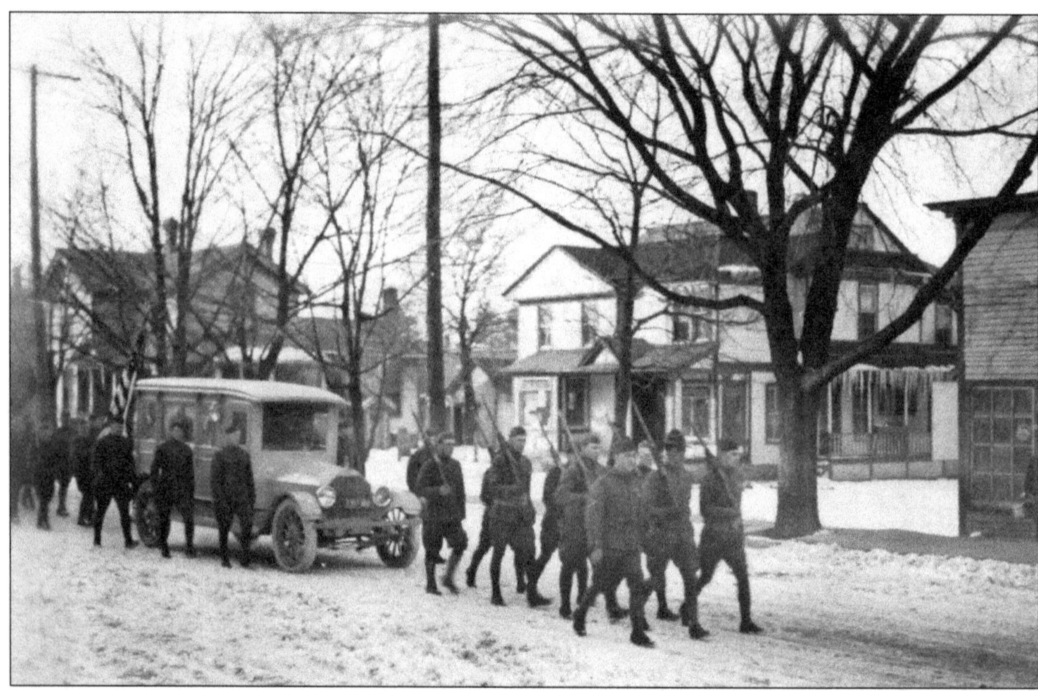

Sparta lost several men in battle in World War I. This fallen soldier is being carried to his resting place in the first motor-driven hearse in Sparta. They are traveling to Myers Cemetery, located east of town, for burial. It looks like this procession is moving east down Division Street. It is not known if all of the men pictured are Sparta veterans.

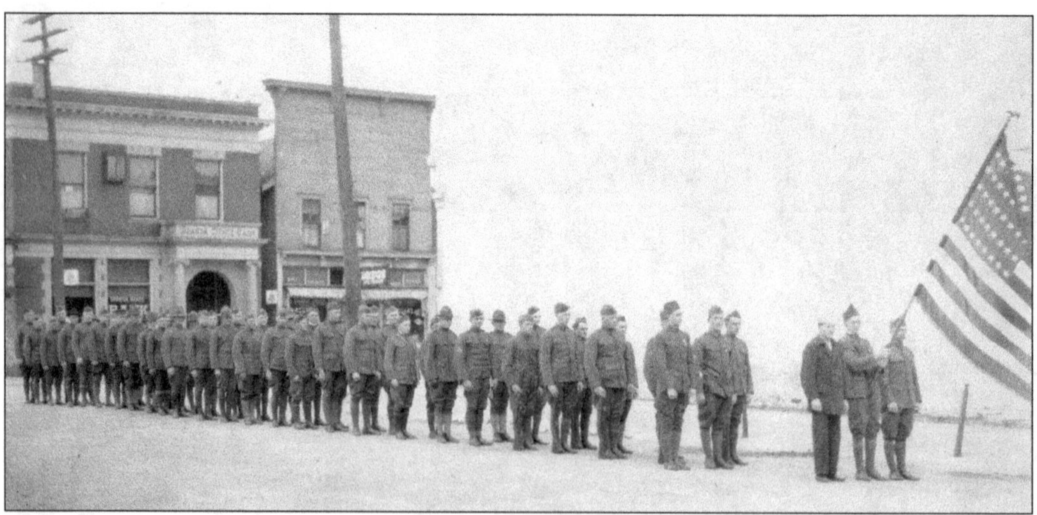

This photograph was taken in 1919 as veterans were lined up for the first military funeral in Sparta after World War I. The funeral was for Nicholas Denhof. It was held at the St. Francis Xavier Church on Thirteen Mile Road, near Crockery Lake. The soldiers are lined up facing south on Union Street where it intersects with Division Street.

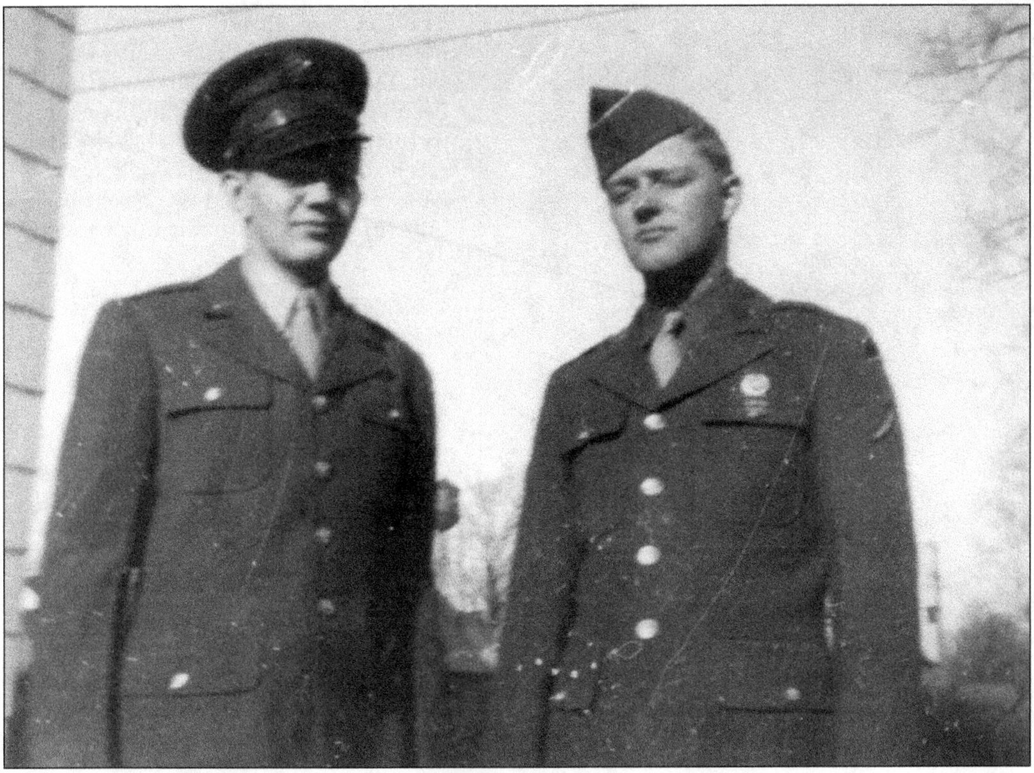

When World War II began, three blue stars hung in the window of the home of Clare and Alice Lamoreaux at 203 Martindale Street. All three of their sons served in the U.S. Army. All three boys were graduates of Sparta High School and were employed locally, prior to the war.

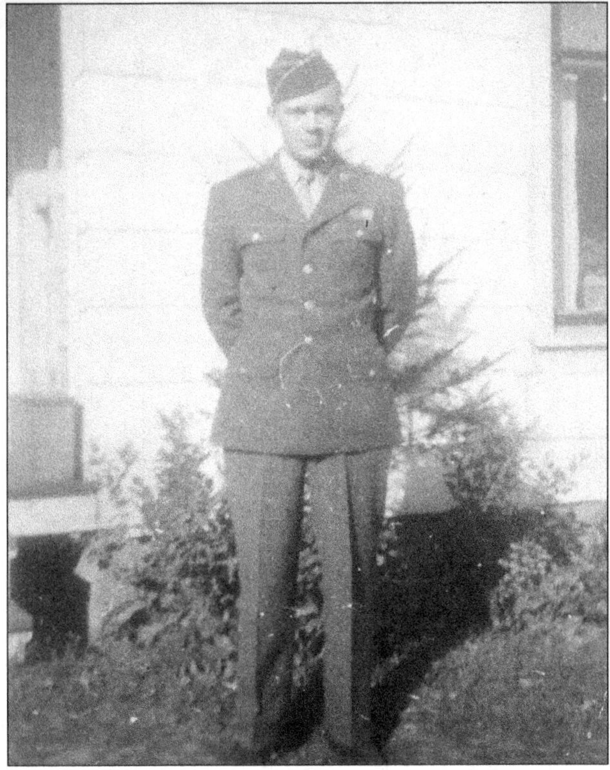

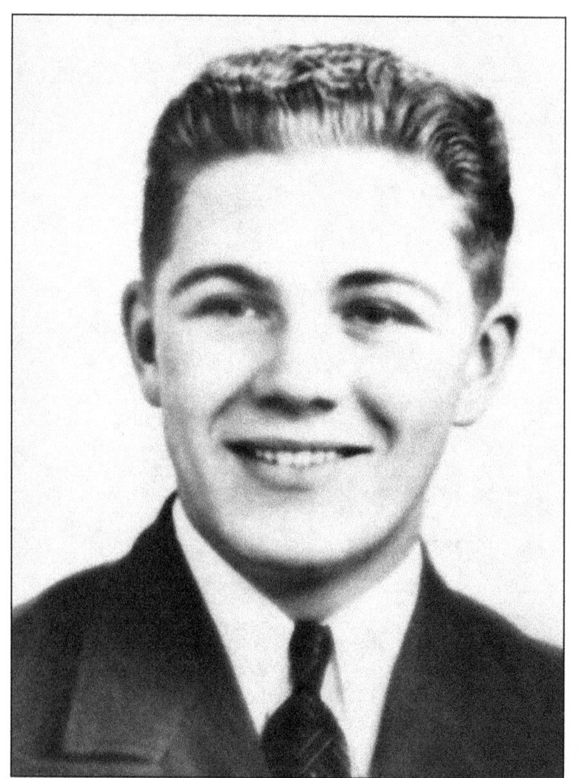

The Lamoreaux family received notification on February 23, 1944, that Pvt. Donald C. Lamoreaux, age 21, had been killed in action in Italy. Donald, pictured, died on January 21, 1944, and received the Silver Star for gallantry. Now one gold star and two blue stars hung in the Lamoreaux family window.

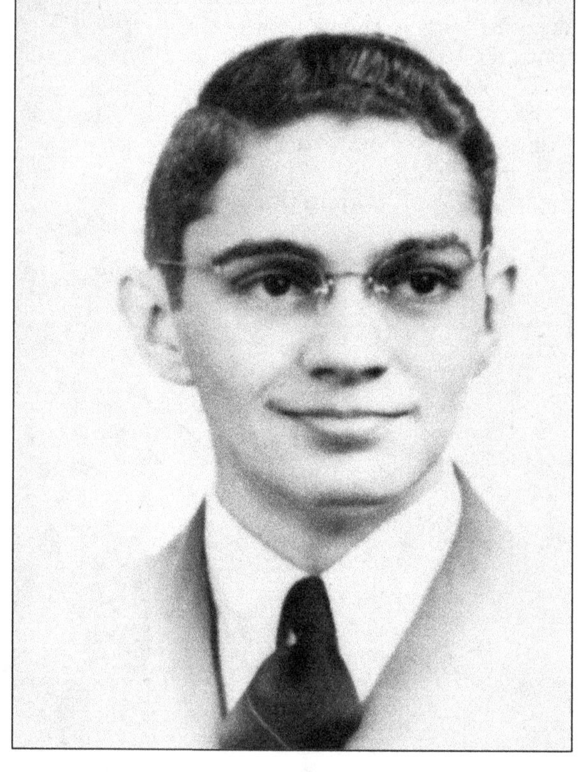

Spring and summer passed, and in the fall, the Lamoreaux family was still receiving letters from sons, Howard, age 20, and Al, age 26. The letters from Howard suddenly stopped. A second notification was received. Pvt. Howard Lamoreaux, pictured, was killed on Leyte Island on November 10, 1944. A gold star replaced another of the blue stars. Now there were two gold stars and one blue star hanging in the family window.

The third notification, a telegram, arrived on Tuesday, February 10, 1945. Sgt. Al Lamoreaux, pictured, was killed in Germany on February 6, 1945. He was the Lamoreaux's third son to die in battle. The following day, the service flag that hung in the Lamoreaux family window was taken down. It was returned, and now three gold stars hung in the window.

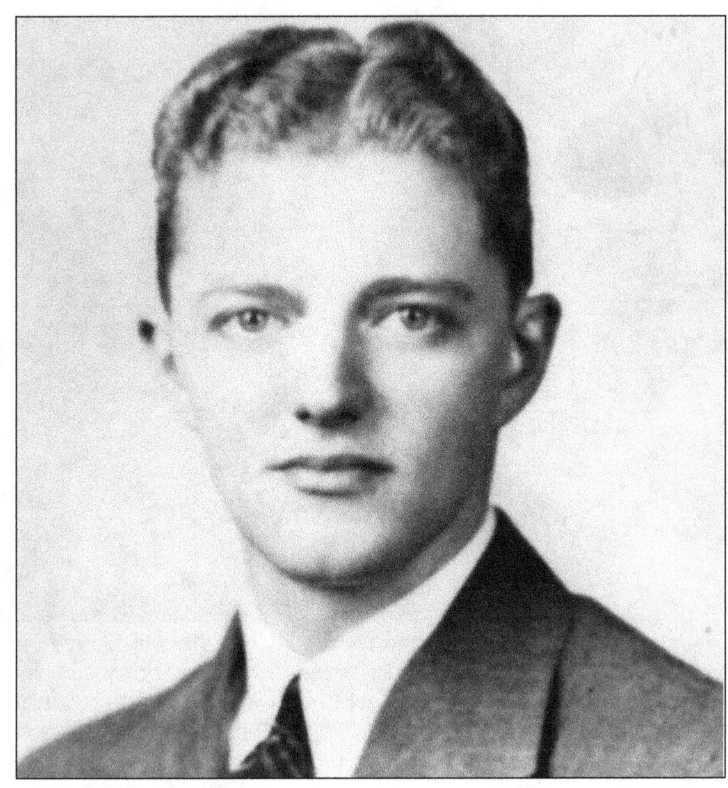

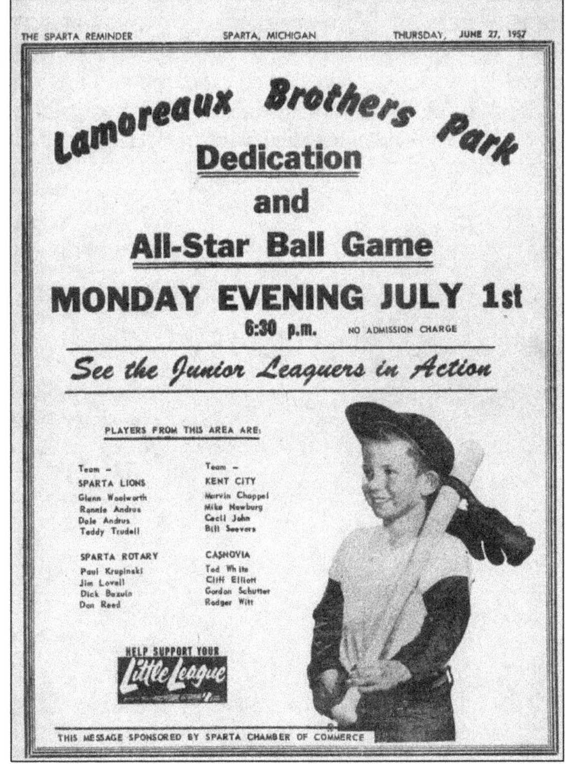

THE SPARTA REMINDER — SPARTA, MICHIGAN — THURSDAY, JUNE 27, 1957

Lamoreaux Brothers Park

Dedication

and

All-Star Ball Game

MONDAY EVENING JULY 1st

6:30 p.m. NO ADMISSION CHARGE

See the Junior Leaguers in Action

PLAYERS FROM THIS AREA ARE:

Team –
SPARTA LIONS
Glenn Woolworth
Ronnie Andrus
Dale Andrus
Teddy Trudell

SPARTA ROTARY
Paul Krupinski
Jim Lovell
Dick Bazuin
Don Reed

Team –
KENT CITY
Mervin Chappel
Mike Newburg
Cecil John
Bill Seevers

CASNOVIA
Tod White
Cliff Elliott
Gordon Schutter
Rodger Witt

HELP SUPPORT YOUR
Little League

THIS MESSAGE SPONSORED BY SPARTA CHAMBER OF COMMERCE

In 1953, a new park was dedicated to the Lamoreaux brothers. For many years the park has served as a gathering place for Little League baseball games, picnics, and a place for children to play on swings and slides. In 1995, a permanent granite monument was dedicated on Memorial Day.

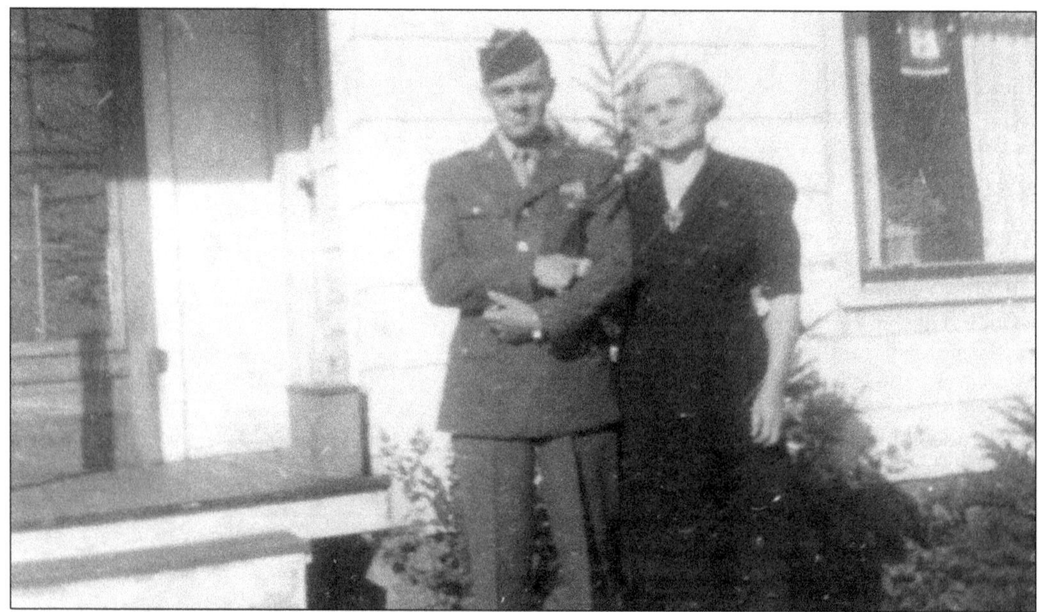

In October 1946 in an interview for the *Sentinel Leader*, Clare Lamoreaux said, "When the boys were living at home, they didn't pay rent, of course, but whenever they found an unpaid gas or electric bill, they took care of it without a word. They were always bringing home presents for their mother. You know, it's those little things that hurt the most when I think of them now." Donald Lamoreaux is pictured with his mother, and notice the flag in the window still had three blue stars on it. Memories of Donald, Howard, and Al, known as "the Lamoreaux boys," are still shared in Sparta. The local post of the Veterans of Foreign Wars was named for them, as was Lamoreaux Park. The boys are survived by their sisters, Edna Lamoreaux Topping and Joanne Lamoreaux Dake. Below from left to right, Joanne Lamoreaux Dake, Alice Lamoreaux, Howard Lamoreaux, Francis Topping, Edna Lamoreaux Topping, Arnold Lamoreaux, Anita Lamoreaux, and Al Lamoreaux gather for a photograph taken by Clare Lamoreaux in the yard of their home.

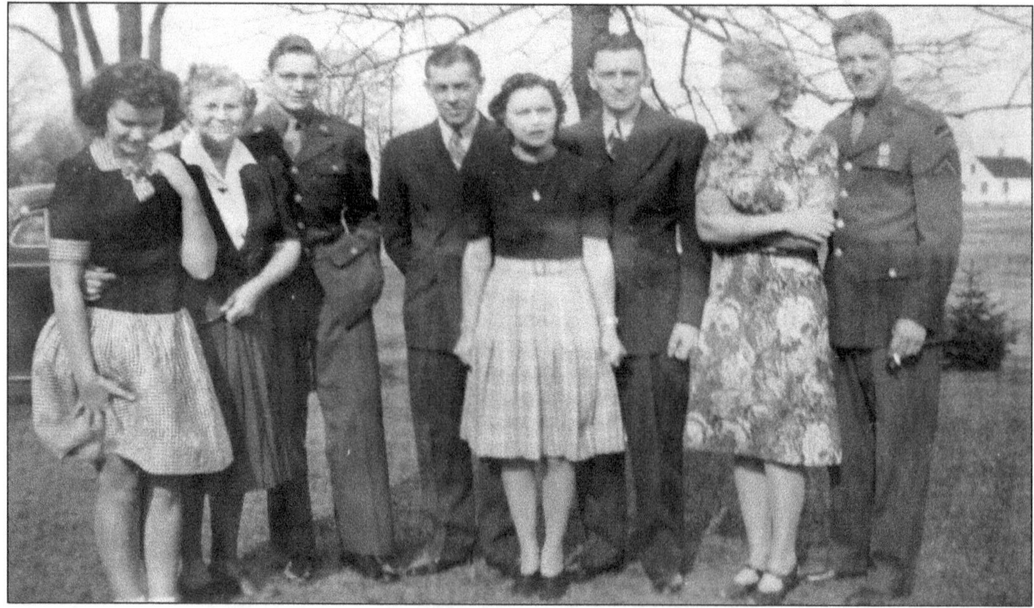

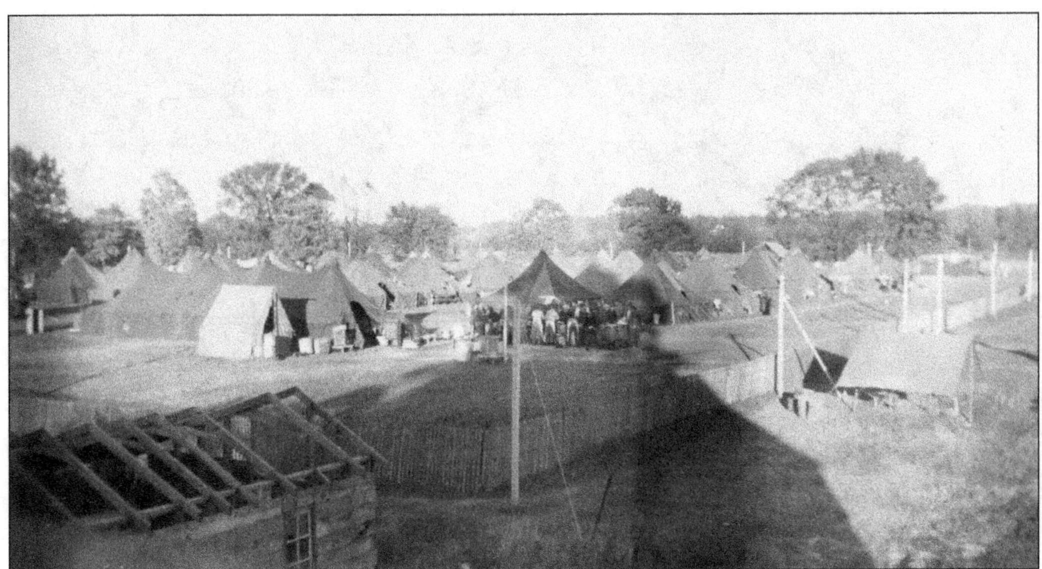

In August of 1944, a prisoner of war camp was set up on East Gardner Street, east of Martindale Street. Over 400 German prisoners were moved there to help harvest the fruit crop. The farmers would pick up the prisoners to work for the day. Many of the farmers were German and were able to communicate with the prisoners. Ironically, the camp was across the street from the Lamoreaux family home.

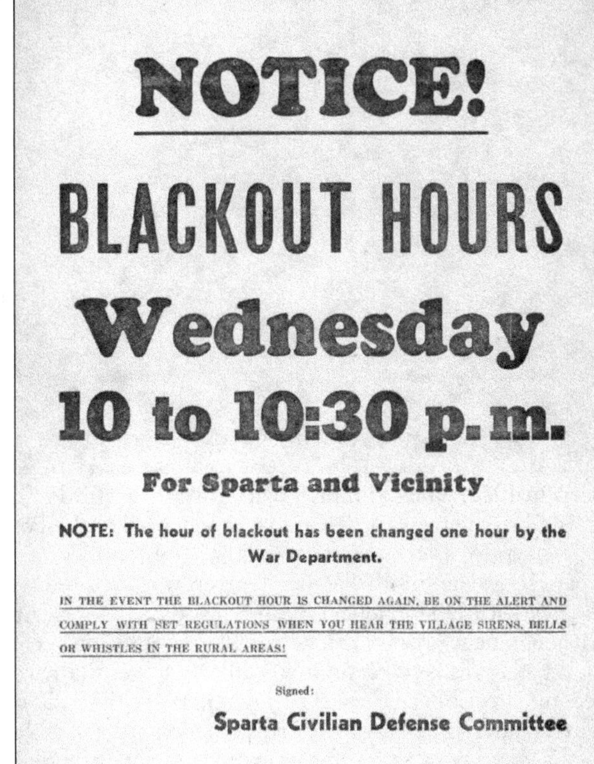

NOTICE!

BLACKOUT HOURS

Wednesday

10 to 10:30 p.m.

For Sparta and Vicinity

NOTE: The hour of blackout has been changed one hour by the War Department.

IN THE EVENT THE BLACKOUT HOUR IS CHANGED AGAIN, BE ON THE ALERT AND COMPLY WITH SET REGULATIONS WHEN YOU HEAR THE VILLAGE SIRENS, BELLS OR WHISTLES IN THE RURAL AREAS!

Signed:

Sparta Civilian Defense Committee

Pictured is a notice of a change in the blackout hours. During World War II, people were expected to cooperate with government orders to hang dark curtains over their windows to keep the light from escaping at night, so that homes across the country would not become targets during an enemy air raid.

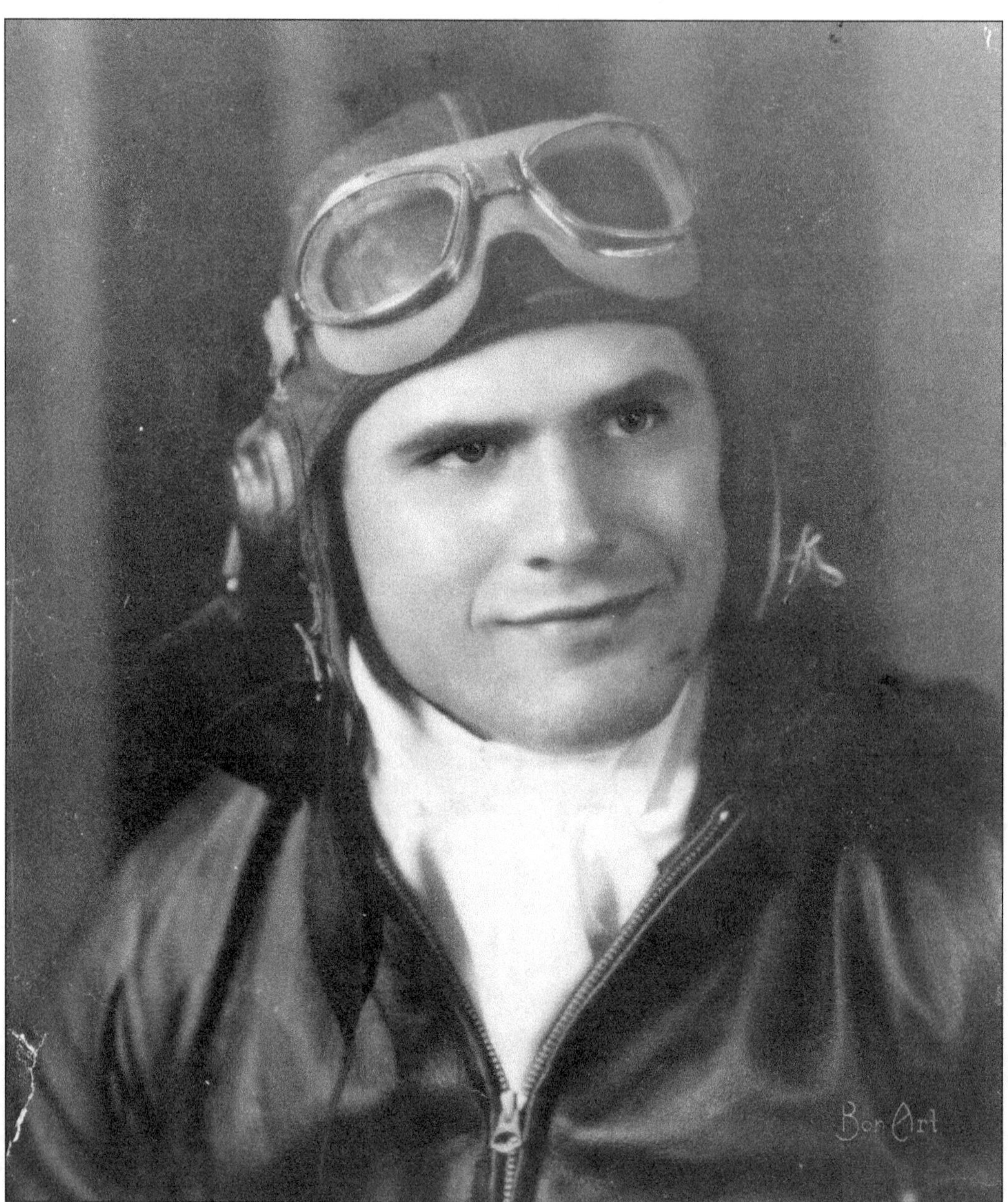

Born in 1920, James "Jimmy" Warren was the third child born to Charles and Rose Warren. He enlisted in the navy in 1942 and was accepted to the Pensacola Naval Academy. At the academy, Warren trained on aircraft carriers as a fighter pilot and was assigned to a navy fleet fighting the Japanese in the South Pacific. Warren was credited with destroying the first Japanese Zero in the new Grummen Hellcat fighter. Just days before Christmas in 1943, his plane was shot down. Although he was wounded, he parachuted into the ocean, where he swam to the shore of a nearby island. Natives kept him safe initially, but eventually the enemy discovered his location, and he became a prisoner of war. On June 3, 1944, the lack of food and medicine ultimately claimed Warren's life as he lay in the arms of fellow pilot Joe Nason. It would be more than a year before the Warrens were sure their son was dead. They would never learn where he was buried. For his bravery, Warren was awarded the Distinguished Flying Cross. (Courtesy of Steve Warren.)

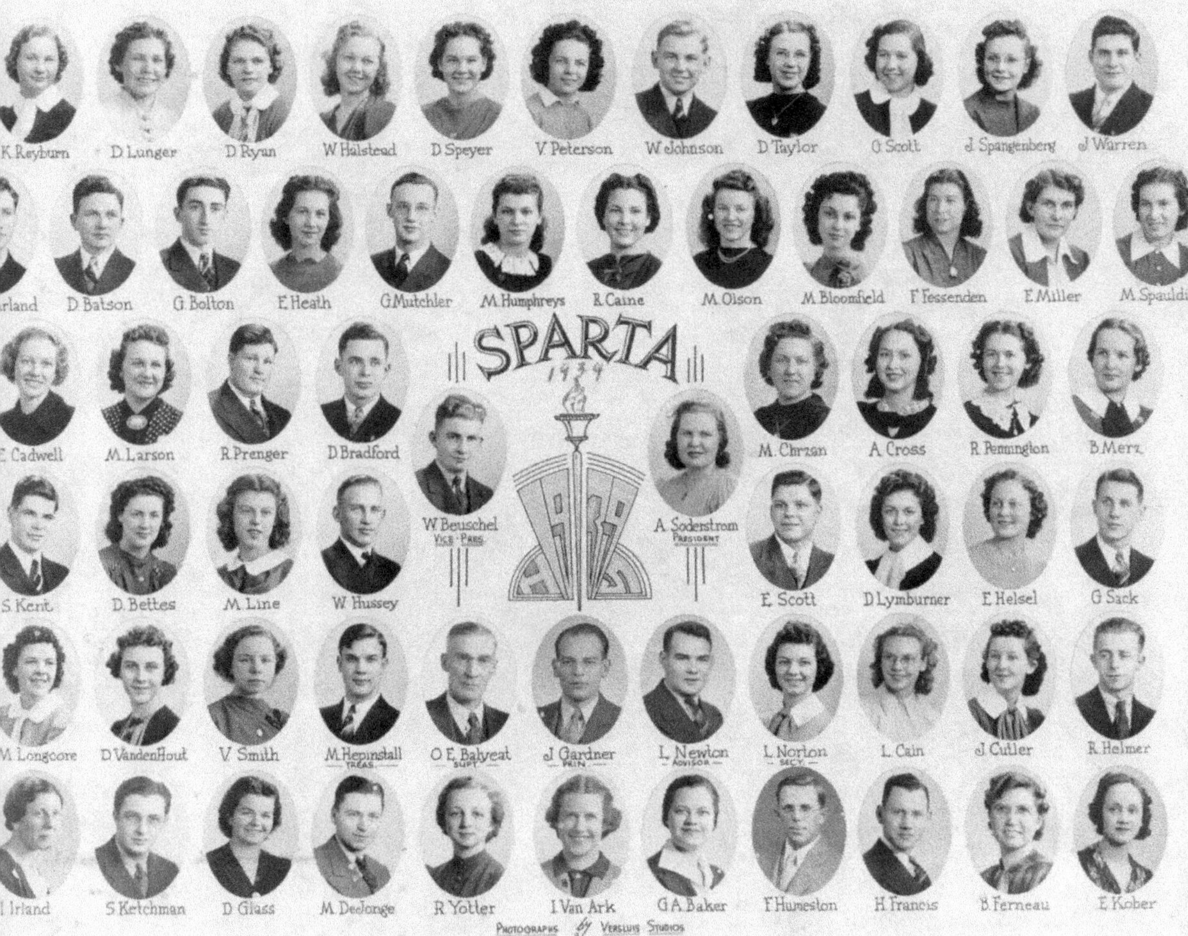

Jim Warren, upper right, graduated from Sparta High School in 1939. He was a running back and the captain of his football team. Warren led his team to the cochampionship of the Ken-O-Wa League. He also played basketball and competed in the pole vault and high jump for the track team. He went on to play football for Grand Rapids Junior College and Michigan State College, but with war looming in 1941, Warren was ready to join the fight. In 1960, Warren's friend and football teammate Dean Bradford requested that a memorial award be established in Warren's name to honor his lost friend. Each year since then, the James Warren Athletic Award has been awarded to Sparta High School's most outstanding athlete. Warren was one of many remarkable young men from Sparta to serve the United States and to die a hero's death. Warren's sister-in-law Dorothy Warren McCready said, "Jim would be proud of each recipient."

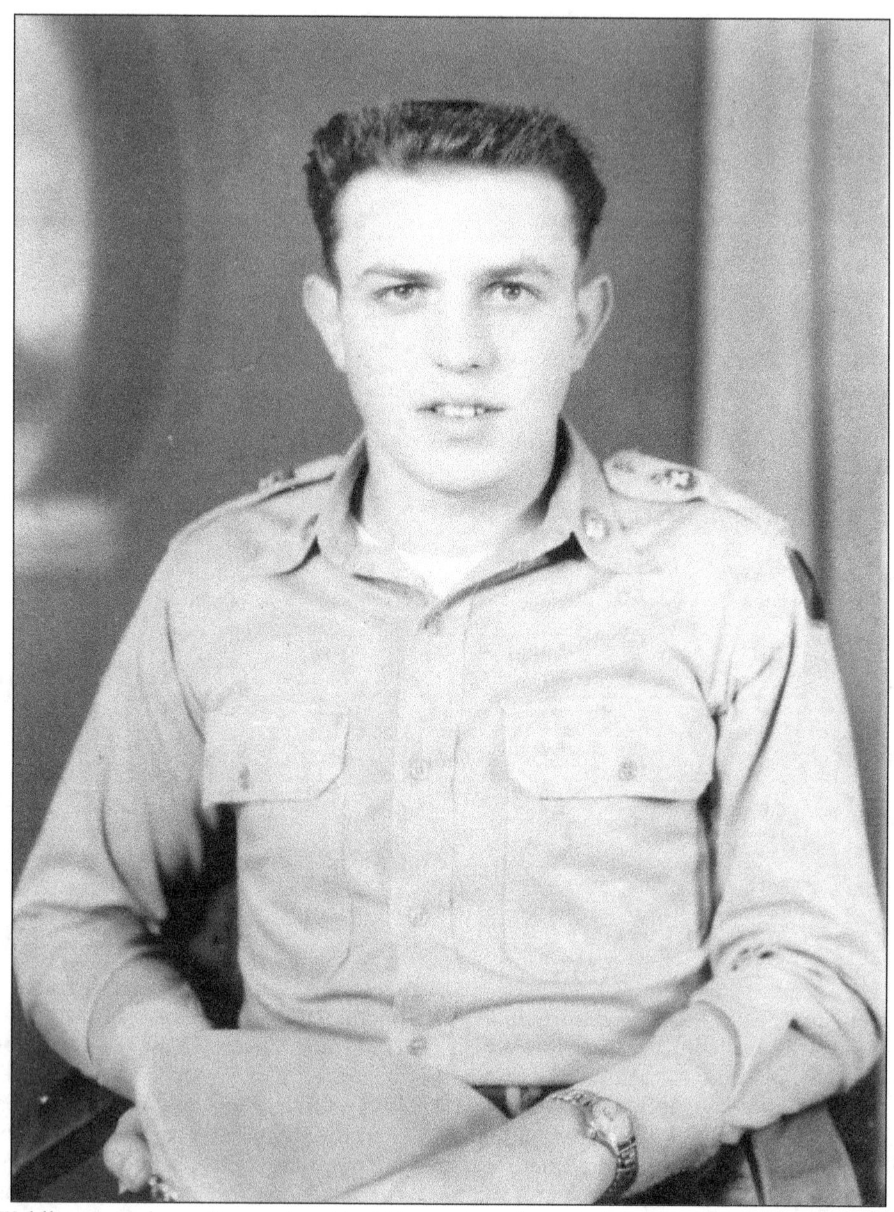

Max Waldherr was born September 13, 1929, and graduated from Sparta High School in 1947. He joined the army in September 1948. Max was wounded in September 1950. He recovered and was sent back to the front line to help take Seoul. In a letter written to his sister Mary on October 24, 1950, Max writes, "I'm glad I have so many people praying for me because it's only God's will that I'm living today." Max was reported missing December 2, 1950. After his mother spent years seeking comrades who may have known what happened to Max, the family held a funeral service. A letter from the Department of the Army dated October 24, 1955, states, "That information has now been received that your son was killed in action in Korea on December 2, 1950." Sergeant Waldherr's body was returned to the United States and was buried in Arlington National Cemetery where his mother believed he would receive more recognition. However, his sister believes the reason they had him buried in Arlington and not Sparta was that her parents could not bear to have another funeral. (Courtesy of Mary Waldherr Dunneback.)

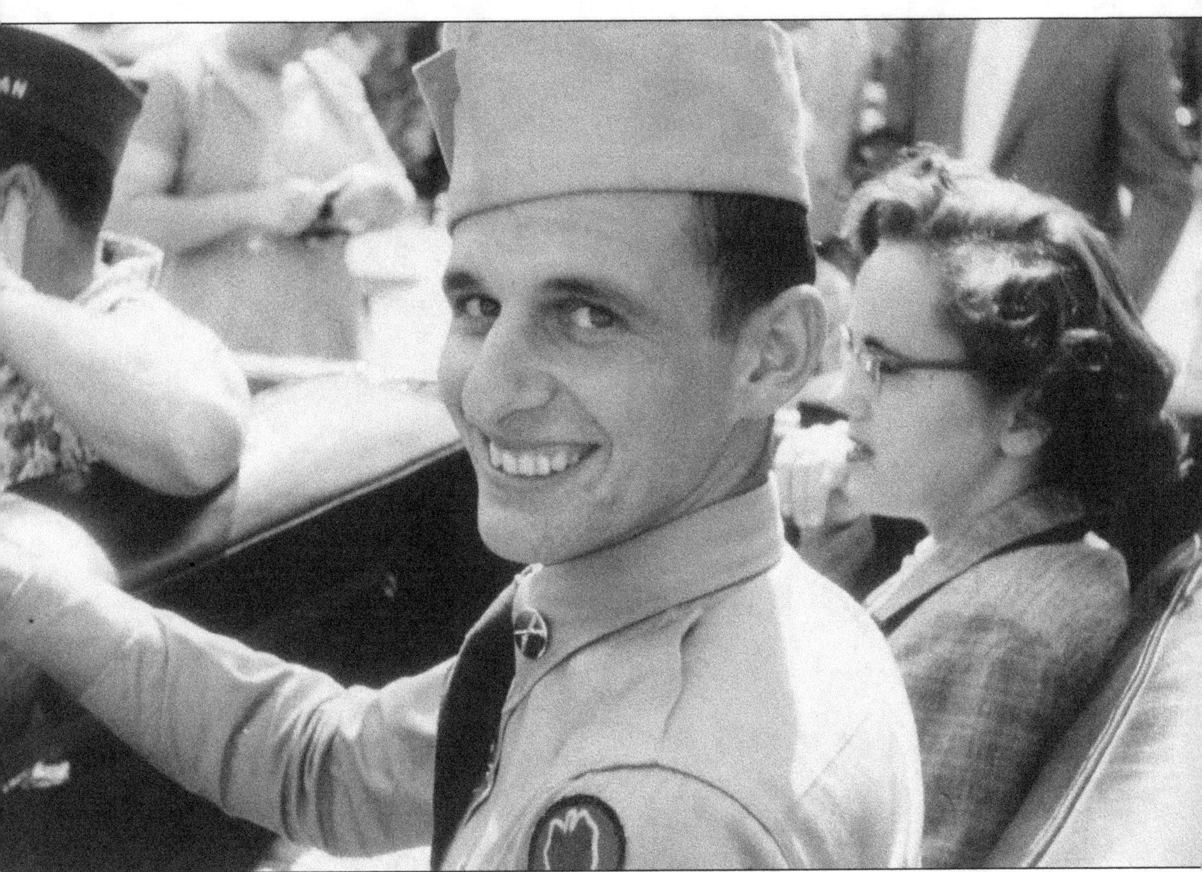

Pvt. Carl Woolworth, a 1947 graduate of Sparta High School, was drafted into the Korean War in October 1950. A member of the 24th Infantry Division, he was captured during the Chinese Communist Force's Spring Offensive, the largest battle of the war. He was forced to march over 200 miles to spend the next 28 months in a prisoner of war camp. Dick Darling and Al Keck, also of Sparta, were captured and held in another camp. Woolworth, son of H. M. and Mary Woolworth, once said he kept his sanity by keeping his faith. The armistice was signed July 26, 1953, on Carl's 25th birthday. Later the Woolworths received a telegram from Carl in Tokyo, which read, "Am on the right side of the bamboo curtain and I am free. Am on the boat. Tell everyone. One look at your faces and I will be alright." More than 1,000 citizens of Sparta were on hand to welcome Pfc. Carl Woolworth home on Labor Day 1953. He won seven bronze stars.

This is it!

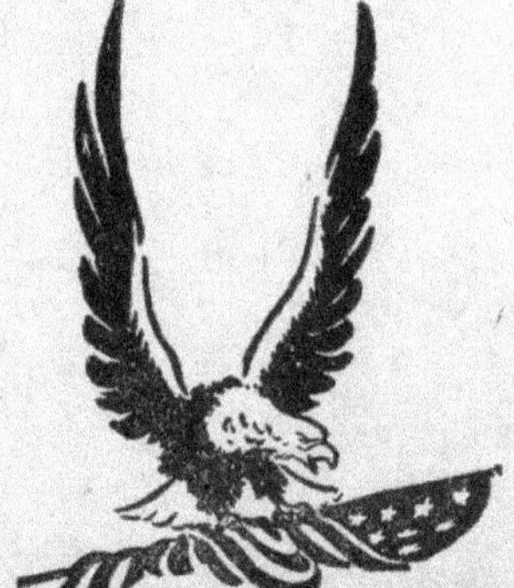

V-J DAY

SURRENDER OF JAPAN

WILL COME SOON

let's be ready

AT SOUND OF FIRE SIREN, WHISTLES AND BELLS, GO AT ONCE TO VILLAGE PARK. PLANS HAVE BEEN FORMULATED FOR A PROGRAM CONSISTING OF PARADE, NOISE, TRUCKS, SINGING, MUSIC, ICE CREAM, ETC.

V-J. COMMITTEE

"Most terrible of all wars ends," screamed the headline in the *Sentinel Leader* on August 16, 1945. The official announcement of the unconditional surrender of Japan had been received on Tuesday evening, August 14, 1945. Sparta's citizens gathered for a joyful celebration, led by school superintendant William H. DeHart. A victory program was staged at the village park on Tuesday night. Reverend Coxon prayed for permanent peace, the high school band played under the direction of Jack Davis, and singing the "Star Spangled Banner" was Georgia Bettes. A big parade was led by members of the local legion post, followed by an especially noisy group of young boys on a foundry truck banging on a huge piece of sheet metal. Sparta's fire truck was loaded with kids, and there were many marching civilians. To quote the article that day in the *Sentinel Leader*, "To you who have sent your sons to battle for us, and got back only a telegram or medal in his place, we owe our lives and liberty!"

Four

CHURCHES

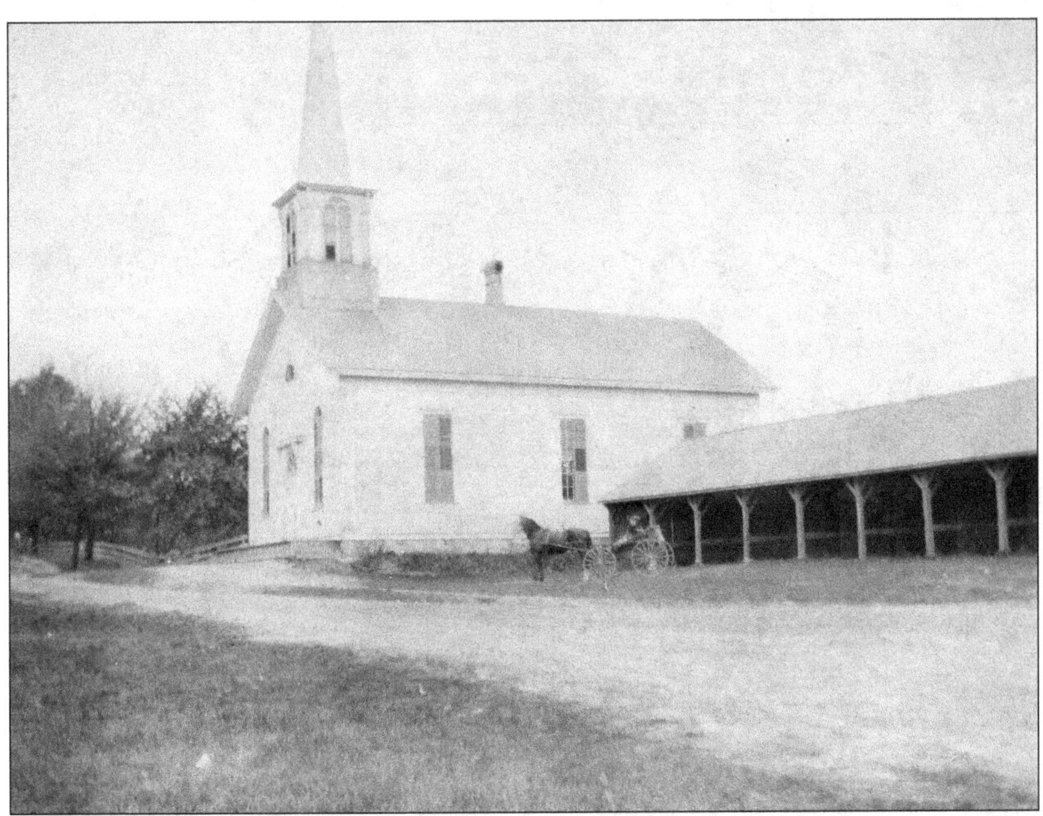

The First Church of Alpine and Sparta, as it was originally named, was built in the late 1860s. It was built on land donated by Lyman and Lusina Ballard, at the adjacent three corners of Ten Mile Road and Sparta Avenue. Built on their land, a schoolhouse and a general store were also constructed in addition to the church. The Ballard Church of Christ at Ballard's Corner is a landmark for its steeple, because it is visible for miles around.

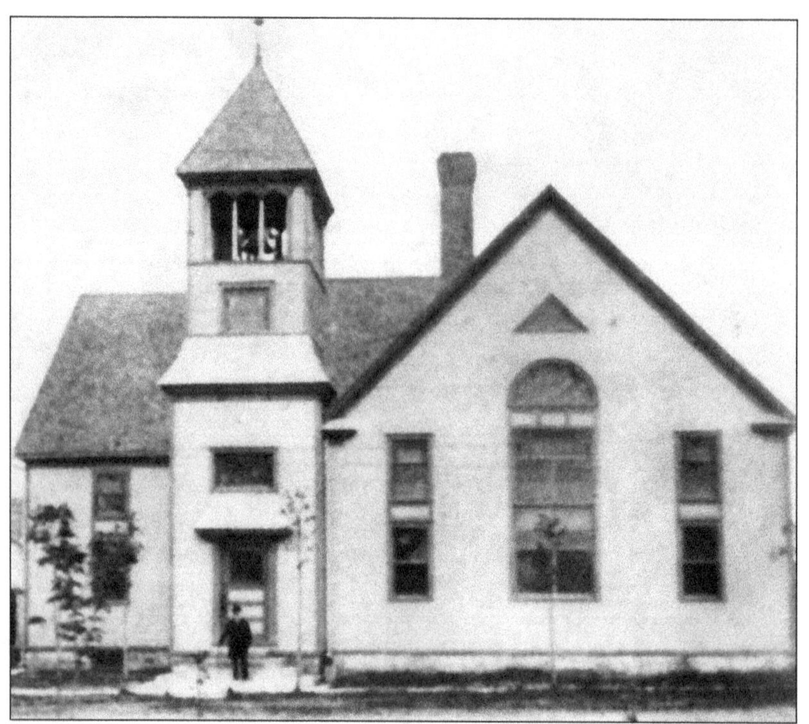

At some point before 1853, the Free Will Baptist Church Society was organized. While there are no records to show where the newly formed congregation met, it is believed they held services in the Nash Schoolhouse. Rev. Erastus W. Norton was called to serve both the Baptist church and Ballard Church of Christ.

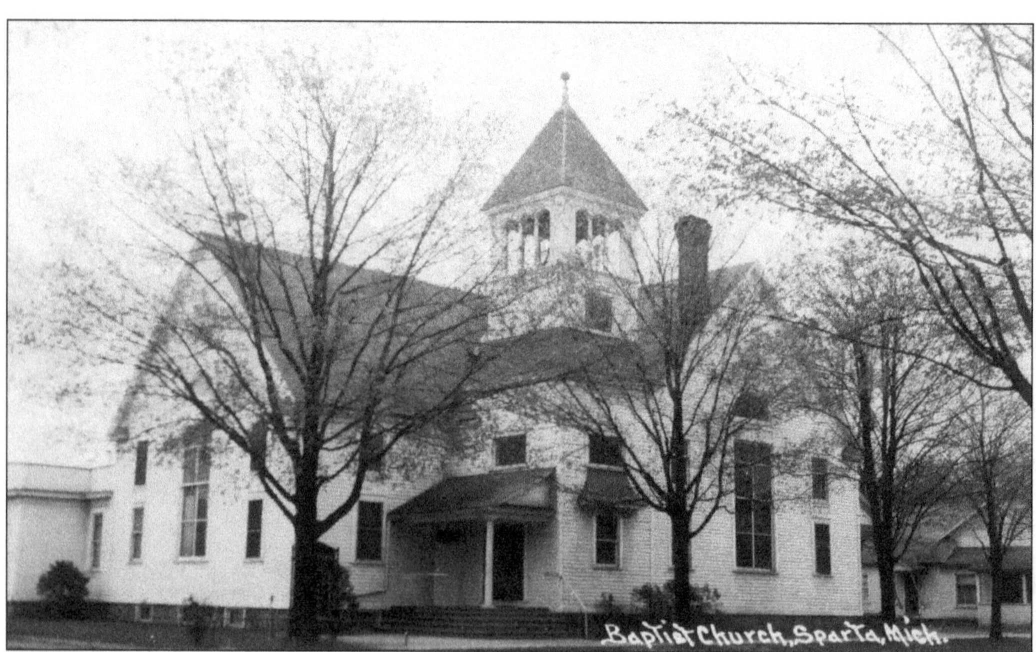

Records show the Sparta Baptist Church was built in 1866 for $3,000. It is believed that the plans used for the Baptist church may be the same plans used years later for the Methodist church, as the original church buildings are strikingly similar. Over the years, many changes and additions were made to accommodate the growing church congregation.

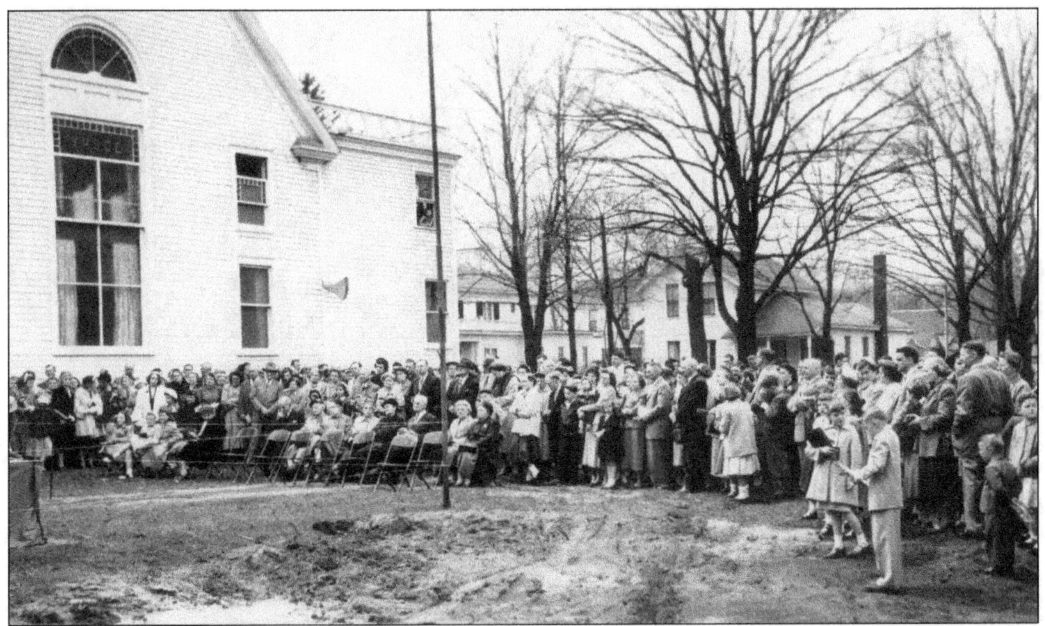

In 1912, Dwight M. Warner sold his lot, located at the corner of Division and State Streets, to the Sparta Baptist Church. The church used the Warner house as the parsonage until 1953. In 1954, a new parsonage and educational building were completed. Pictured above is the ground breaking for the new Sparta Baptist Educational Building.

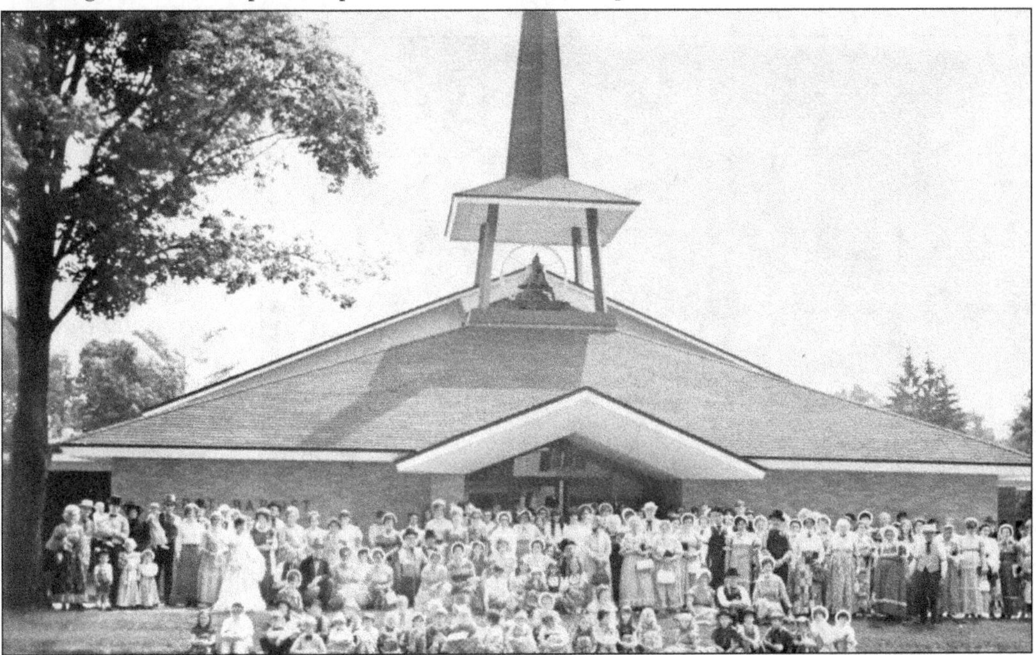

In 1969, the old church was torn down to make way for a new church, which would house the growing Baptist congregation. Leaving only the old bell and the pulpit furniture, a brand new church was constructed. On December 6, 1970, the new church was dedicated. Members of the Baptist congregation are posing in their quasquicentennial finery in front of the new building in 1971, celebrating Sparta's 125th anniversary.

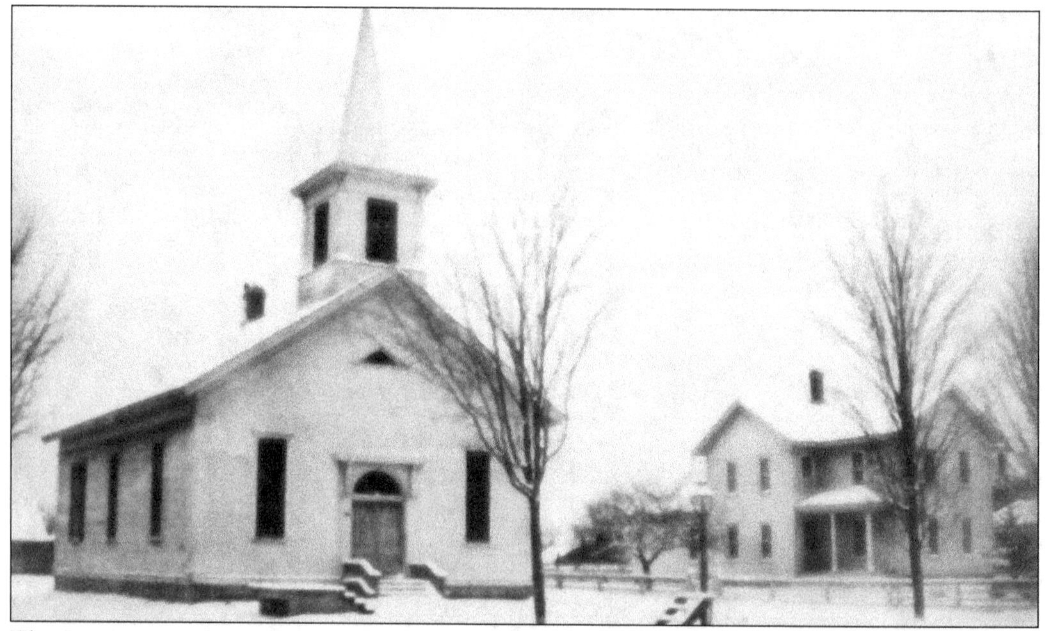

The Sparta United Methodist Church was organized in 1852 as the Methodist Episcopal Church. It initially met in various homes and later in a schoolhouse. In 1859, the church purchased land for $25 from Jonathan and Augusta Nash to house a new church building. Due to the Civil War, a new sanctuary was not completed until 1868. This wooden church stood until 1901.

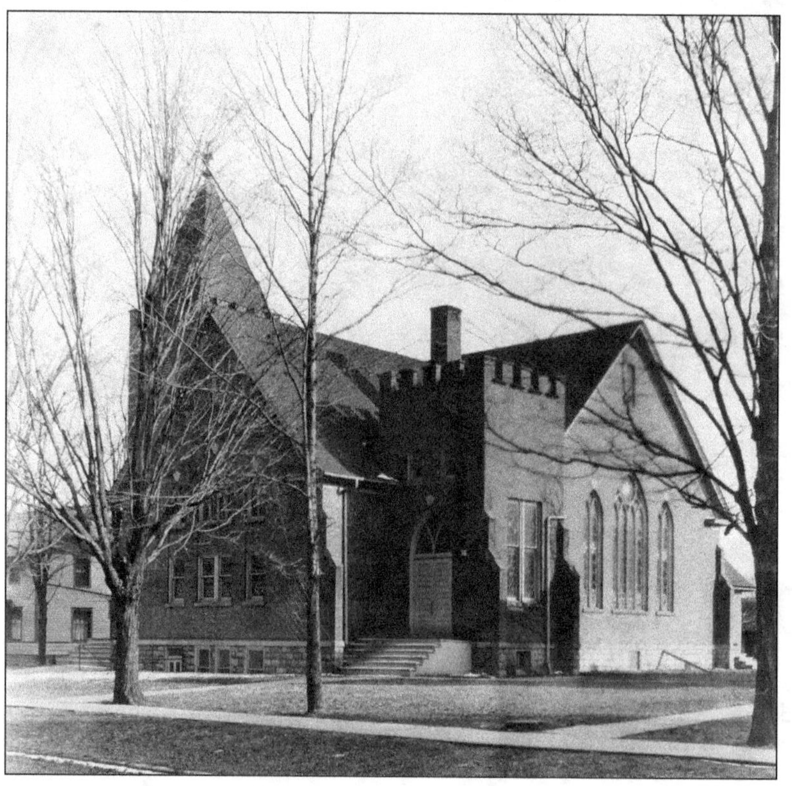

In 1901, the wooden church was torn down, and a redbrick sanctuary was built in its place. On January 30, 1927, this structure was destroyed by fire, threatening the town and requiring assistance from the Grand Rapids Fire Department. Tragically, Martin M. Murray, the 78-year-old church caretaker, perished in the blaze.

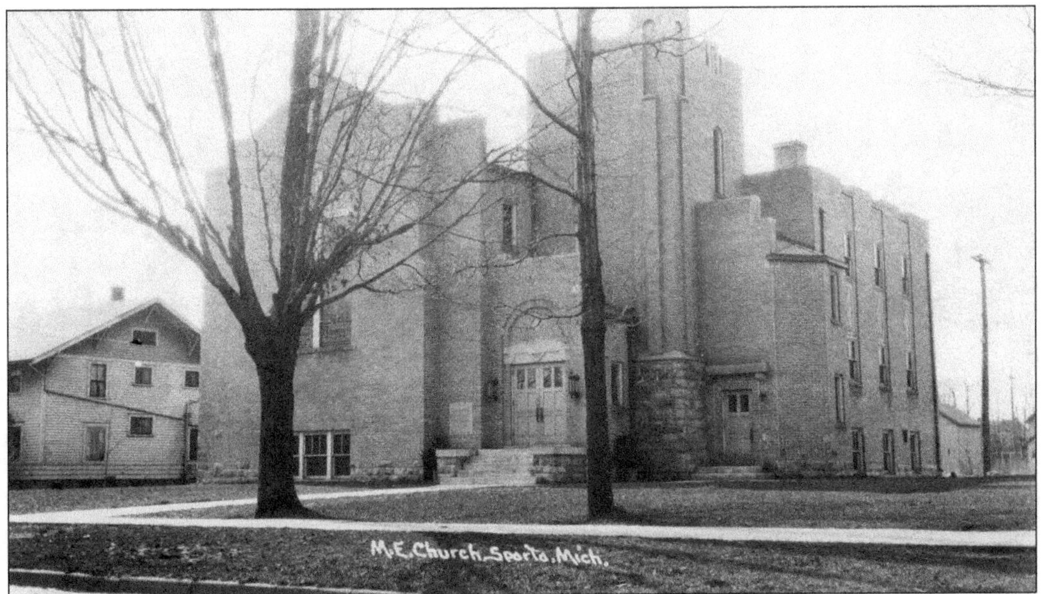

The current two-story brick structure was built and dedicated on October 16, 1927. In 1956, a 5,000-square-foot educational building was completed. In that same year, plans began to complete a new parsonage. On February 1, 1960, the old frame parsonage was torn down, making way for a new brick structure.

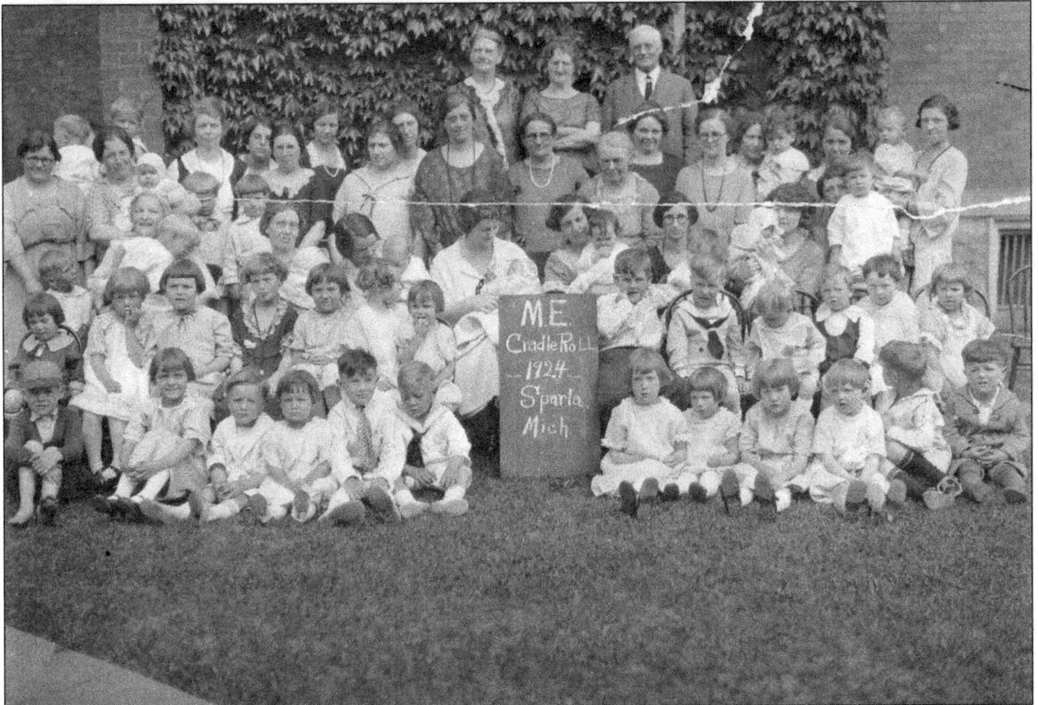

Pictured above is a photograph of the children and mothers of the 1924 Methodist Evangelical Cradle Roll. At one time a common practice among churches, cradle rolls were comprised of children grouped from birth to three years old who had been baptized or dedicated in the church, in this case the Methodist Evangelical Church.

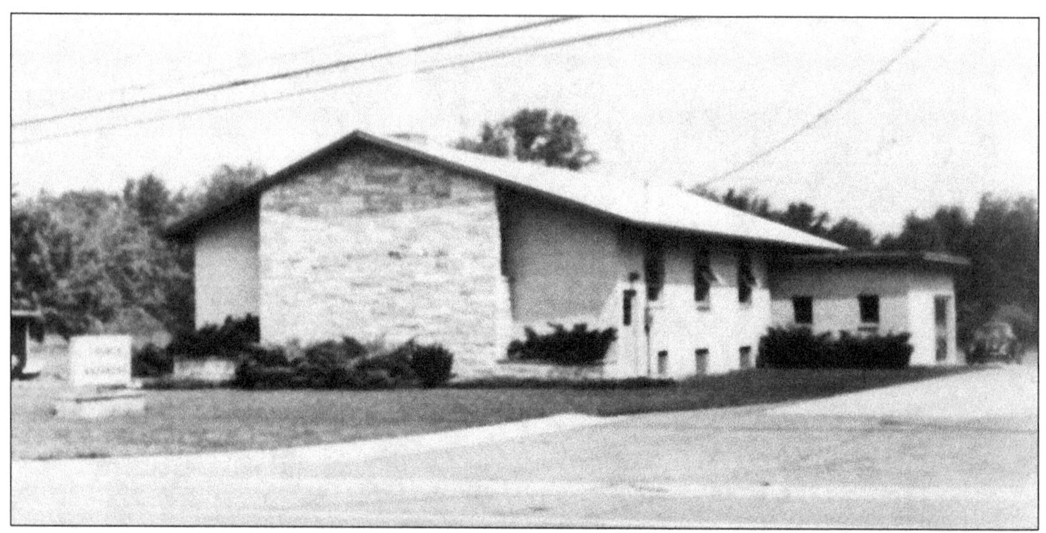

Organized in 1946, the Church of the Nazarene first held services in a structure located on Grove Street. In November 1961, the current location on Thirteen Mile Road was purchased. Building of the sanctuary was completed in April 1966. The new sanctuary was dedicated Sunday, May 15, 1966.

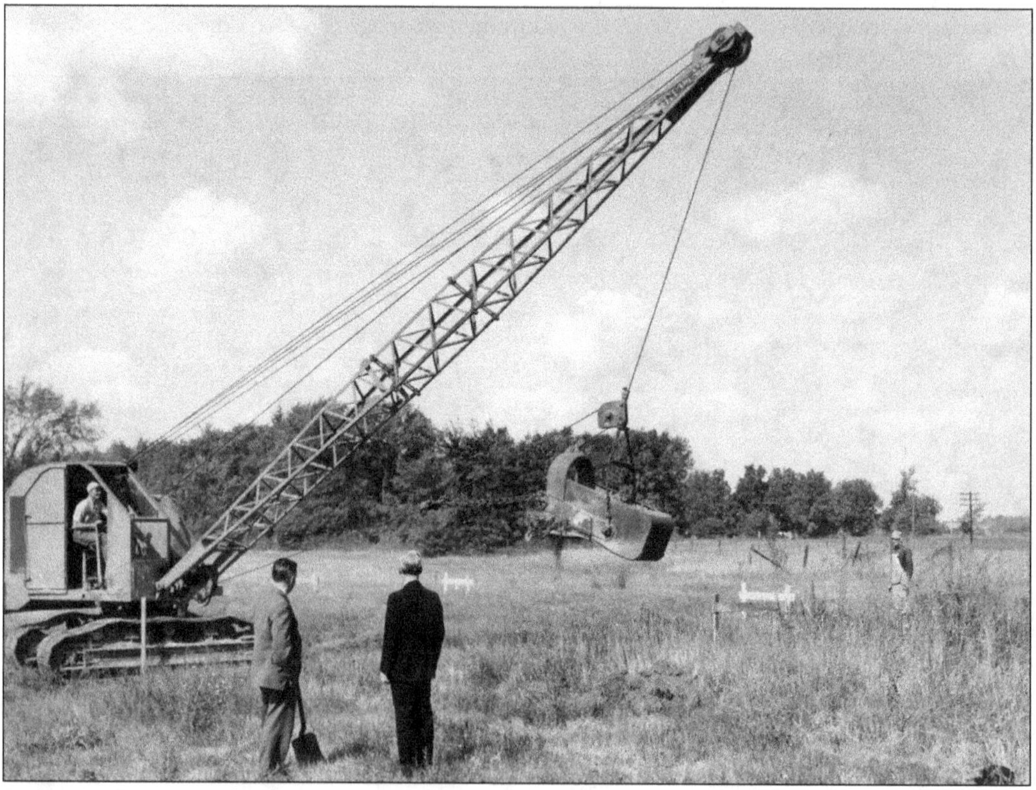

Father McKenna is shown observing the progress of the new Holy Family Church building. Construction was approved for a new church in June 1962 at an estimated cost of $230,500. The first Mass was celebrated on Thursday, August 15, 1963. It was not until October 27, 1963, that a diocese-wide open house was held.

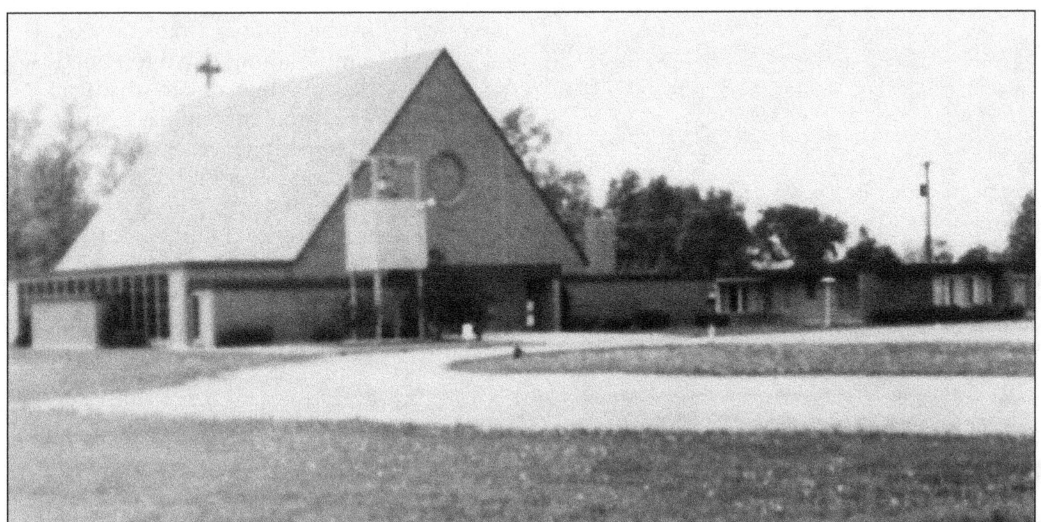

Established in 1947, Holy Family Catholic Church is located on Sparta Avenue, just south of downtown Sparta. As Sparta's only Catholic church, Holy Family is home to an active and large congregation. Before the church was built, Mass was held in Sparta's Township Hall, located on North State Street, just north of Division Street.

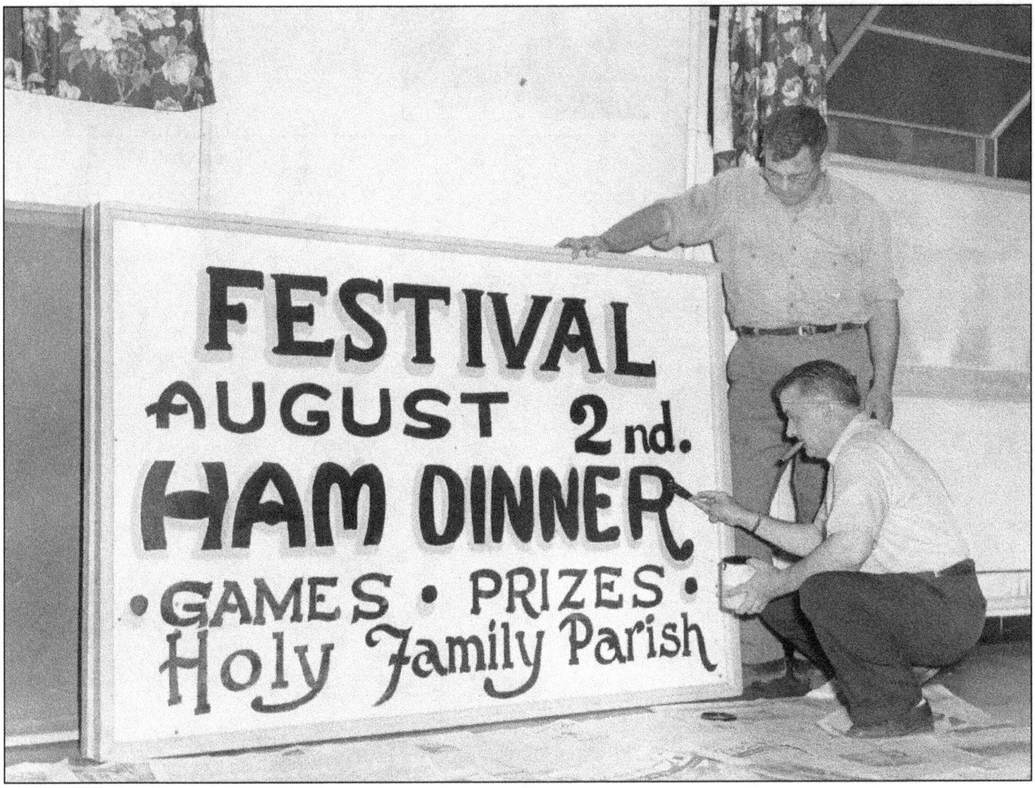

More than 2,000 meals were served by the kitchen committee for the Holy Family's ham dinner and festival on August 2, 1955. Winner of a 1,100-pound Hereford steer named Hector and a Frigidaire Deep Freeze was Henry Smolenski of Grand Rapids. The general chairman, John VanLeeuwen, is shown painting the festival sign.

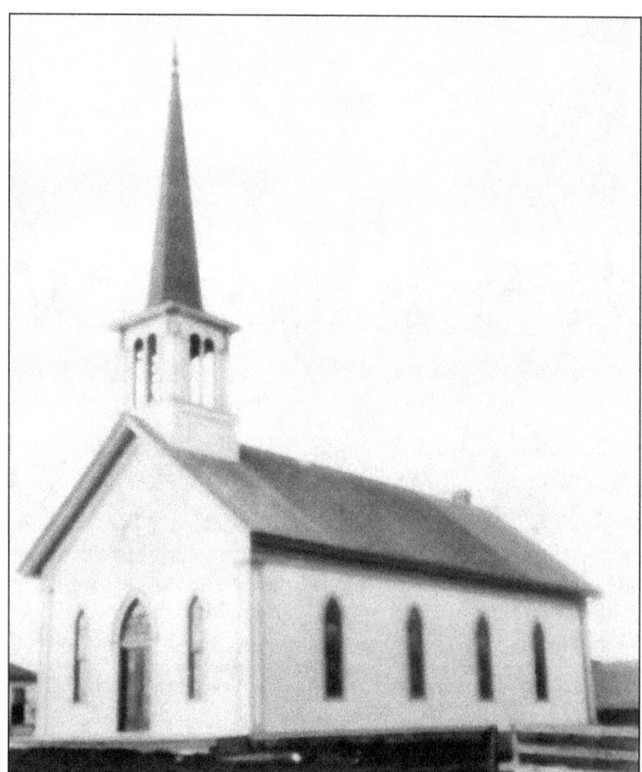

In the 1850s, a group of Swedish families immigrated to America, making their way to Michigan. This group of families began to worship together. In 1872, the congregation built a new house of worship and named it Mamrelund Lutheran. In 1957, the sanctuary, located on the corner of Fruit Ridge Avenue and Lutheran Church Road, was completed.

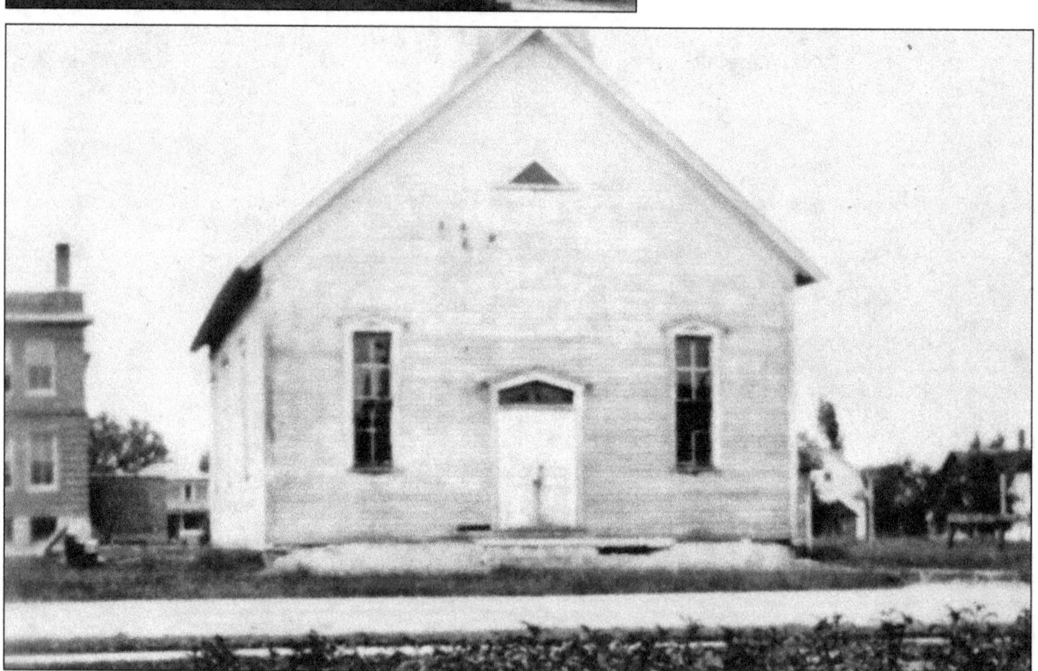

The Sparta Free Methodist Church was organized on August 15, 1884. First gathering at the Sparta Town Hall and later at the location of the fire station on North State Street, the church eventually moved to its present location in 1912. Located on the corner of Union and Grove Streets, the church still stands today.

Five

Education

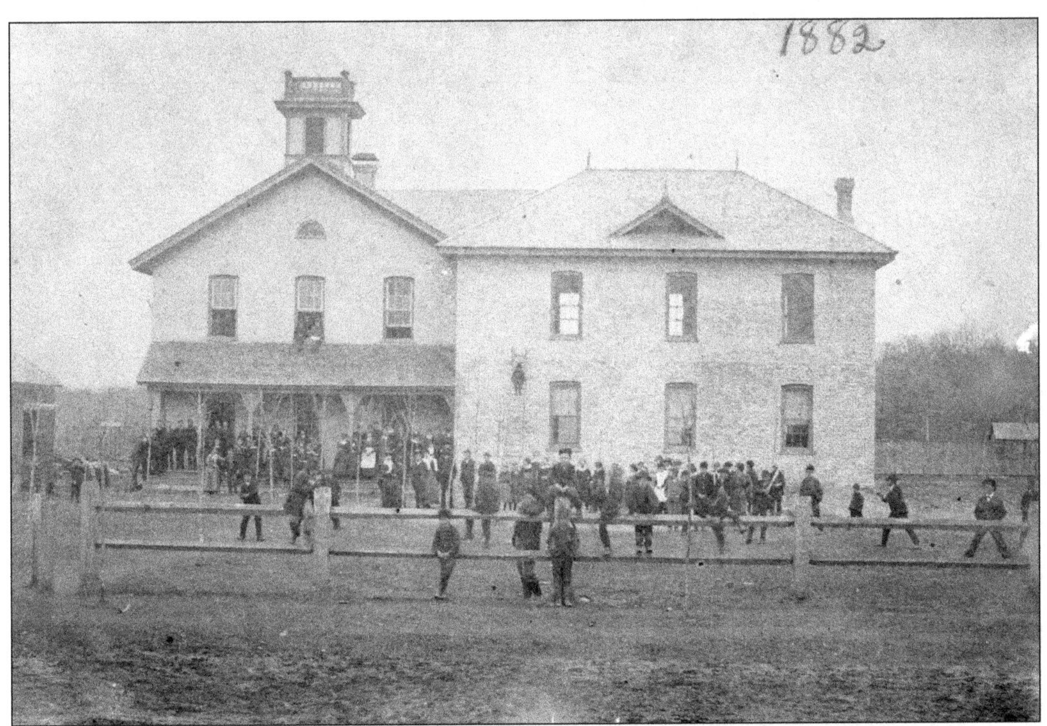

The first public high school building in Sparta was constructed in 1875. Sparta's first classes were taught by Harriet Symes in her log cabin in the late 1940s. In 1893, Sparta became a 12-grade school, with the first graduating class in 1894, which consisted of Charles Hallack, Mable Ballard, Delbert Biddleman, Mattie Dart, L. D. Purdy, Lulu Hardy, Edith Davis, and Mae Sharp.

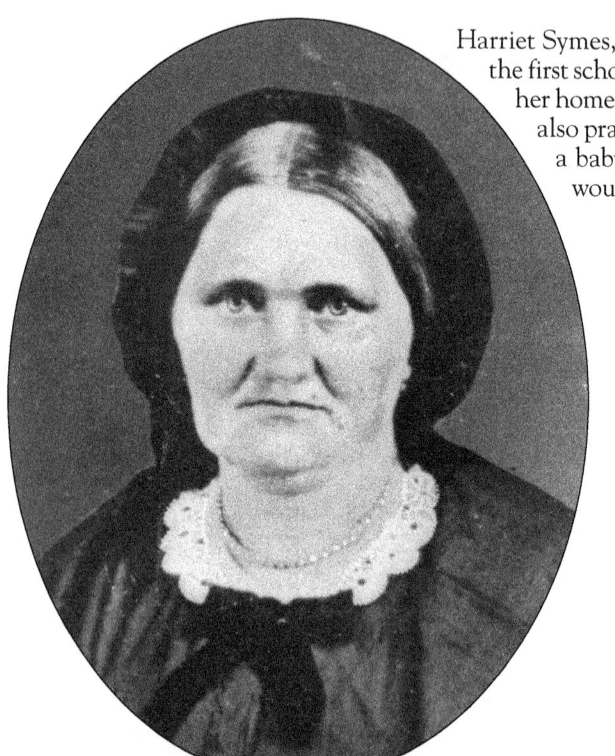

Harriet Symes, wife of John Symes, was the teacher of the first school in Sparta Township. Class was held in her home, a log cabin, just south of Sparta. Symes also practiced obstetrics, and when the birth of a baby kept her from her work, her husband would step in and teach for her.

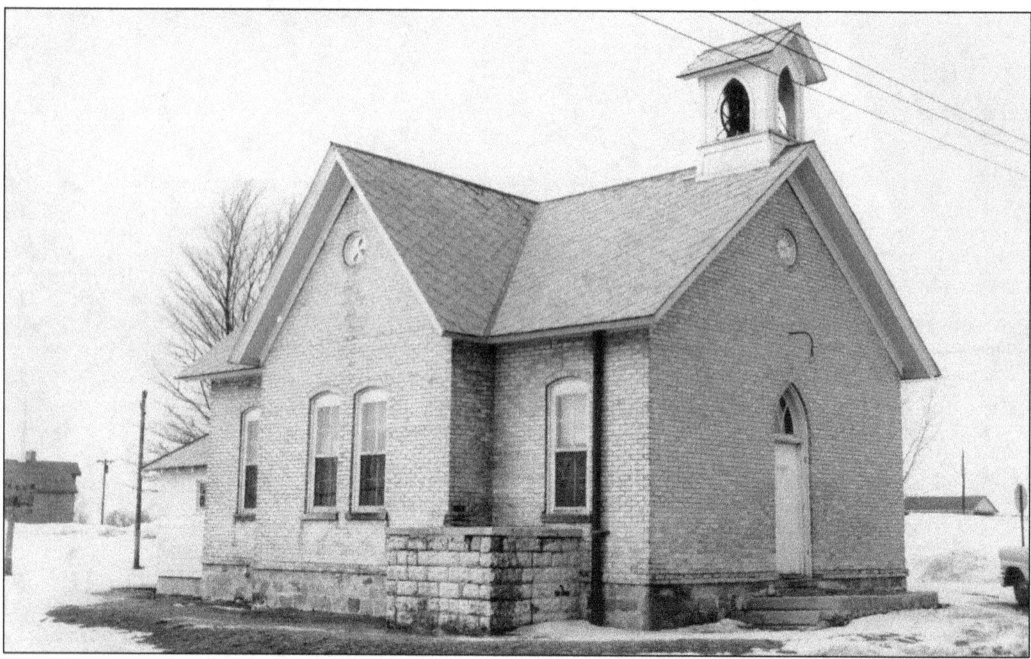

Manchester School was located on the corner of Fruit Ridge Avenue and Lutheran Church Road, near Mamrelund Lutheran Church. During recess, students would go to the church to play kickball. The building was a one-room schoolhouse with wooden desks and a hook for each student to hang his or her personal things.

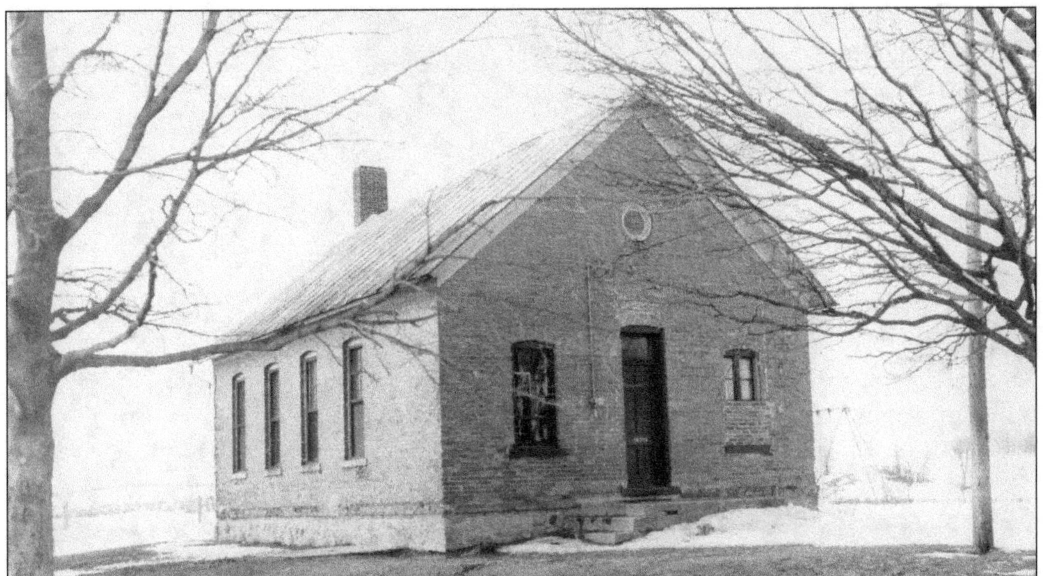

Located on Peach Ridge, between Twelve and Thirteen Mile Roads, Spangenburg School was one of many country elementary schools that fed into the Sparta school system. Originally the one-room schoolhouse enrolled kindergarten through the 10th grade, but later it would become limited to just the first and second grades.

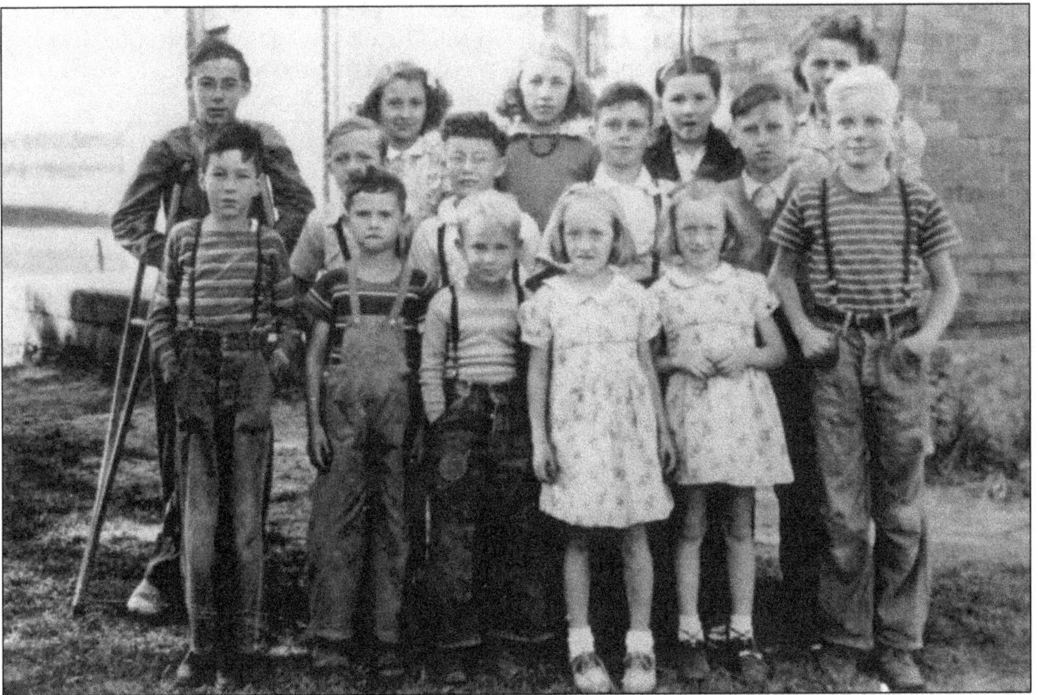

This photograph of the Spangenburg School was taken during the 1946–1947 school year. Those pictured are, from left to right, (first row) Jerry Johnson, William Longcore, Onalee Simons, Monavee Simons, and Russell Coster; (second row) Lloyd Oberg, Leon Simons, Ken Simons, John Johnson, and Leo Simons; (third row) Lowell Coster, Aloe Longcore, unidentified, Janette Longcore, and teacher Geraldene Coster.

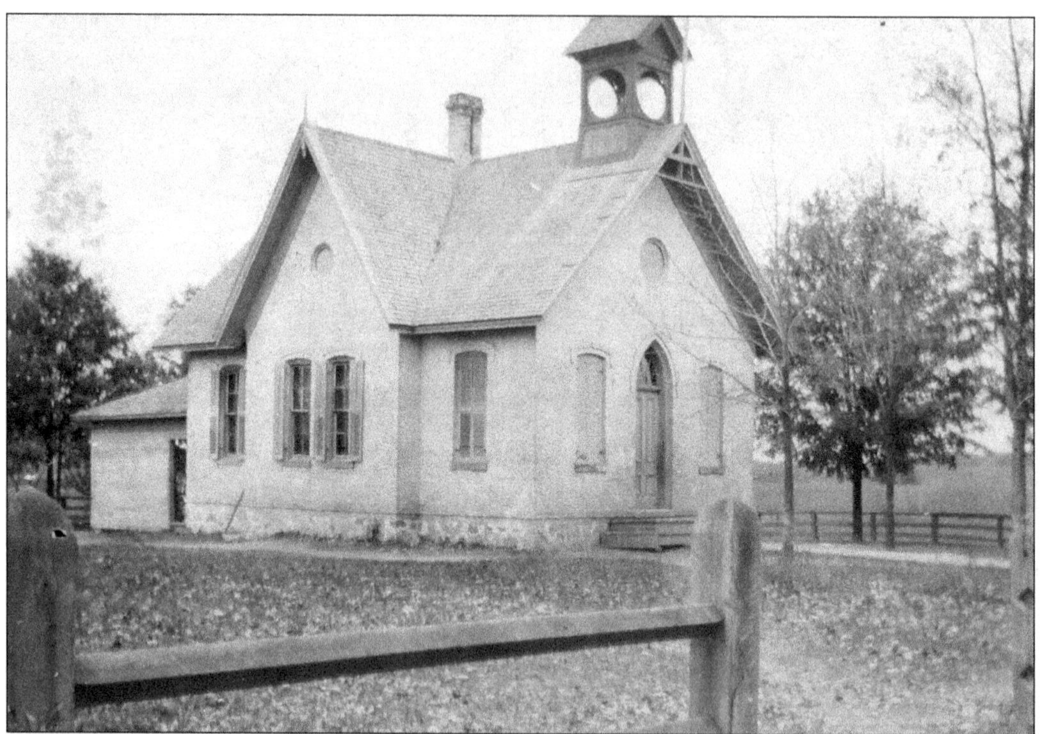

Ballard School was located on the south side of Ten Mile Road, west of Sparta Avenue. In 1850, a meeting was held to organize a school district. It was decided that the school was to be built on land donated by the Ballard family at what is known as "Ballards Corners."

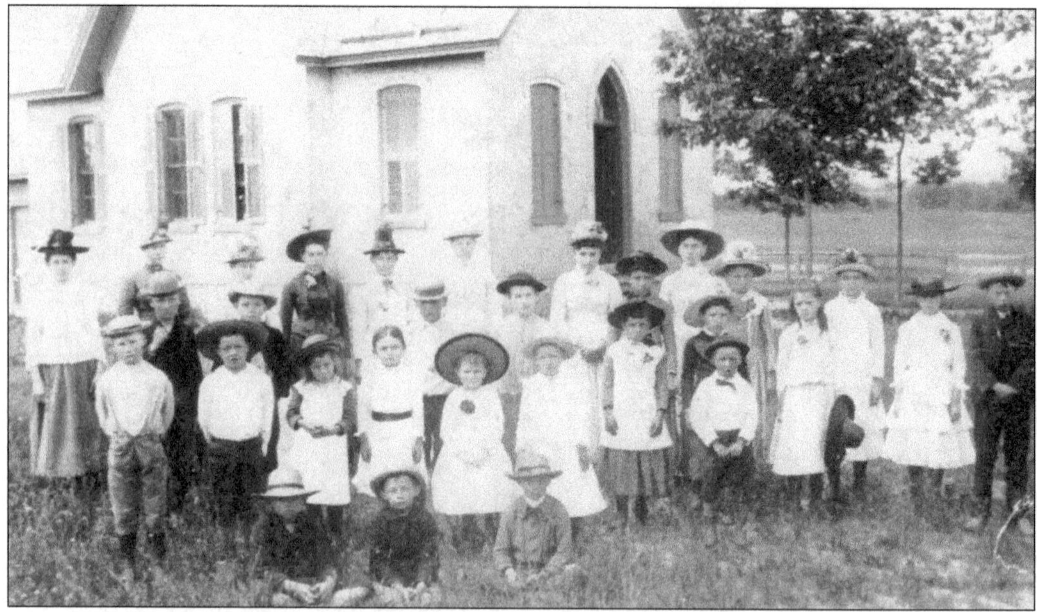

Lyman S. Ballard came to Sparta in 1850 from New York, where he was born. He and his wife, Lusina, owned three corners of the intersection at Ten Mile Road and Sparta Avenue where they opened a general store, post office, church, and the Ballard School. These students were photographed in 1888.

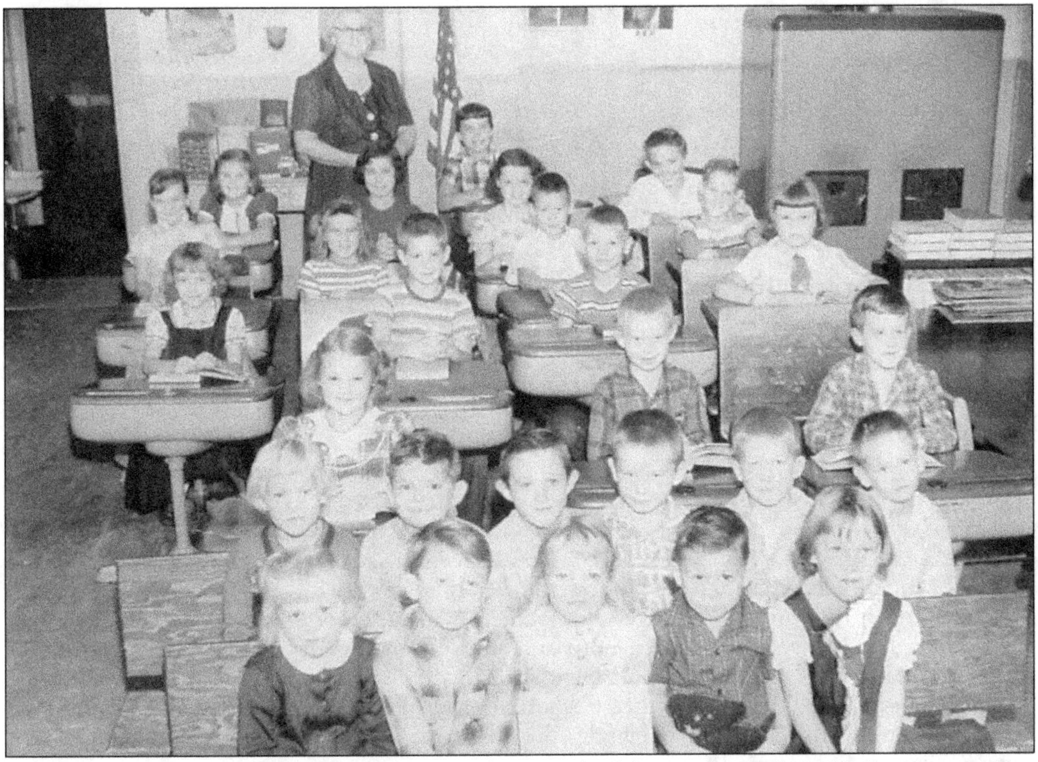

Bass school teacher Gladys Stinson's class was photographed during the 1955–1956 school year. Class members included, from left to right, (first row) unidentified, Ricky ?, Dianne Scheidel, unidentified, and Susan Burelson; (second row) Judy Procter, Billy Clark, Ed Scheidel, Tom Kotcha, Dan McCaig, and Joe Kotcha; (third row) Janet Davenport, Jimmy Swartz, and Keith McCaig; (fourth row) Kathy Burelson, Terry Beaucamp, Dan Procter, and Linda Townes; (fifth row) Sandy Hiler, Vicki Beaucamp, Jim Procter, and Jim Sargent; (sixth row) Pam Beaucamp, MaryLou Swartz, Barb Davenport and unidentified; (seventh row) teacher Gladys Stinson and Beverly Pope.

This picture is of a class reunion held at Norton School sometime in the 1920s. The Norton School building was located near the northeast corner of Phelps Avenue and Fifteen Mile Road, west of Sparta. In the 1960s, one of Sparta's principals converted this school into a home for his family.

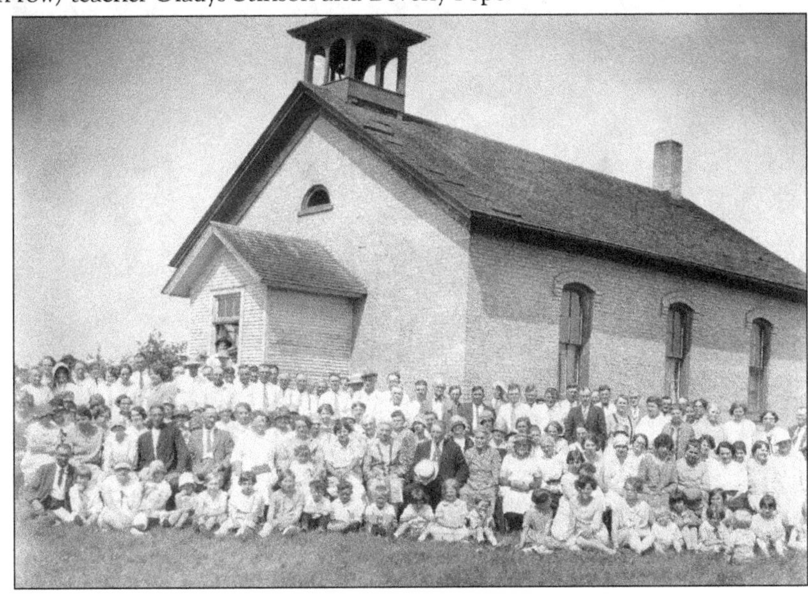

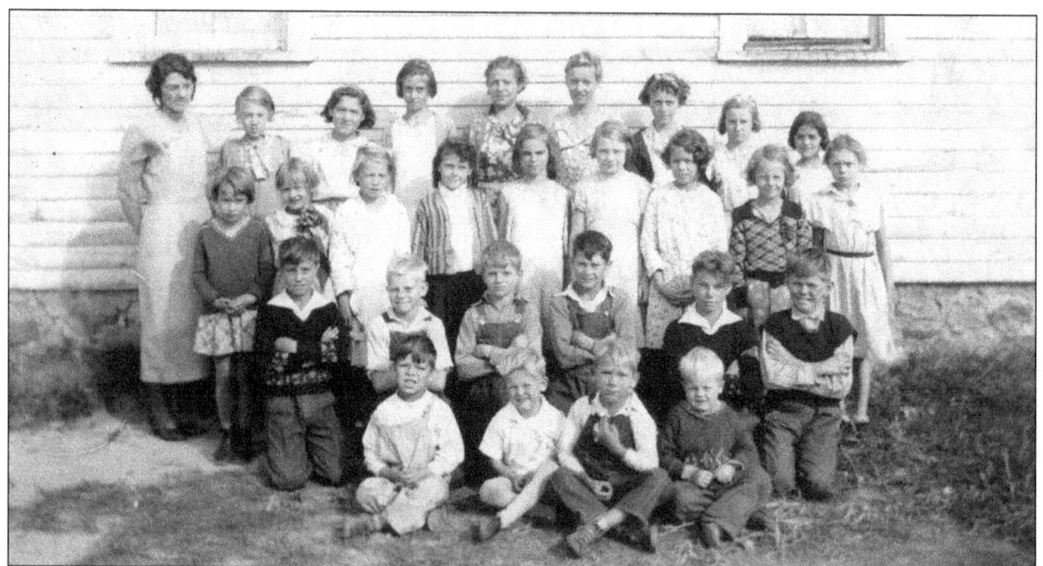

The following people, pictured from left to right, were students at Hull School during 1934–1935: (first row) Robert Reyburn, Robert Peters, Junior DeBruyn, and George Fraser; (second row) Roger Towns, Douglas Henderson, Richard DeBruyn, Tom Nestle, Dale Towns, and Bernard Reyburn; (third row) teacher Ivah Carlson, Norma Henderson, Jean Bowers, Erma Finch, Carol Lymburner, Marian Sorenson, Ireta Johnson, Dorothy Reyburn, Dorothy Fraser, and Lena Reyburn; (fourth row) Ruth Early, Ruth Pennington, Mary Henderson, Phila Finch, Gladys Bowers, Donna Lymburner, Kitty Reyburn, and Virginia Pennington.

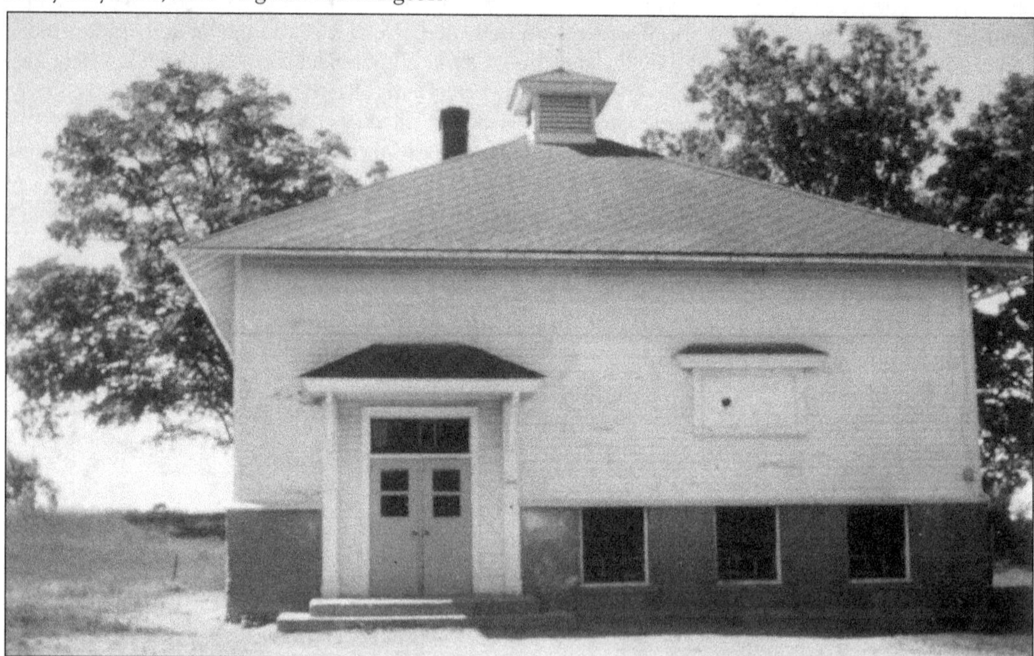

Another of Sparta's country feeder schools, Koon School, was located south of town near the intersection of Eight Mile Road and Vinton Avenue. While the school was not technically located in Sparta Township, some of the children who attended this country school did eventually transfer to Sparta High School to complete their education.

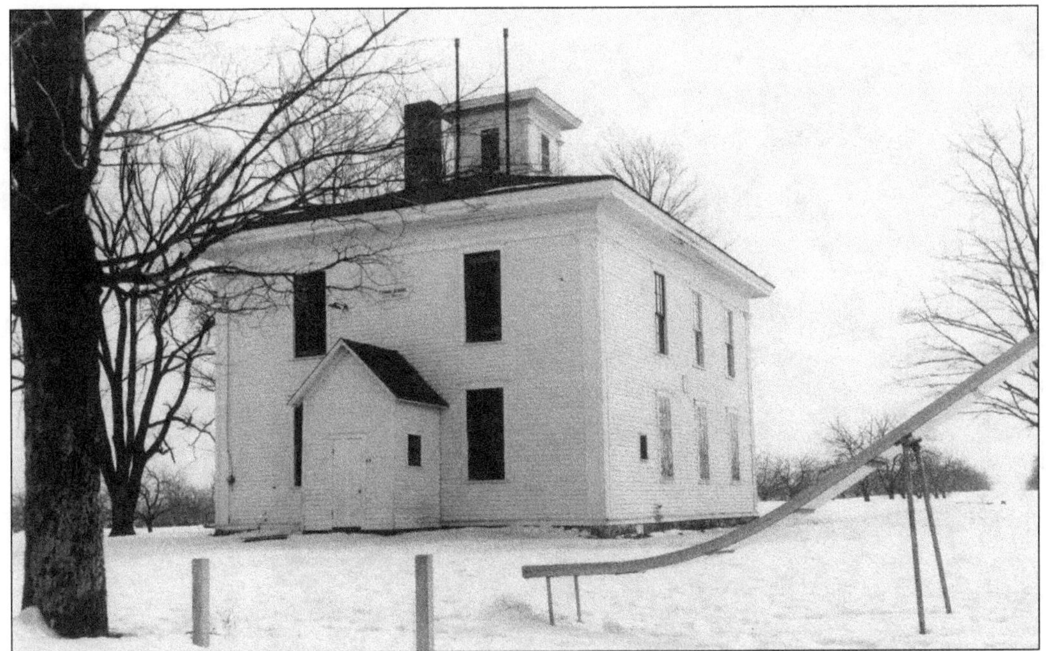

Lisbon School was located on the southwest corner of Kenowa Avenue and Twelve Mile Road. It was unique because it was a two-story schoolhouse. Music teacher Virginia Bettes Barnum came to Lisbon as well as other country schools for music education. At recess, the students sometimes played in the Schaefer's orchards nearby or used the basketball hoop in the schoolyard.

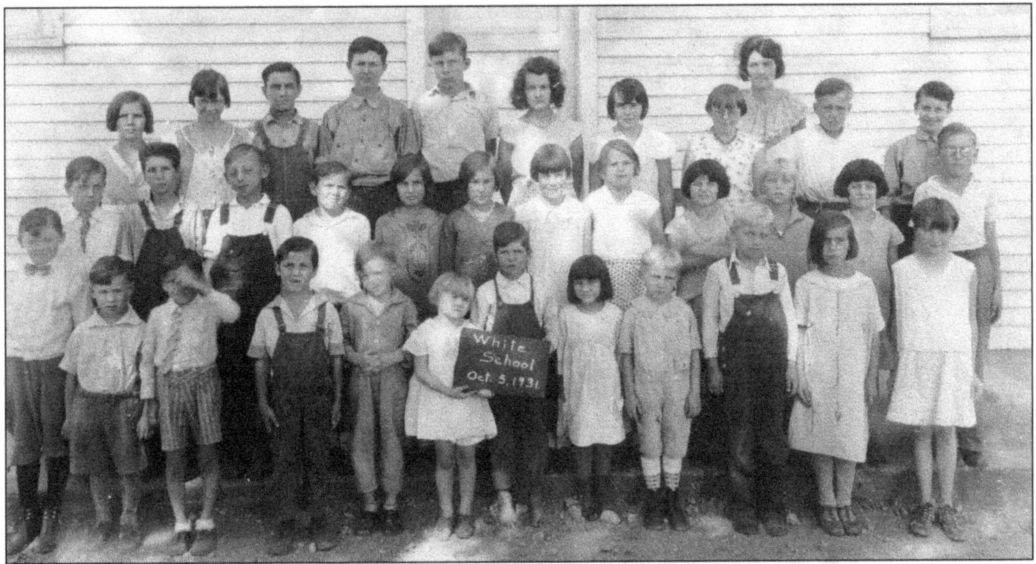

Those pictured are, from left to right, (first row) James Goodfellow, Gerald Myers, James Mullen, Harvey Hamblin, Gordon Goodfellow, June Goodfellow, Junior Morgan, Ivan Hamblin, Curtis Olson, Dominic Galinis, Emogene Hamblin, and Mildred Olson; (second row) Jack Carlson, Henry Morgan, Willie Galinis, Vernon Lewis, Irene Hamblin, Mona Lewis, Janice Goodfellow, Bernice Lewis, Louise Rice, Anna Galinis, Elaine Rice, and Gerald Lewis; (third row) Wanetta Morgan, Eleanor Dutton, Kenneth Hamblin, Carlton Rice, Hugh Olson, Marie Runyon, Irene Goodfellow, Wanda Carlson, Arthur Braford, and Lawrence Rice.

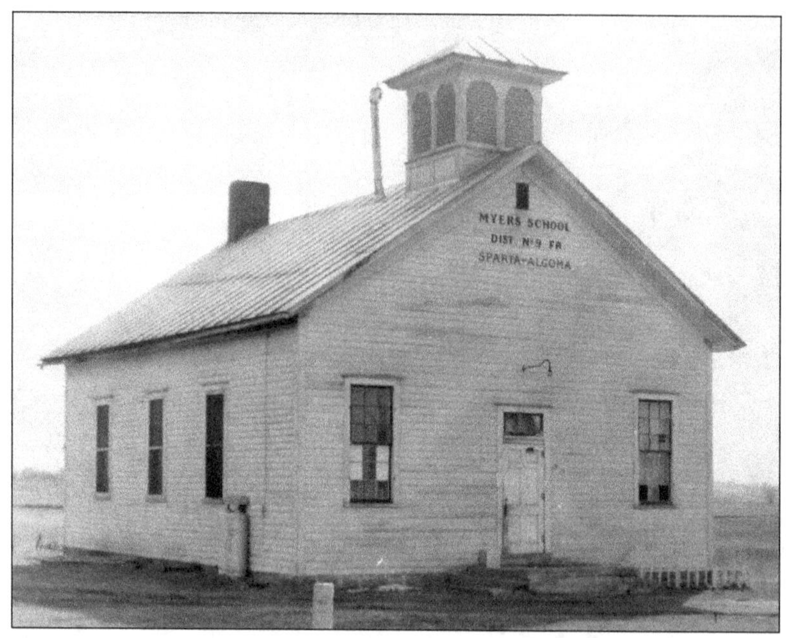

Myers schoolhouse, located on the corner of Thirteen Mile Road and North Division Avenue, is one of the most recognizable schoolhouses from the early Sparta Area School District. Named for Hiram Myers, who donated the land for the schoolhouse, the first building was constructed of logs and included a split-log teacher's desk.

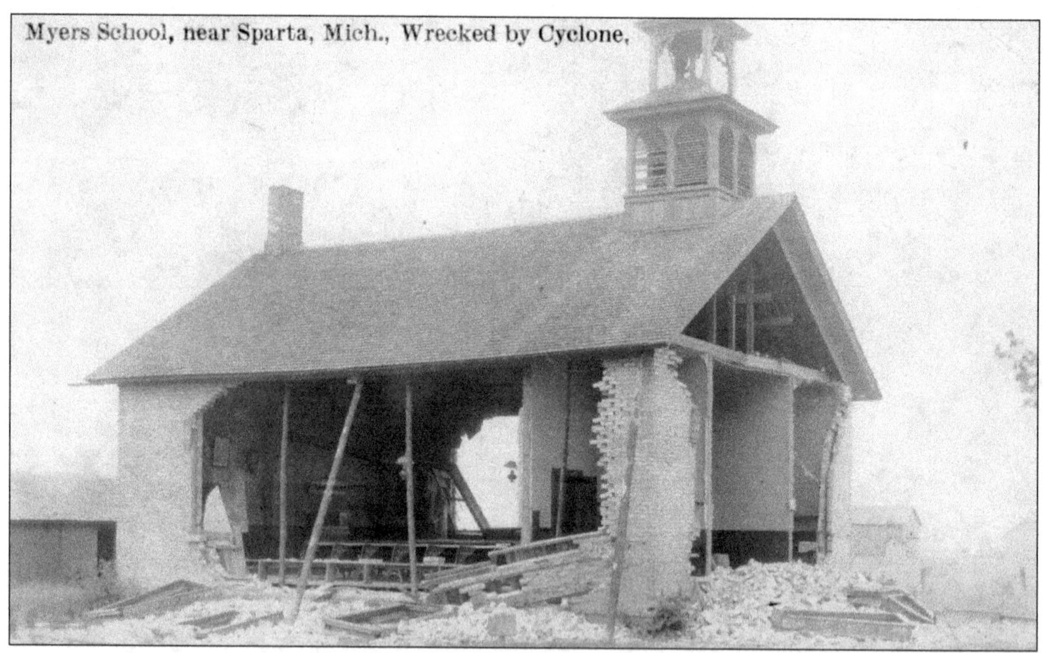

Myers School, near Sparta, Mich., Wrecked by Cyclone.

In 1890, the original log Myers schoolhouse was destroyed by fire. A new brick school building was constructed to replace the log schoolhouse. In 1921, the brick schoolhouse was completely destroyed by a tornado. A frame lumber schoolhouse was then constructed to replace the destroyed brick building.

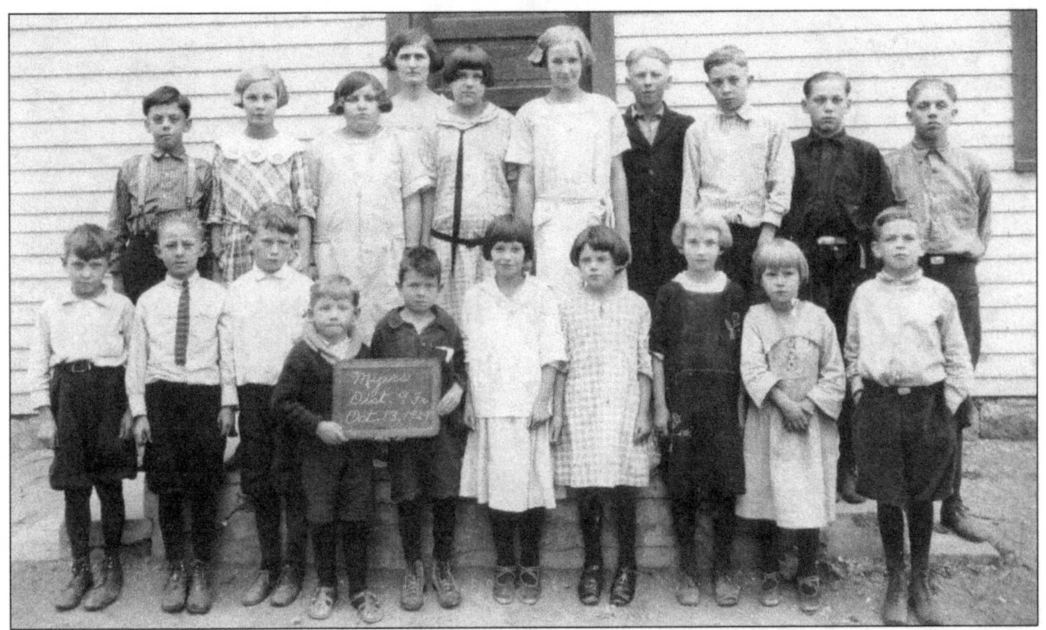

The 1924 class photograph was taken in front of the Myers schoolhouse. The students are, from left to right, (first row) Lloyd Trum, Ted Meidema, Lowell Ingersoll, Kenneth Cumings, Burt Vander Meer, Cecal Leaf, Carrie Cumings, Irene Wiersma, Evelyn Leaf, and Jesse Vander Meer; (second row) Floyd Guiles, Rolena Wiersma, Rose Cumings, teacher Sally Carlson, Nettie Clark, Mae Wiersma, Ed Chrzah, George Meyers, Albert Saur, and Howard Cumings.

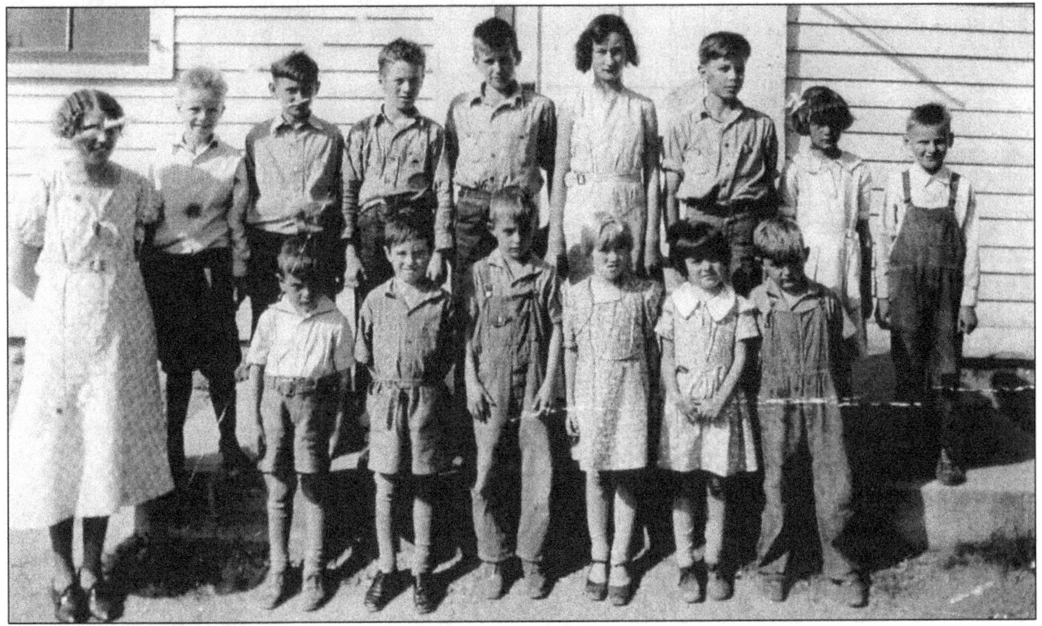

Buck School was located on the corner of Ten Mile Road and Peach Ridge Avenue. Pictured above is the class of the 1935–1936 school year. They are, from left to right, (first row) Jack Erhart, Richard Thome, Alvin Hubert, Dolores Thome, Patty Scheidel, and Orville Hubert; (second row) unidentified teacher, Donald Heft, Marvin Heft Jr., Donald Thome, Bill Platte, Dorothy Armock, Calvin Scholten, Barbara Erhart, and Richard Heft.

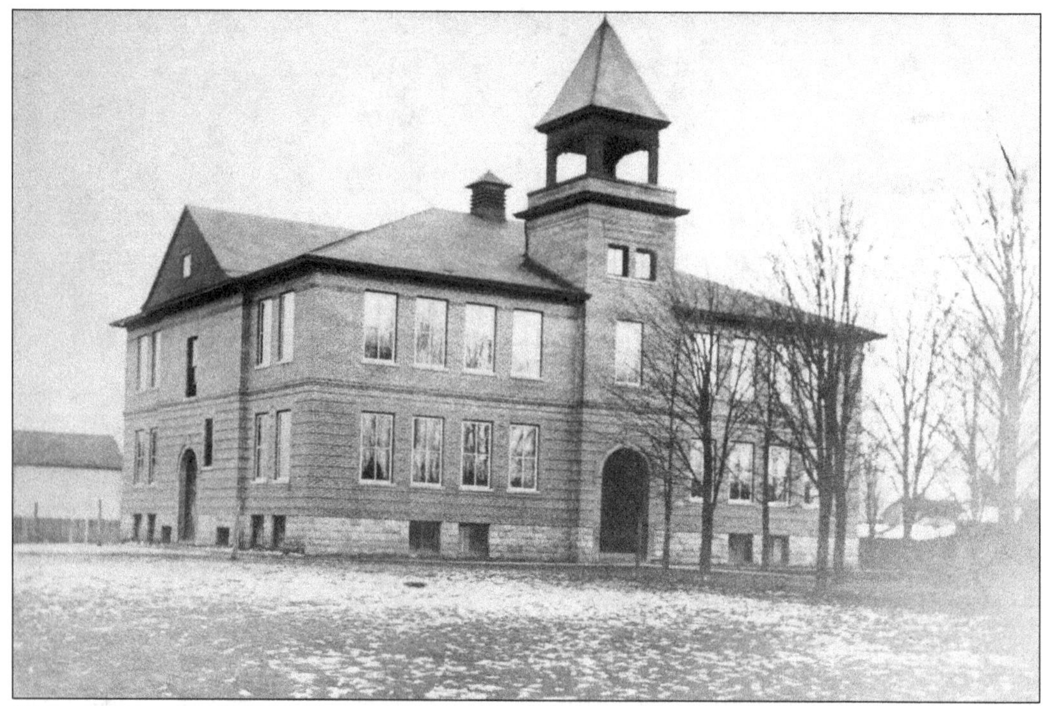

Here is a photograph of the Sparta Public School built in 1901. This school housed the in-town students from kindergarten through the 12th grade. Some of the country schools would feed into the high school at the ninth grade. The country students would leave their one-room schoolhouses to resume their studies in this large, brick building.

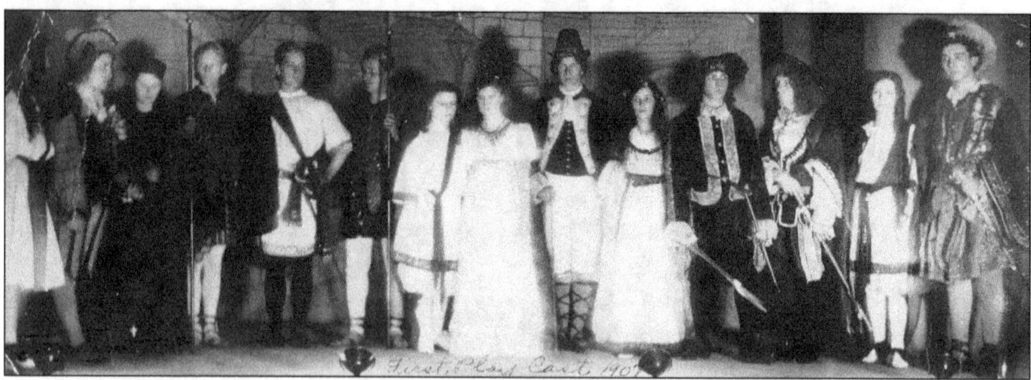

The senior class of the Sparta Baptist Church produced Shakespeare's *Twelfth Night* in 1907. The class did not want to have baccalaureate service that year, so instead of that, the students put on a play. Those pictured are, from left to right, Zoe Porter, Hazel Doyle, Maude Outhwaite, Lancy Dunn, Elmer Caukin, Miner Purdy, Fay Norton, Elva Bolender, Tracy Bloomer, Blanche Bradford, George Bettes, Clarence Moore, Lola Norton, and C. Loomis.

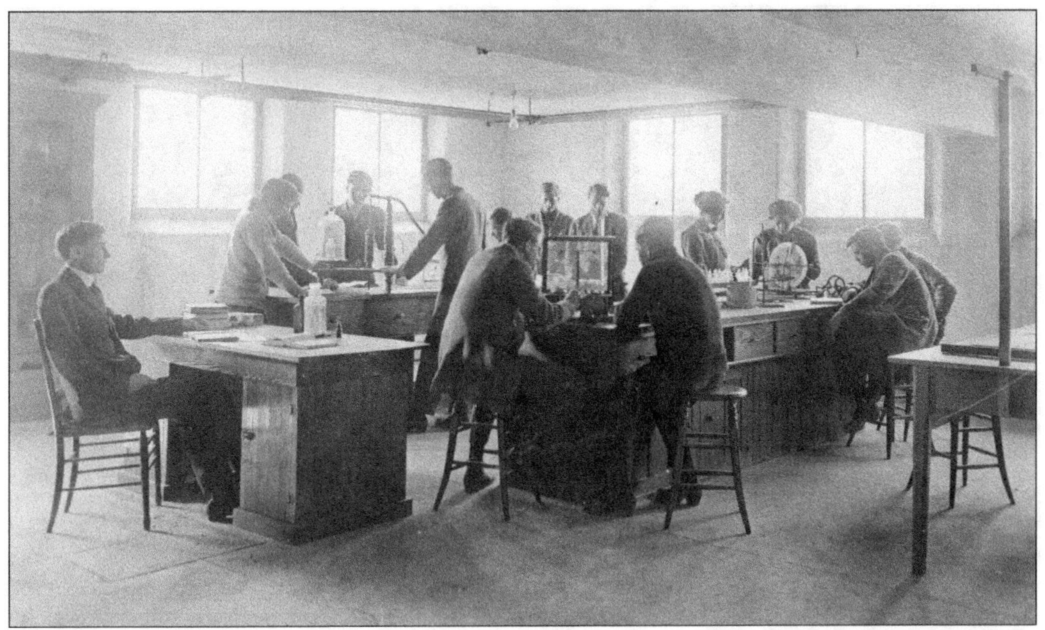

This photograph offers a unique look into an early Sparta High School chemistry class. These students are hard at work while their teacher keeps a watchful eye. Those pictured include, from left to right, superintendent Orley E. Balyeat, Robert Fonger, L. D. Myers, Clifford Gillett, Olga Hilton, Era Haines, Wilfred Cumings, Carl Bradford, Oscar Johnson, Fred Walcott, Frank Walcott, George Nelson, D. J. Moore, and John McInis.

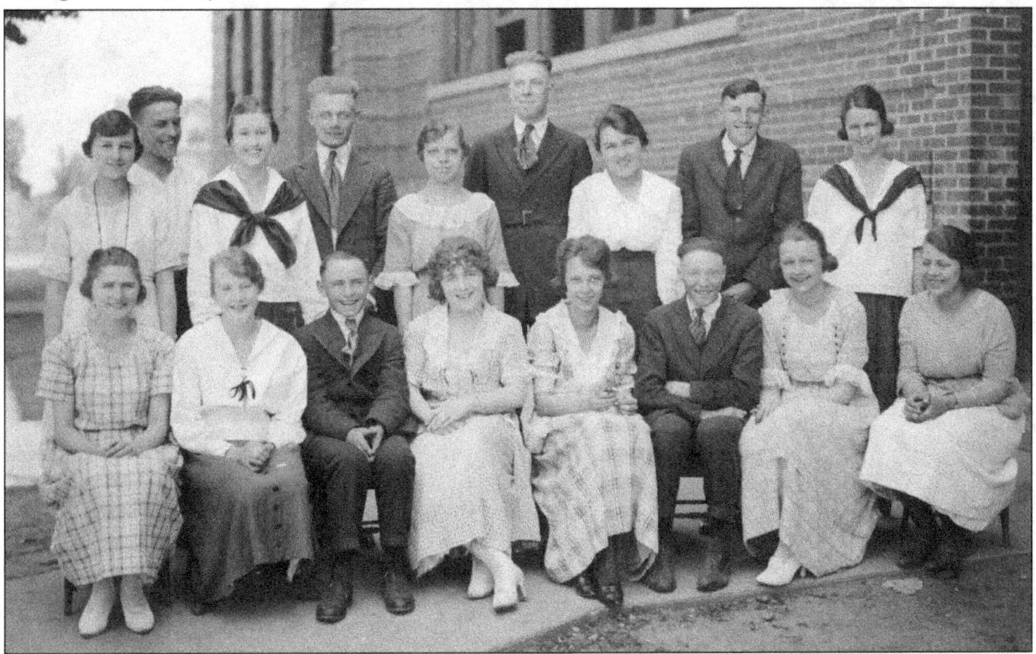

The Sparta High School class of 1920 is pictured above, from left to right, (first row) Sally Carlson, Mary Saur, John Parks, Merle Hodgins, Marietta Blossom, Nathan Snyder, Edna Johnson, and Burnadette Dutmer; (second row) Donna Meeker, Herbert Miller, Margaret Fox, Earl Ryder, Lena Dargie, Lawrence Johnson, Leona Montgomery, Howard Gillett, and Thelma Kellogg.

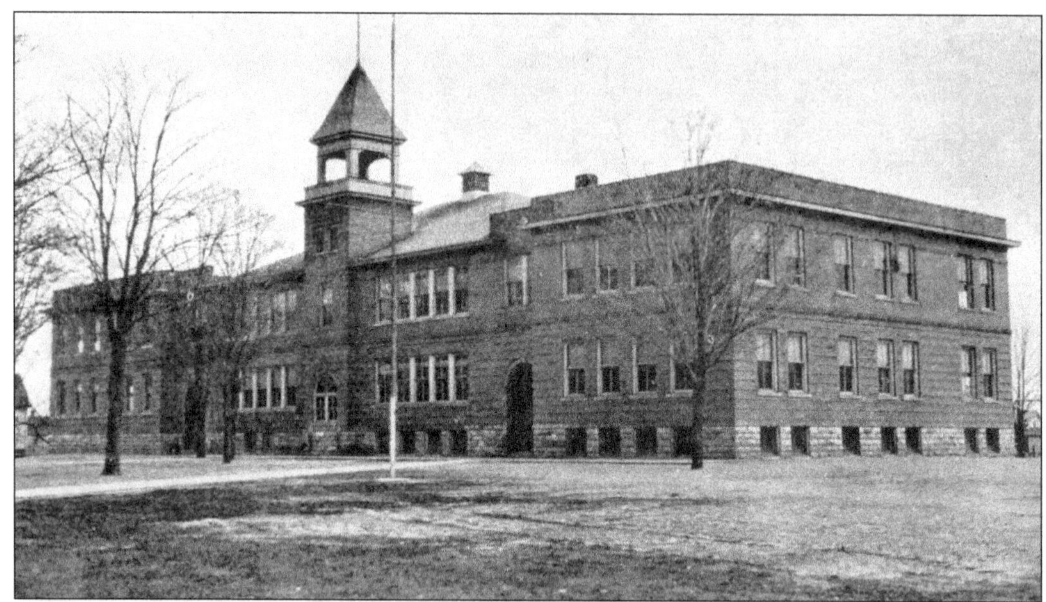

The Sparta Public School is pictured sometime after 1936. Lemuel Coates was the superintendent of the school district when students moved into the brand new building in 1901. To accommodate a growing student body, additions to the original structure were completed in 1910, 1925, and 1936. By 1910, Orley E. Balyeat was superintendent of the schools.

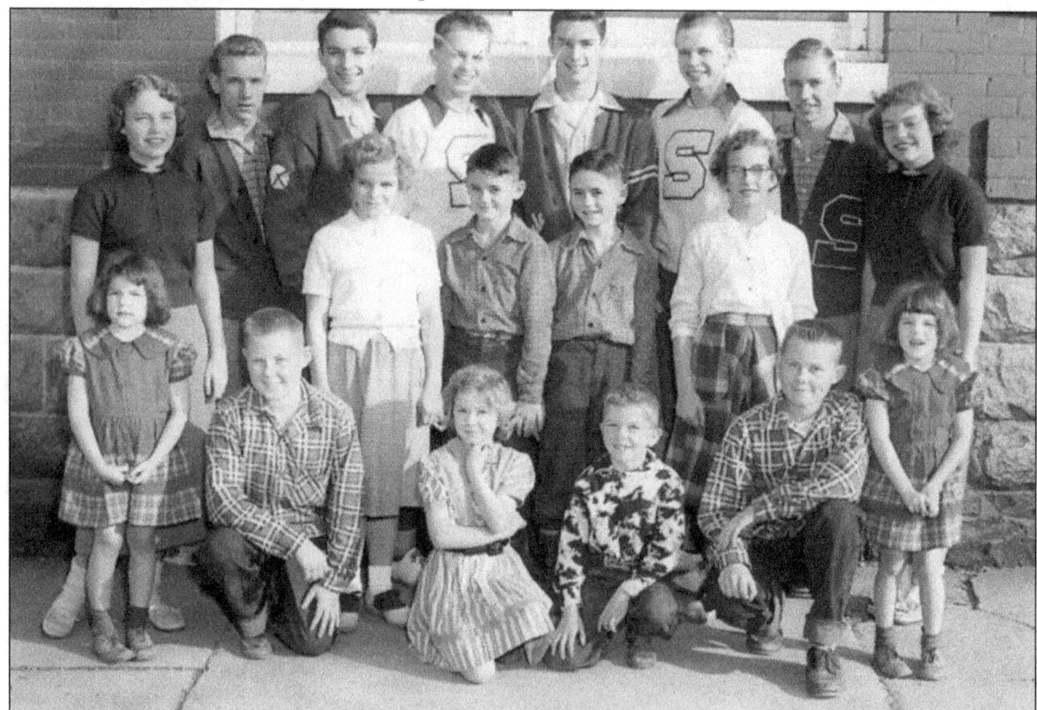

In 1953, there were nine sets of twins in the Sparta Area School District. Pictured in front of the old high school are twins Barber, Bradford, Frank, Houk, McCready, Swanson, Trimble, unidentified, and Wiersma. Most of these twins are identical, which makes it difficult to identify them by their full names.

Proudly displaying what looks to be some type of championship trophy, the 1922 Sparta High School girls' basketball team looks to be exceptionally pleased with the accomplishments of the season. Included in this photograph are, from left to right, (first row) Alma Anderson, Gladys Saur, and Nina Stauffer; (second row) Nyla Witt Feerick, Althea Klenk, Leah Rice, and Lillian Culver Bradford; (third row) Clara Fox.

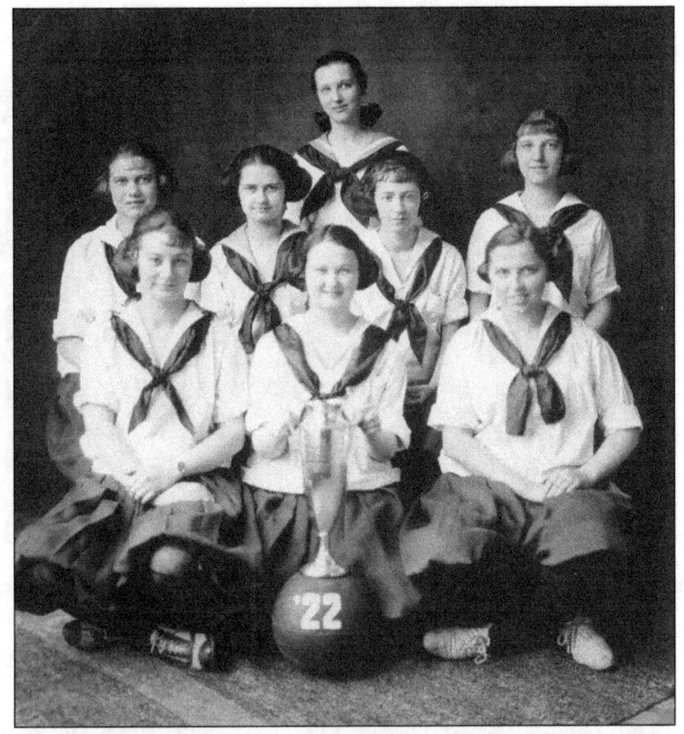

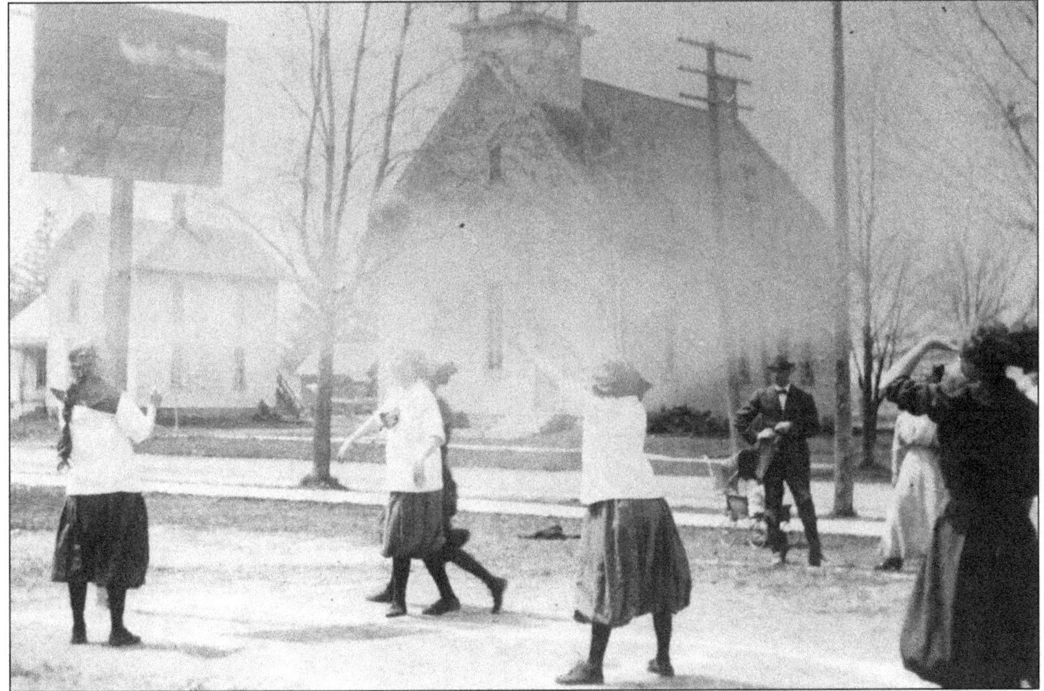

This fuzzy photograph shows one of the early Sparta High School girls' basketball teams. The girls appear to be enjoying themselves, playing a lively game of basketball; the skirted uniforms were typical of this era. Shown around 1908, this game takes place on an outdoor basketball court at the high school across the street from the Free Methodist Church.

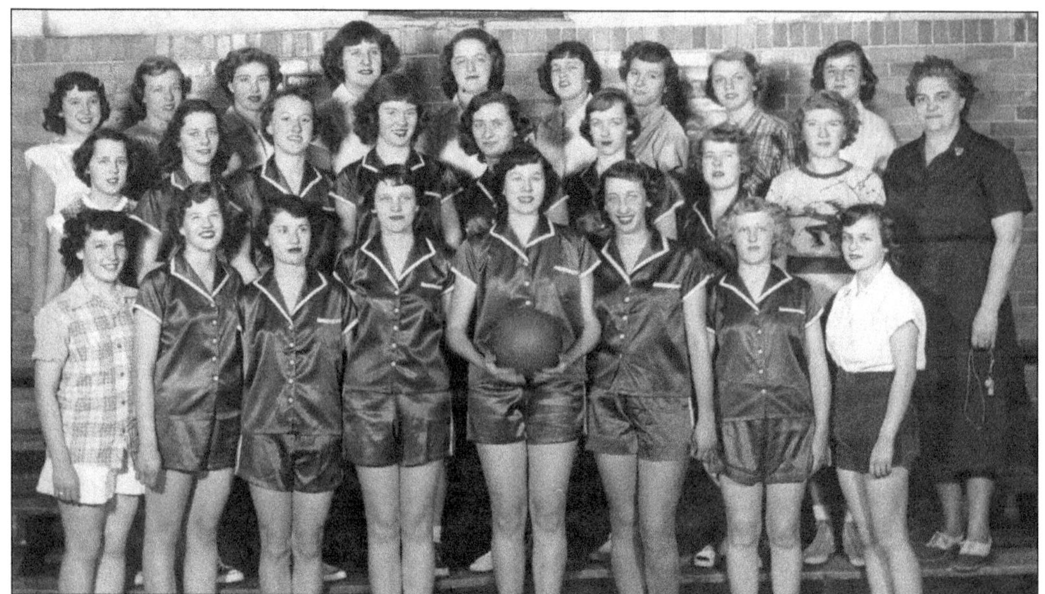

The 1950–1951 girls' basketball team includes, from left to right, (first row) Nena Meginley, Jean Kay Nason, Lois Klenk, Janice Miller, Delores Moody, Sharon Lowring, Ruth Elve, and Eleanor Kirk; (second row) Myrtle Anderson, Janet Amburgey, Janice Anderson, Donna Dufort, Ethyle Krewson, Shirley Forwood, Luanne Fahling, Betty Trudell, and coach Thelma Russell; (third row) Carol Bellamy, Shirley Hanna, Margaret Amidon, Ann Schoolmaster, Lorna Amburgey, Nancy Miller, Joyce Carpenter, Emily Anderson, and Ann Fraleigh.

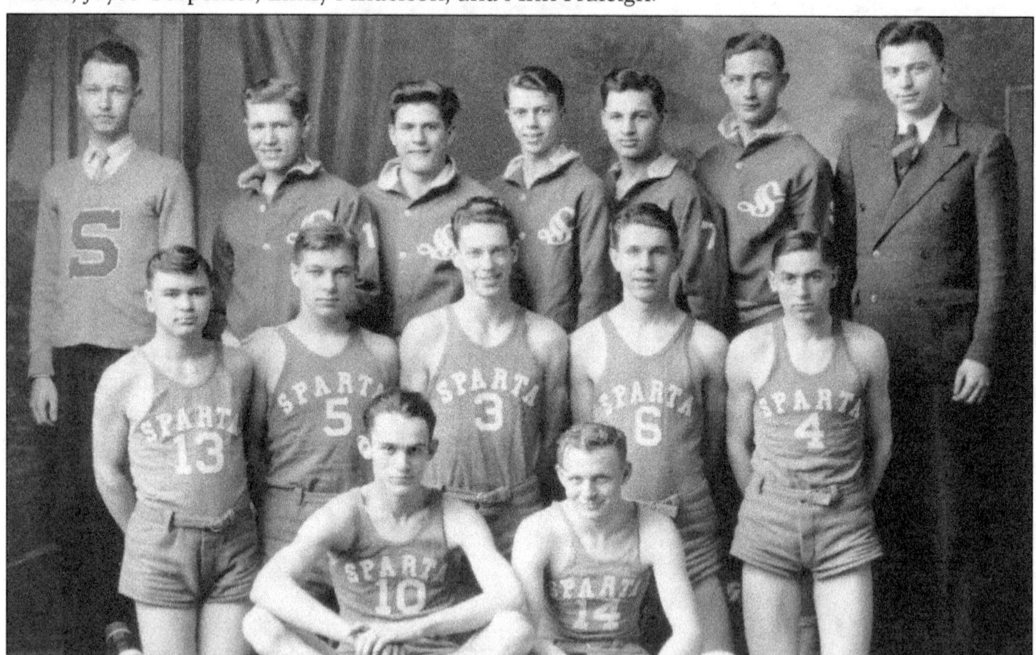

Pictured is the 1936–1937 Sparta High School boys' basketball team. From left to right are (first row) John Powers and Glenn Inman; (second row) George Leary, Kenneth Johnson, Elmer Smith, Gordon Sack, and LaVerne Bockman; (third row) Edmund Nequist, Merlin Robinson, James Warren, Barth Carlson, Harvey Stebbins, Norman Bradford, and Marcellus DeYoung.

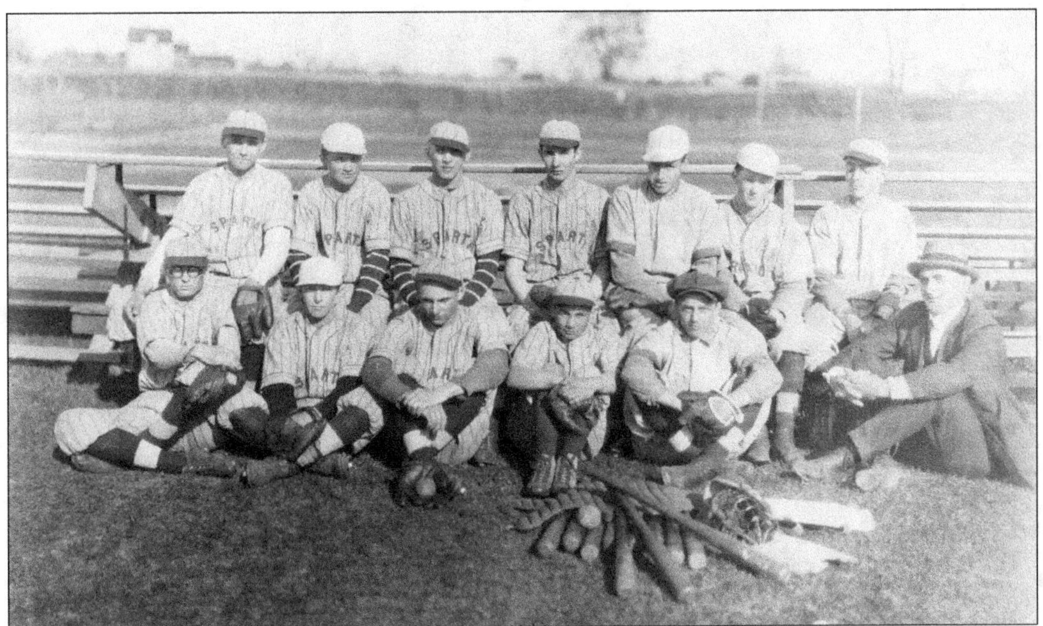

A shining example of what old-time baseball looked like, pictured above, is the 1925 Sparta High School baseball team. Shown are, from left to right, (first row) Clark East, Alvin Reister, Elmer Cain, Hazel Anderson, Vernon Hussey, and coach Howard Passage; (second row) Gustave Dahlin, Van Lundquist, Lawrence Bodell, Clarence Anderson, Stanley Pierson, Clarence Post, and George Felt.

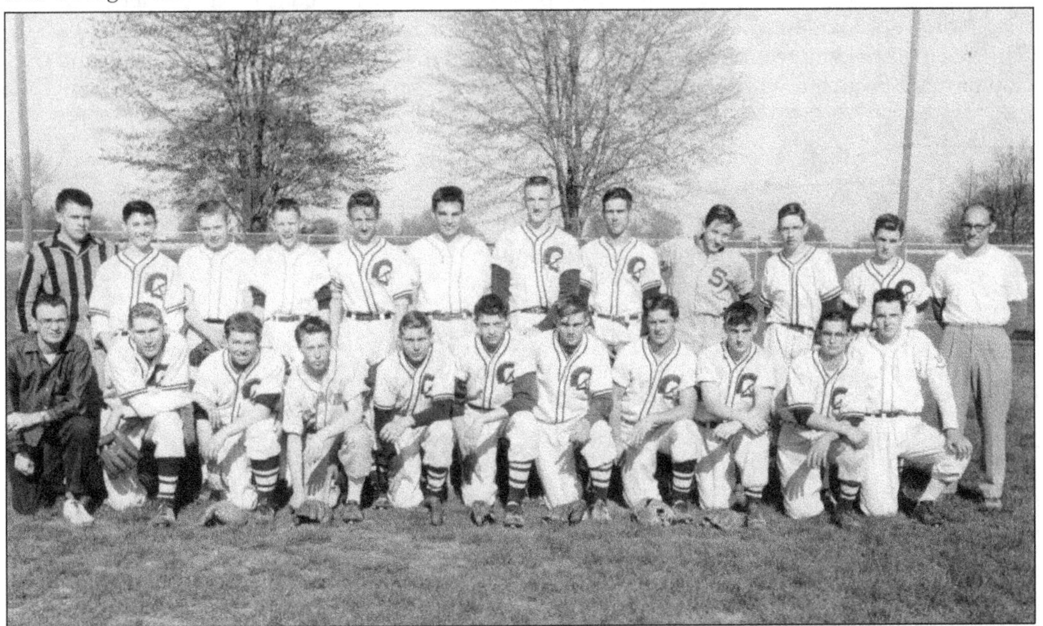

The 1957 Sparta High School baseball team was comprised of, from left to right, (first row) assistant manager Hugh Krewson, Brian Longcore, Bruce Pike, Danny Ferguson, Duane Witt, Larry Bradford, Jim Kline, Russ Thayer, Randy Rouse, Jim Simmons, and Leslie Gray; (second row) manager Jim DeVoogd, Doug Lee, Dennis Bromley, George Kleibusch, Pete Wolters, Bob Carpenter, Dave Mutchler, Jim Dood, Jerry Norton, Gordon Couturier, Roger Kik, and coach Finch.

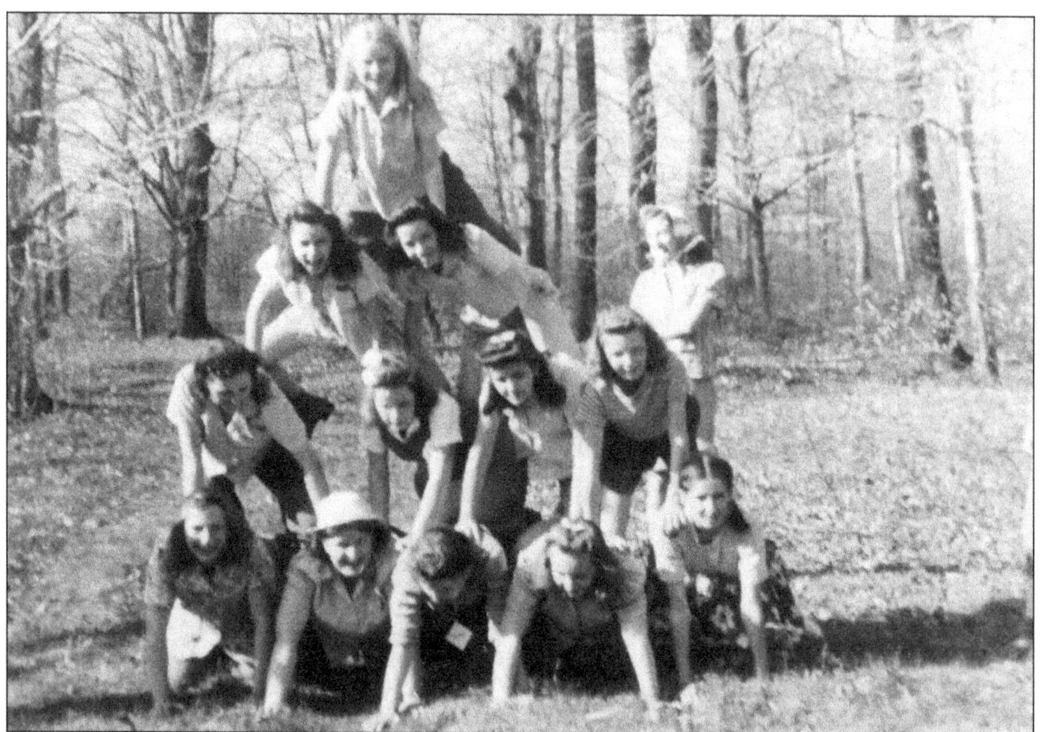

These eight girls are enjoying some free time during physical education class in 1942. Those pictured are, from left to right, (first row) Iris Stedman (physical education teacher), ? Smith, Frieda Johnson, Margaret Kelly, and Elizabeth Anderson; (second row) Norma Morgan, Dorothy Gardner, Joanne Lamoreaux, and Marilyn Miller; (third row) Joyce Pennock, June Dake, and Lois Zimmerman; (fourth row) Evelyn Lavine. (Courtesy of Elizabeth Anderson Mason.)

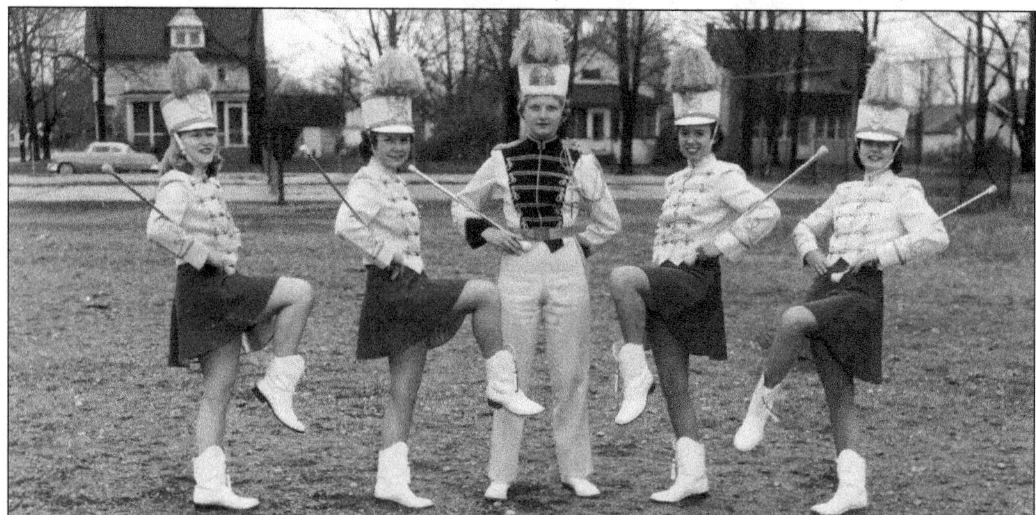

The Sparta High School drum majorettes and drum major are shown above in 1957. Providing both direction for the band and entertainment for the crowds during football games, the drum major and majorettes were an important part of Sparta High School sports seasons. Those pictured are, from left to right, Barbara Patterson, Marilyn Humeston, Terry Averill, Sandy Anderson, and Joyce Cooper.

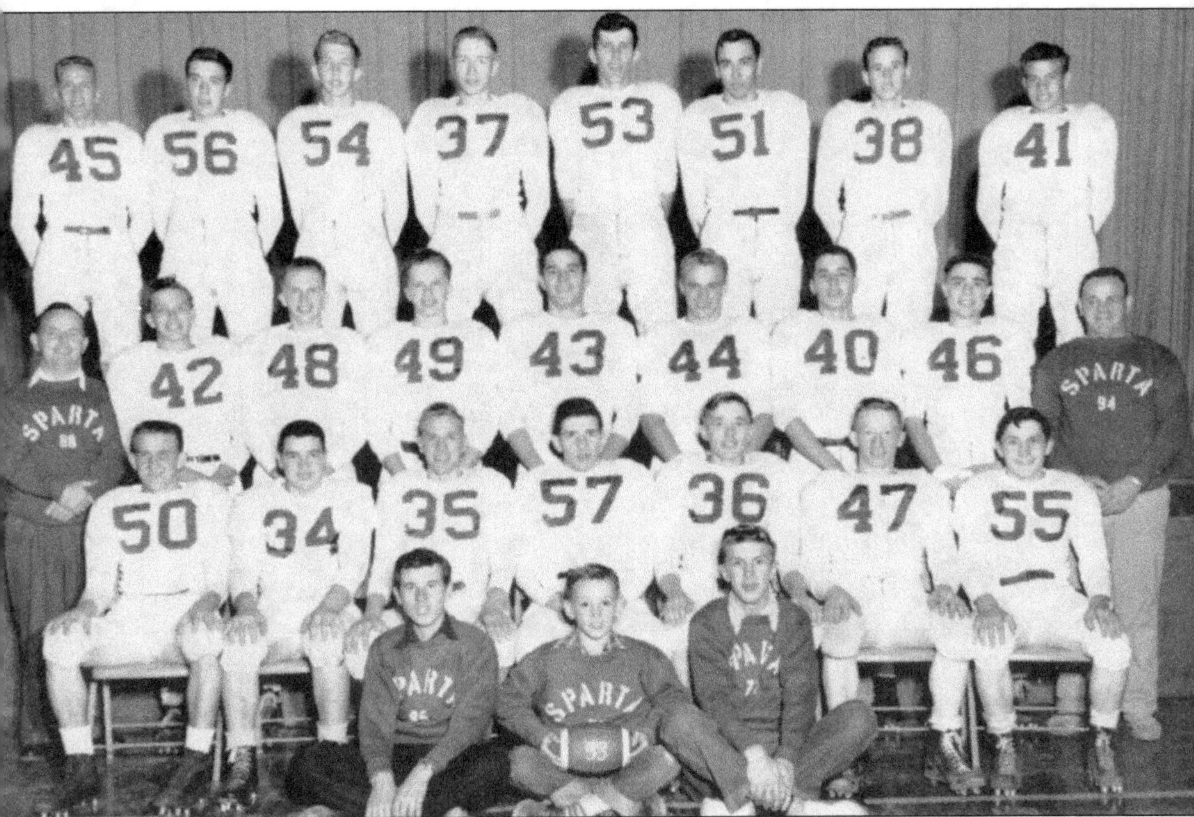

The 1953 Spartan football team combined speed, skill, student spirit, and a will to win, and the result was one of the best teams in Sparta history. Bolstered by 13 seniors, the Spartans fought their way to an undefeated season and the Ken-O-Wa League Championship. No Sparta team to date has had an undefeated, or untied, season since 1953. Head coach Norm Harris and his assistant coach Wes Perrin led the team. The team was equally strong on offense and defense as they scored 275 points while holding their opponents to only 32 points. Not one team scored more than seven points against Sparta during the entire season. Those pictured are, from left to right, (first row) managers Bob Beardsley, Mark Hudson, and Roger Singleton; (second row) Don Shangle, Roger Simmons, Tom Barber, Earl Watkins, Bert Phinney, Jerry Kober, and Ron Klenk; (third row) coach Perrin, Ray Schuiling, Don Bradford, Duane Bradford, Dale Trimble, Glenn Burgett, Gale Trimble, Arlan Lundquist, and coach Harris; (fourth row) Phil Barber, Ted Passmore, Jim Whitehouse, Dick May, Rog Radeck, Tom Stortz, Roger Montgomery, and Ken Shangle. (Courtesy of Don Bradford.)

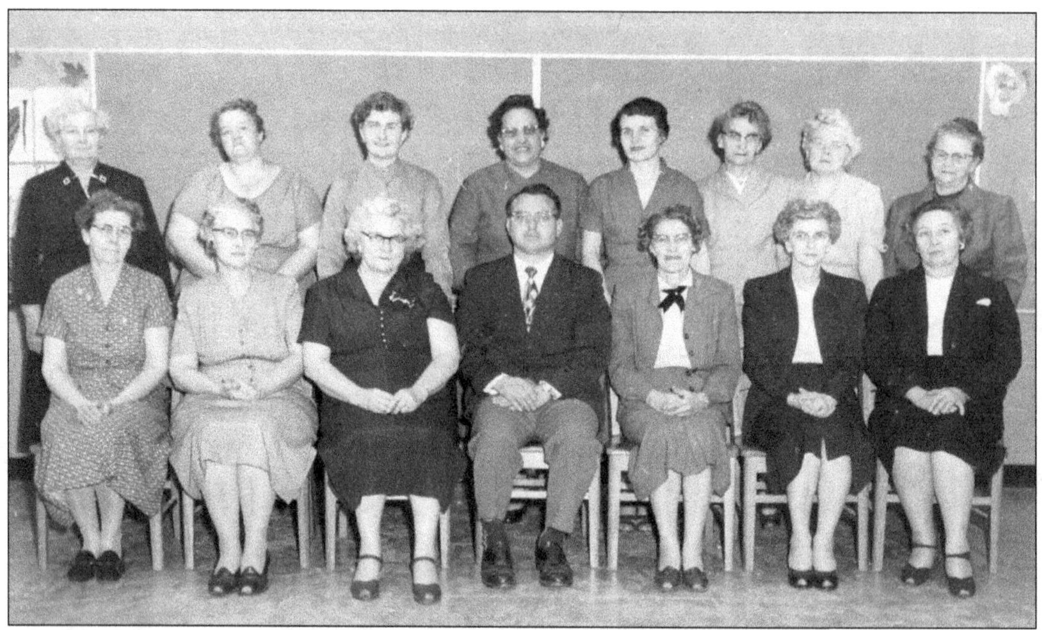

This photograph, presumed to be of teachers from rural schools, was taken in the fall of 1956. They are, from left to right, (first row) Lorraine Nequist, Florence Anderson, Gladys Stinson, Frank Huey, Ivah Carlson, Una Robinson, and Francis Slapinski; (second row) Josephine Beuschel, Helen Bessemer, Joan Furhoff, Constance Frank, Audrey Hunt, Annette Lymburner, Delma Johnson, and Irma VanAntwerp.

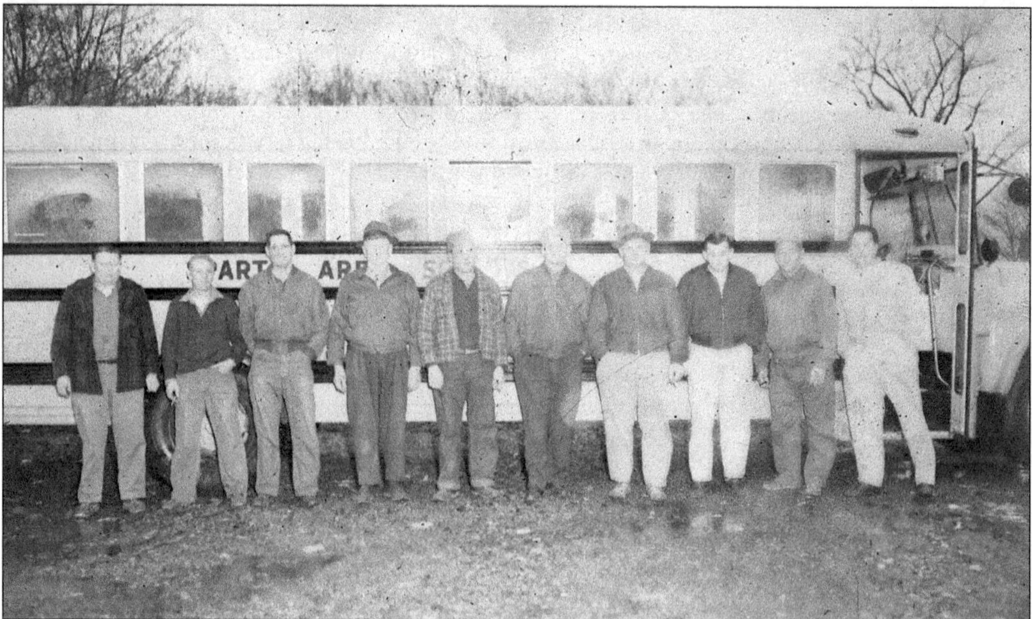

This photograph of Sparta bus drivers was taken sometime in the mid- to late 1950s. Routes at that time were somewhat shorter because drivers only had to transport rural high school students. Elementary students either attended country schools or walked to school in town. Those pictured are, from left to right, Bill Bloom, Bob Schwab, Roycee Wilson, unidentified, John VanOeffelen, Karyl Shangle, Ollie Blumenstein, Bob Blumenstein, unidentified, and ? Premae.

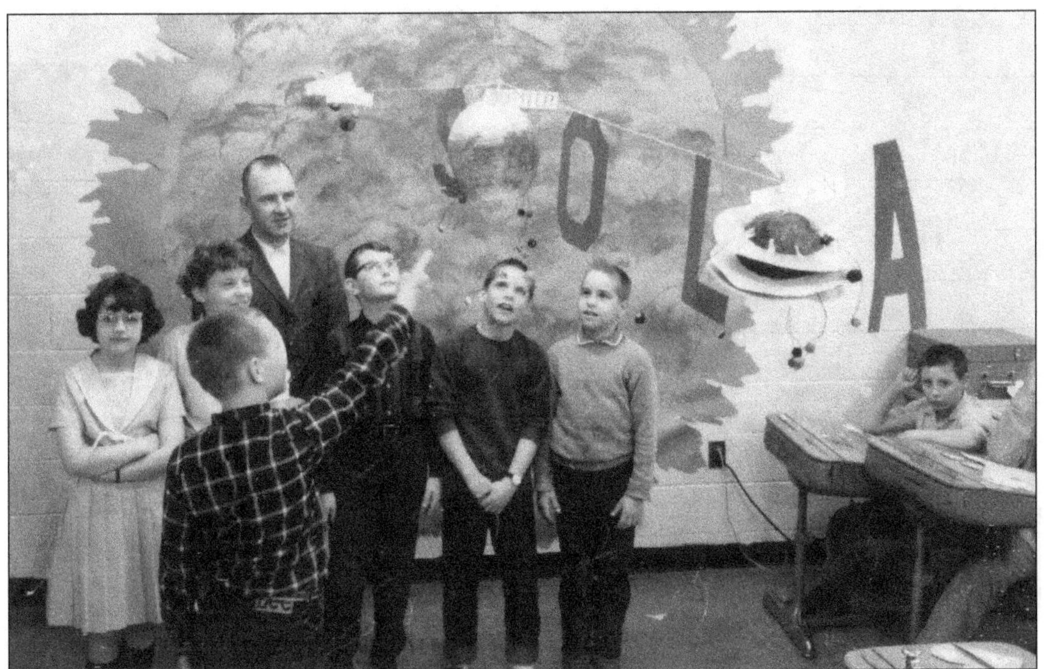

Studying the solar system, from left to right, are (front) Mike VanderHyde; (second row) Elizabeth Montgomery, Connie Balbach, teacher Mr. Rynders, Allen Blackmore, Tom Hammond, and Pat Jazwinski. The student sitting at the desk is Charles Purdy. The photograph was taken at Algoma School, which was located on the corner of Thirteen Mile Road and Algoma Avenue, where these students were in the fifth grade.

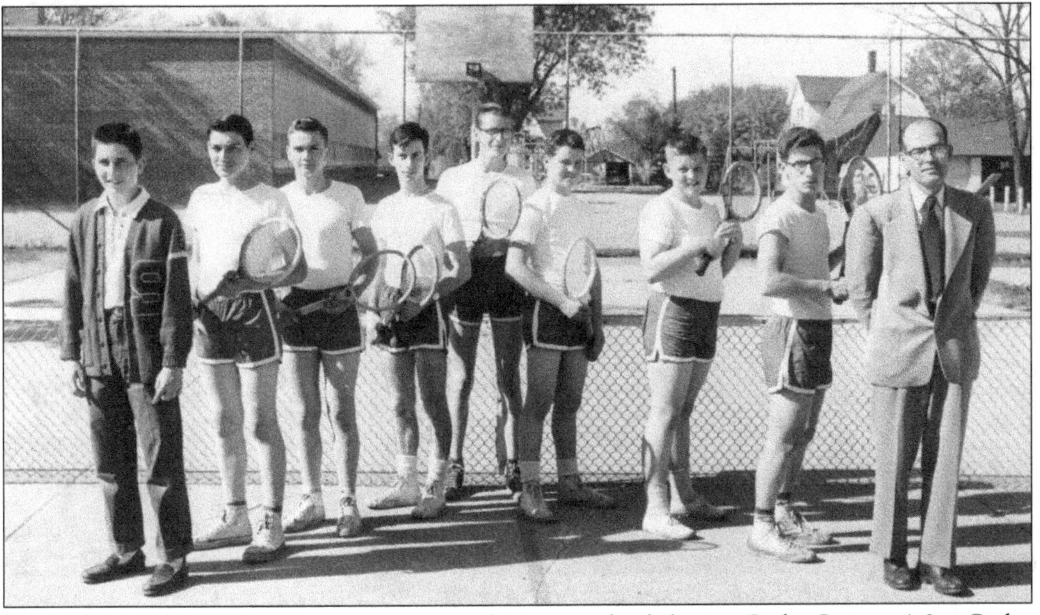

Sparta High School's 1952 tennis team started its season by defeating Cedar Springs 4-0 at Cedar Springs. The record at the end of the season stood at 2-2. From left to right are Ken Graves, Bob Boros, Dale Fitzner, Walt Reister, Ron DeLang, Roger Simmons, Bob Blumenstein, Gordon Fulkerson, and coach Gardner.

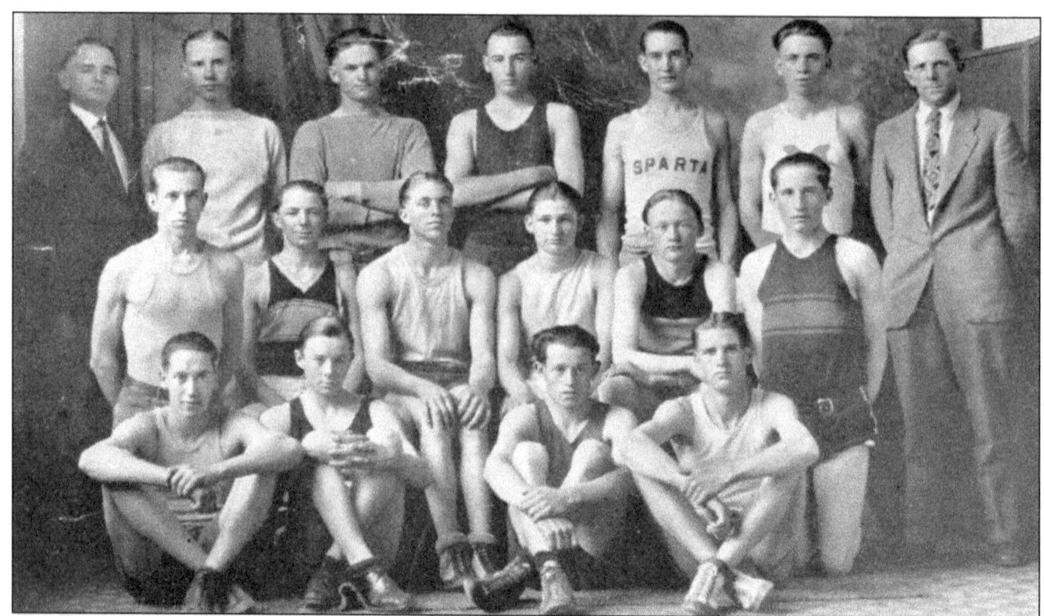

The 1927 *Sparta High School Annual* delights in the abilities of coach Mabie and coach Humeston to create a "real" track team. Competing in four track meets that year, the team consisted of, from left to right, (first row) ? Athearn, ? Stevens, ? Vincent, and ? Ballard; (second row) ? Rogers, ? Olson, ? Cumings, ? Baehre, ? Anderson, and ? Anderson; (third row) coach Mabie, ? Kirschner, ? Ritz, ? Starn, ? Anderson, ? DeLange; and coach Humeston.

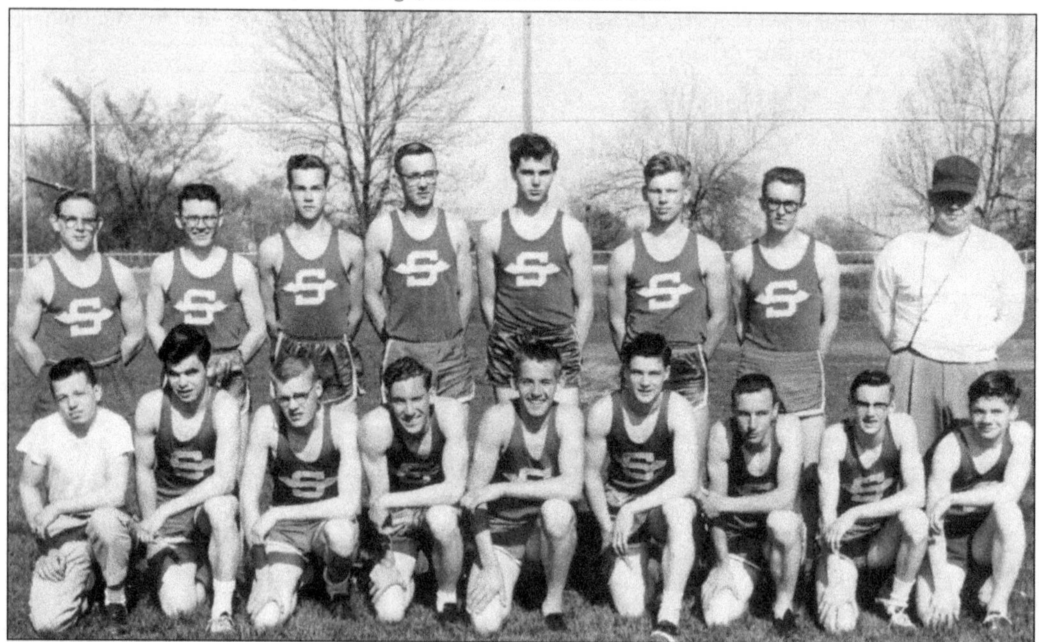

The 1957 Sparta High School boys' track team once again gained the title of Ken-O-Wa League Champions. The championship team consisted of, from left to right, (first row) manager Ron Chapman, Laverne Tawney, John Ekster, Bob Merchant, Dave Whitcomb, Dave Hertling, Don Fries, Gary Jacobs, and Ellis Kober; (second row) John Martin, Harold Keech, Rush Ring, John Mutchler, Dave Andrus, Jim Fryear, Bill McCarthy, and coach Clauss.

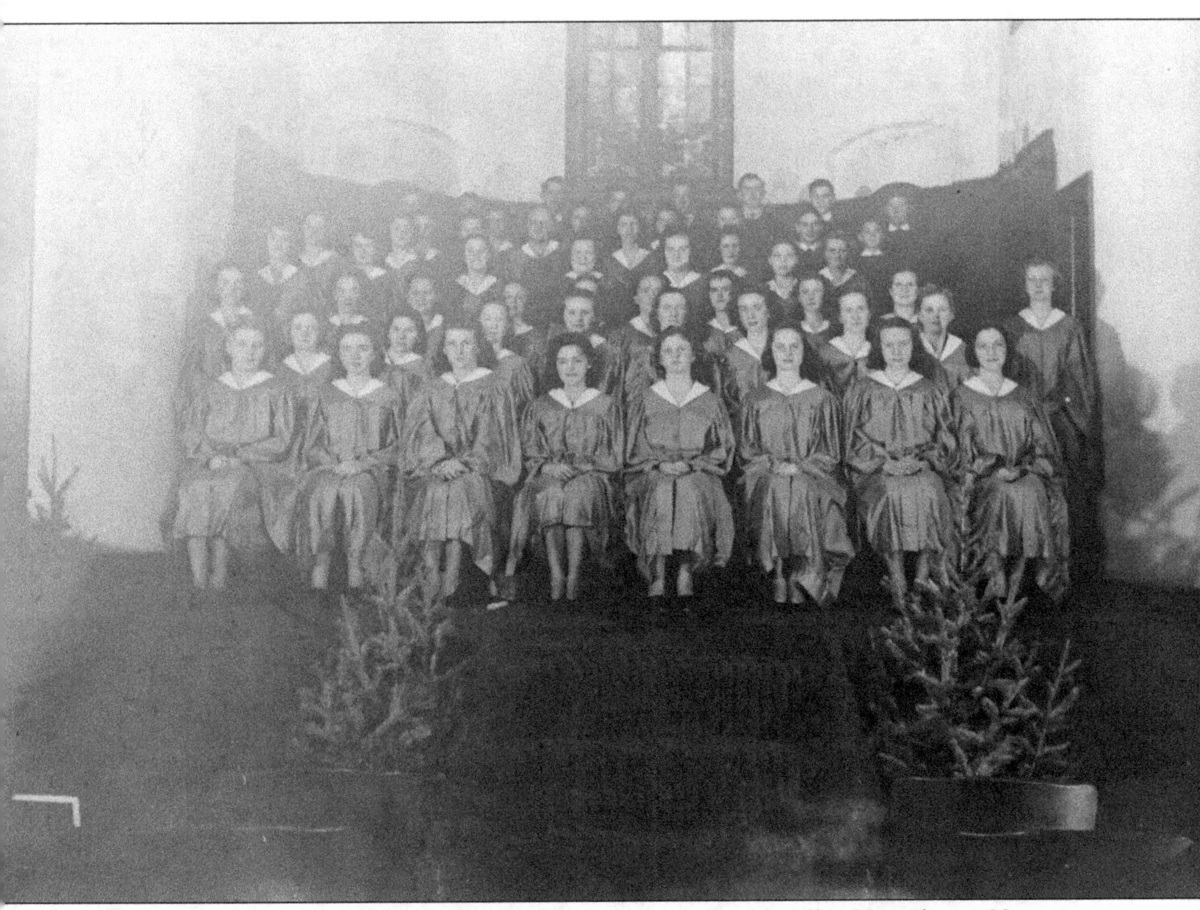

The 1939–1940 glee club consisted of Georgia Bettes, Norma Smith, Ellen Humphreys, Virginia Pennington, Rebecca Durham, Lorraine Rogers, Marijean Gold, Catherine Powell, Lorraine Peterson, Hazel Neilsen, Ione Pinckney, Jean Slapinski, Imogene Rosell, Virginia Edwards, Virginia Heath, JoAnn Lillie, Ruth Yotter, Luella Purdy, Goldie Dingagen, June Gillam, Joy Lonnee, Doris Heath, Pauline Cutler, Dorothy Kyser, Elizabeth Ruth, Eva Mae Watkins, Helen Thorson, Winnifred Johnson, Marian Johnson, Lucile Holmquist, Maxine Brace, Laverne Swenson, Betty Totten, Rena Fonger, Julia Greenhalgh, Charlotte Baehre, Jackie Tindall, Mary Jane Falconer, Clinton Parcels, Howard Lamoreaux, Bob McIntyre, Rudy Lonnee, Maynard DeYoung, Basil Myers, Larry Collins, Charles Saur, Jack Young, and Archie Cumings. By the 1950s, the Sparta chorus had grown to well over 100 members. Each year, both a Christmas concert and spring concert were presented to the community, with selections sung by the girl's glee club (the Spar-Tone-Ettes), and a select male chorus (the Spar-Tones). Managing a chorus of well over 100 voices could be a daunting task, but it also proved to be a lot of fun.

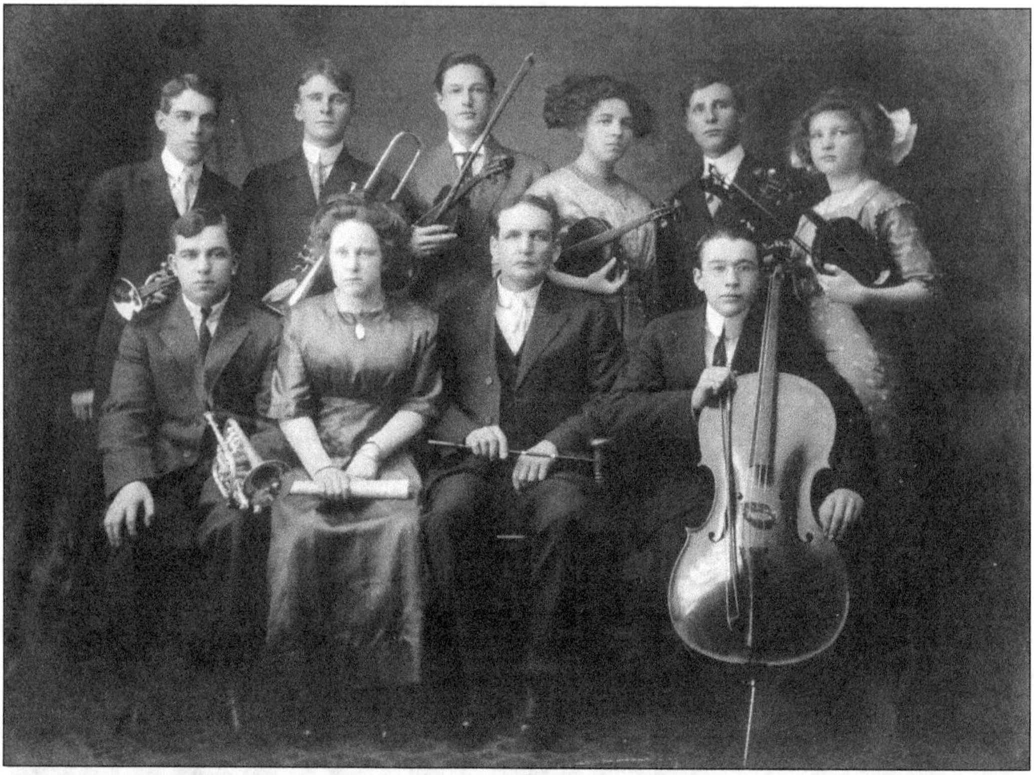

A striking example of an early high school music program, the 1913 Sparta High School band consisted of the following members: from left to right, (first row) D. J. Moore, Olga Hilton, V. Richtee, and Karl Bolender; (second row) Loren Gardner, Frank Walcott, Kenneth Coville, Ruth Beacon, Fred Walcott, and Quida Brown.

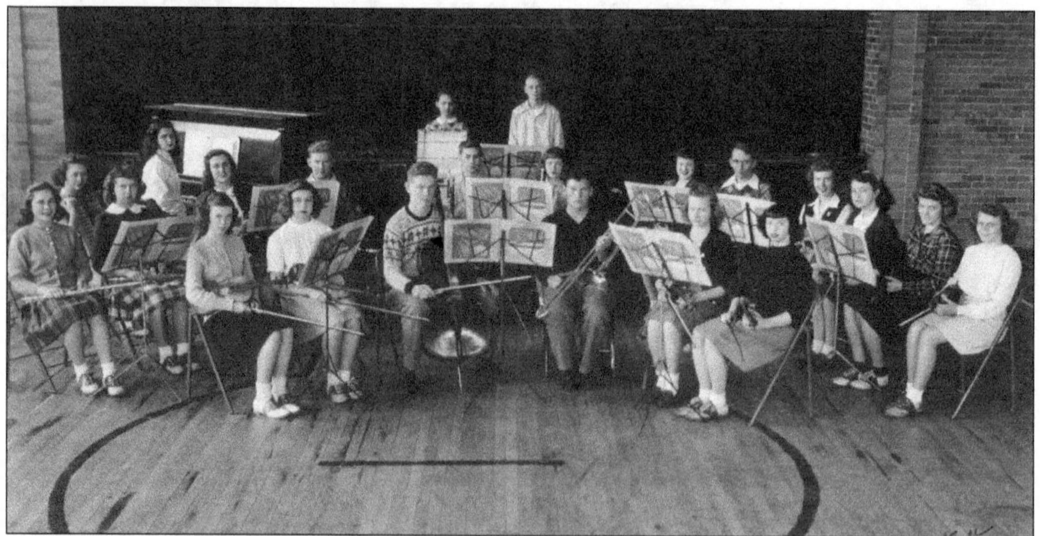

Pictured above are members of the Sparta High School band, taken in 1947. In addition to playing music, the band was responsible for entertaining sports spectators at football and basketball games. To do so, the band members created several formations for football games and formed a pep band to play at basketball games. The band also played in an annual spring concert.

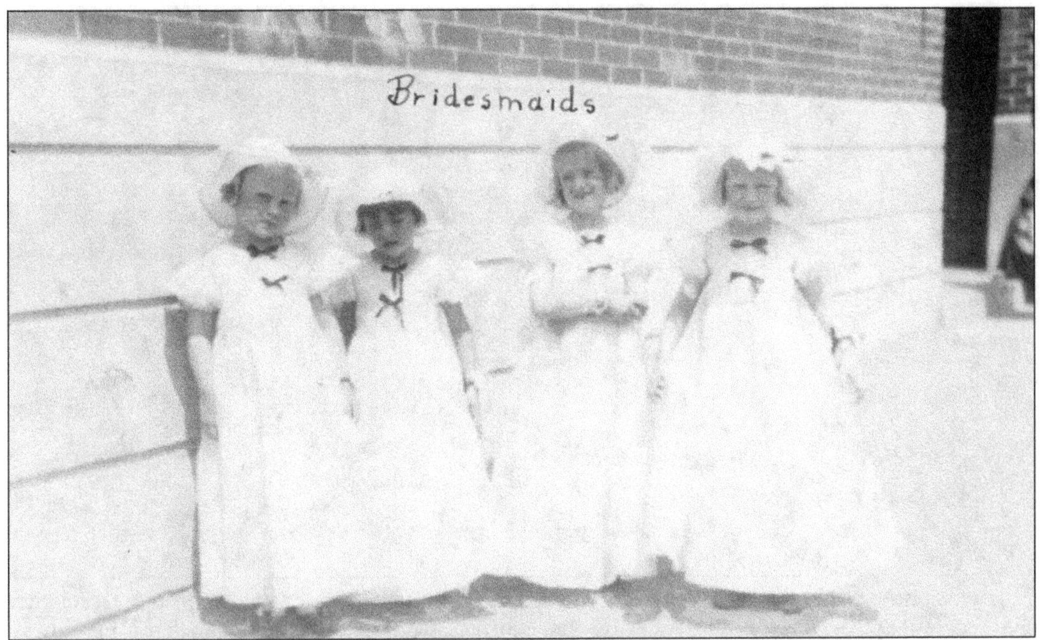

These little girls are dressed in their bridesmaids' best for the kindergarten spring program, "Wedding of Jack and Jill," on May 2, 1938. The groom was played by Jim Mortensen, and the bride was played by Kathryn Rider. Shown here are, from left to right, Gail Brooks, Crystal Proctor, Glenda Hayward, and Dolores Thorson.

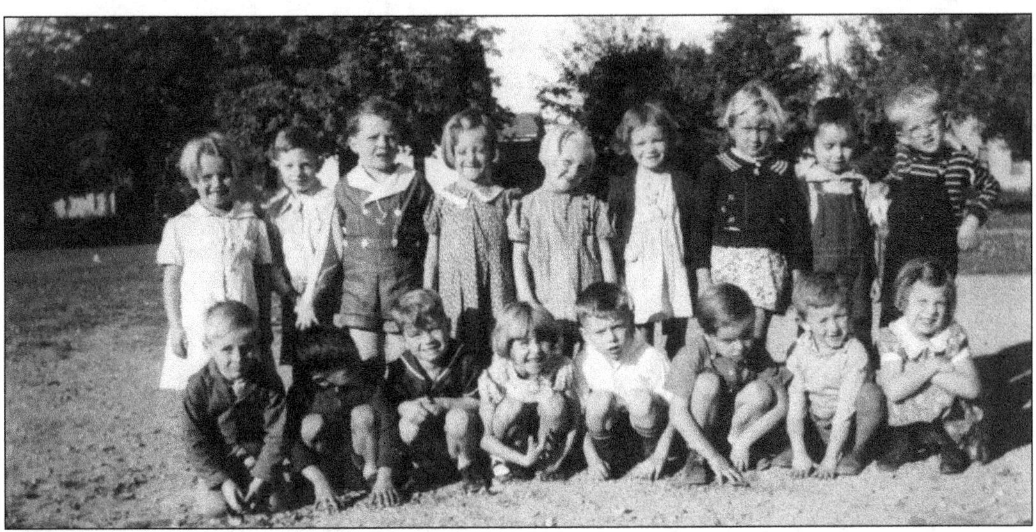

This photograph, taken in 1938, is of a Sparta kindergarten class. These students would be part of the future class of 1950. From left to right are (first row) Bud Balyeat, Carl Mosher, Bob Norton, Crystal Proctor, Jim Mortensen, Warren Guiles, Bob Larson, and Mary Lou Hickock; (second row) Ardith Mutchler, Frank Beuche, Ed Paas, Glenda Hayward, Gail Brooks, Audrey Oxford, Lenore Sterkenberg, Larry Winans, and Gordon Badgerow.

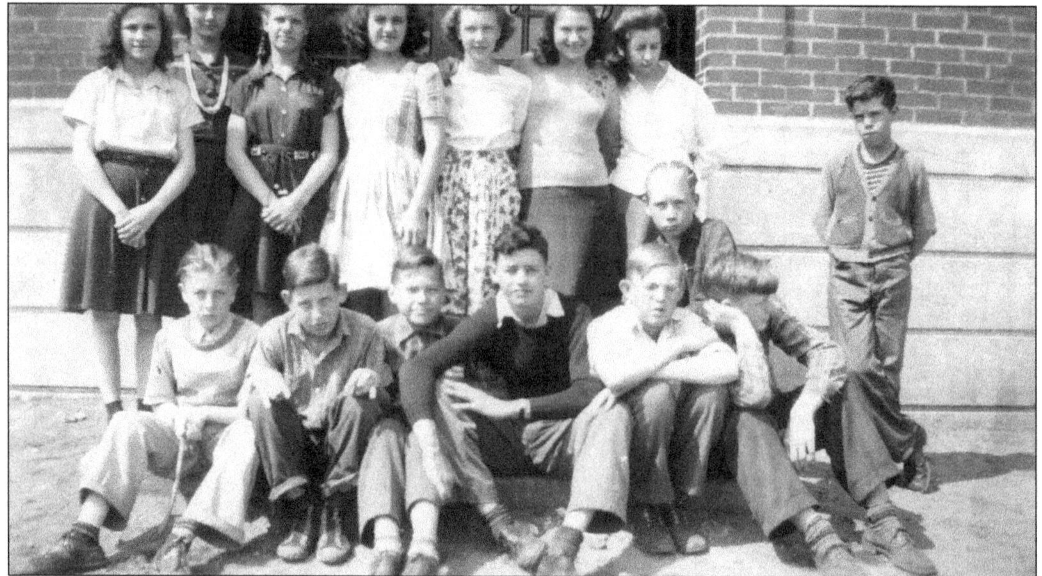

This class photograph details a group of students who completed kindergarten through the eighth grade together at the school in town. After the eighth grade, country school transfers joined these students. This new, larger group then finished their high school careers together. Those pictured above are, from left to right, (first row) Burwell Powell, Lowell Heath, Ted Baker, Ken Colby, unidentified, John Nequist, Arzie Pinckney, and Dick Straight; (second row) Elverna Metzger, Jean Hansen, Lavonna Allen, Barbara Bull, Lorraine Fitzner, Beverly Meyers, and Helen Harper.

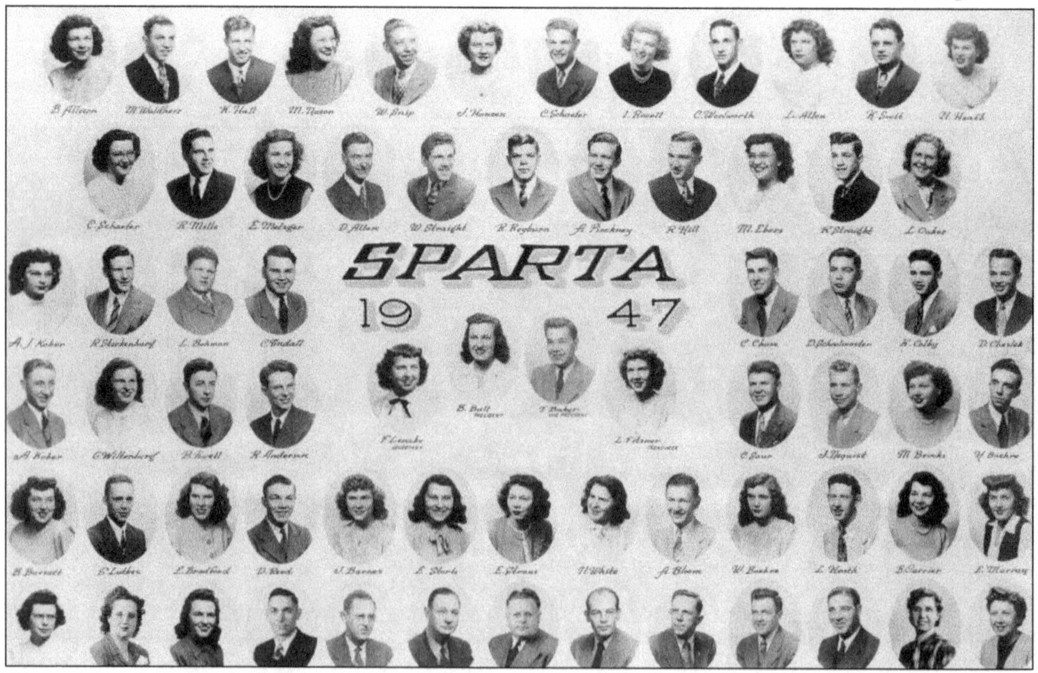

This photograph is of the Sparta High School class of 1947. Included are the original 14 students from the previous photograph that details the group of "in-town" students. Note the size of the graduating class with the country school additions. Also included in this graduating class are Max Waldherr and Carl Woolworth, two local military heroes.

Six

People, Places, and Events

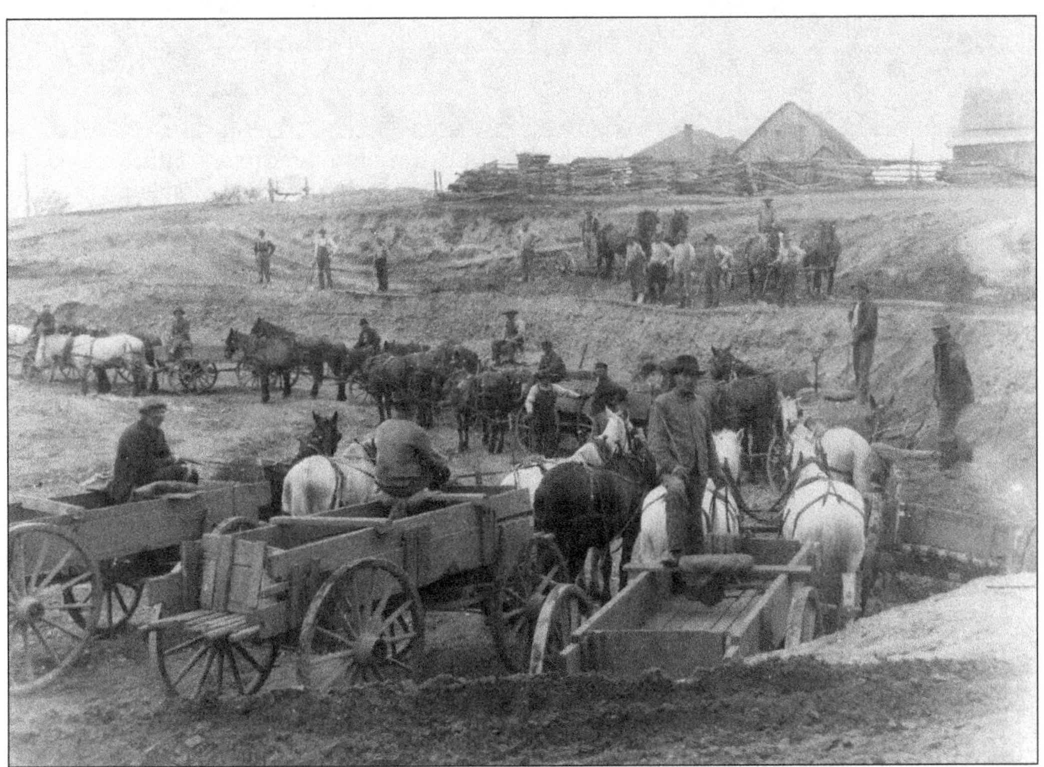

These wagons are headed for a barn raising on the Carlson Farm at the southeast corner of Stebbins Avenue and Indian Lakes Road. Barns were often the largest and most expensive structures on a family farm. The family would have collected materials, and plans would be drawn up. Members of the community would donate their time and skills to erect the barns.

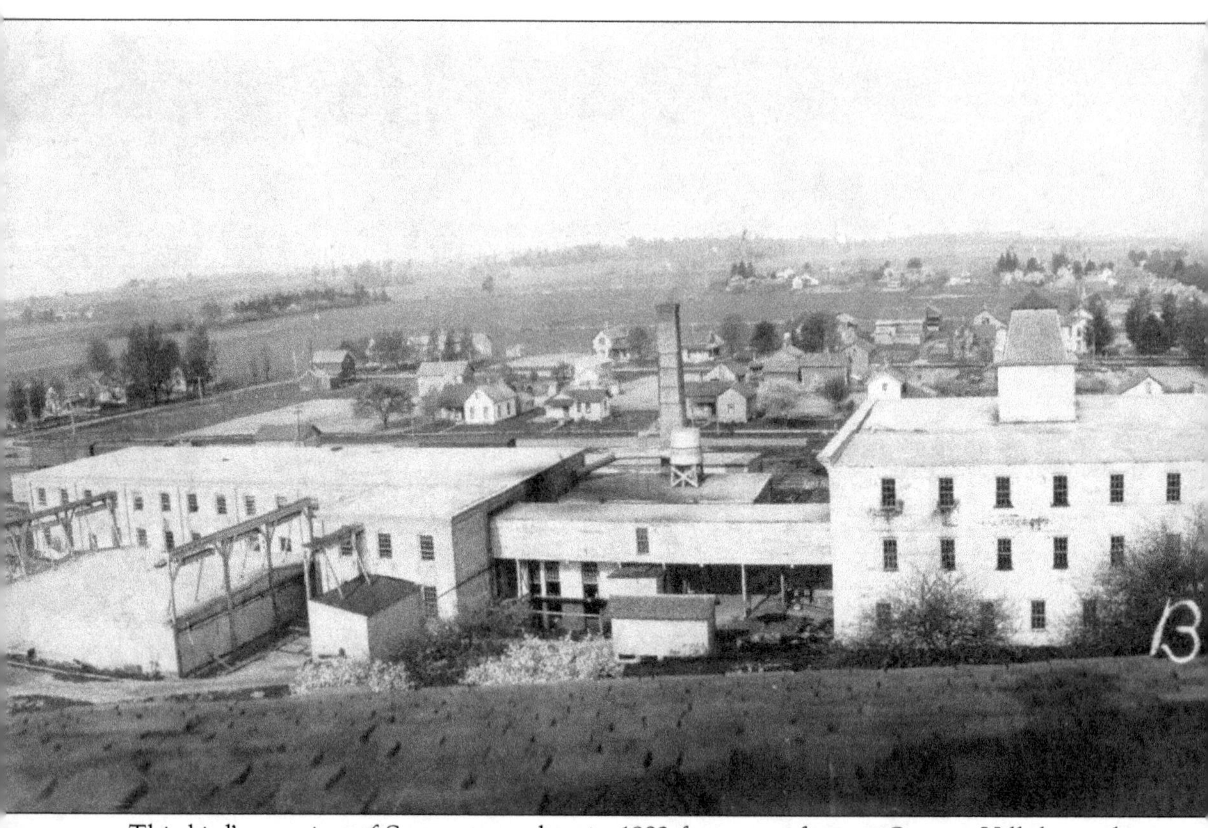

This bird's-eye view of Sparta was taken in 1892 from a rooftop on Simons Hill, located on Prospect Street. The building in the foreground was Welch Folding Bed Company, later to

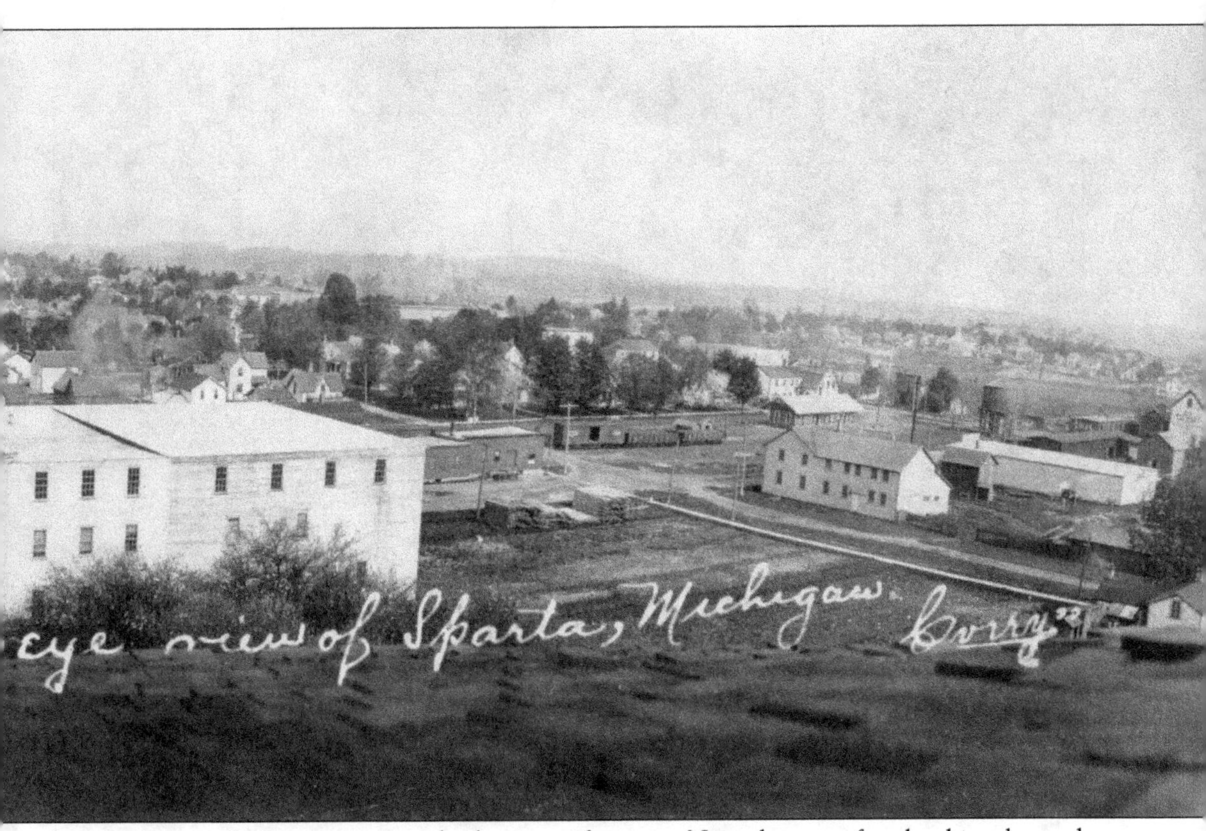

become Extensole Corporation, and other manufacturers. Note the open farmland just beyond the immediate village and the dirt roads to the right of the photograph.

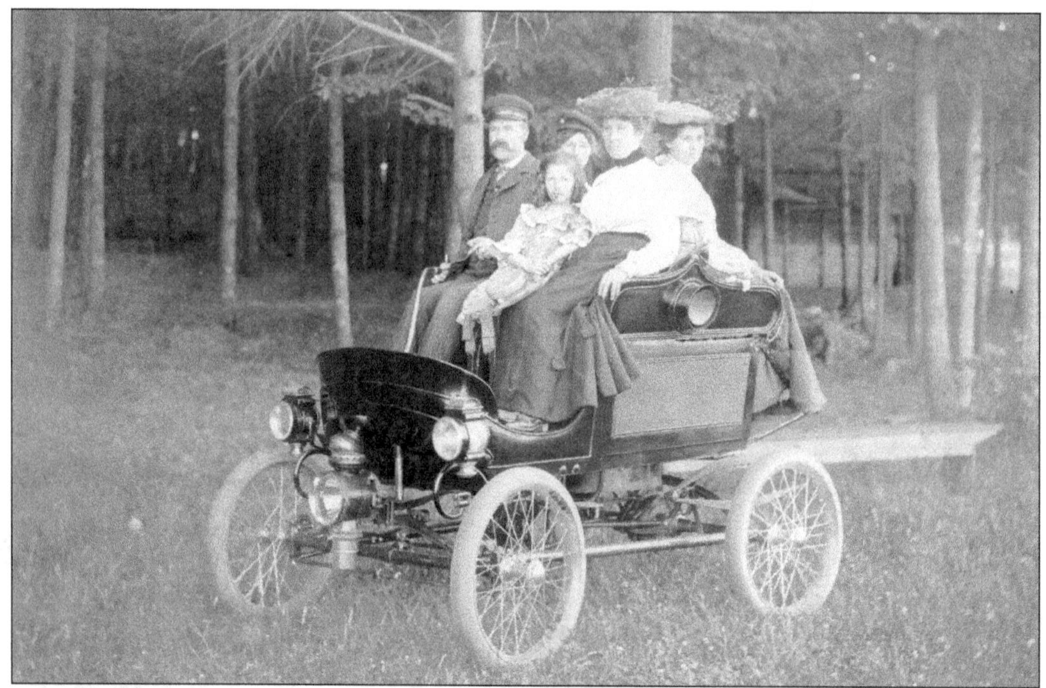

This photograph from 1901 shows one of the very first automobiles in the Sparta area. It was owned by Manley W. Burch, who is in the vehicle with his wife and family. The Burch family was prominent in the Sparta area, as Burch was superintendant of the Welch Folding Bed Company.

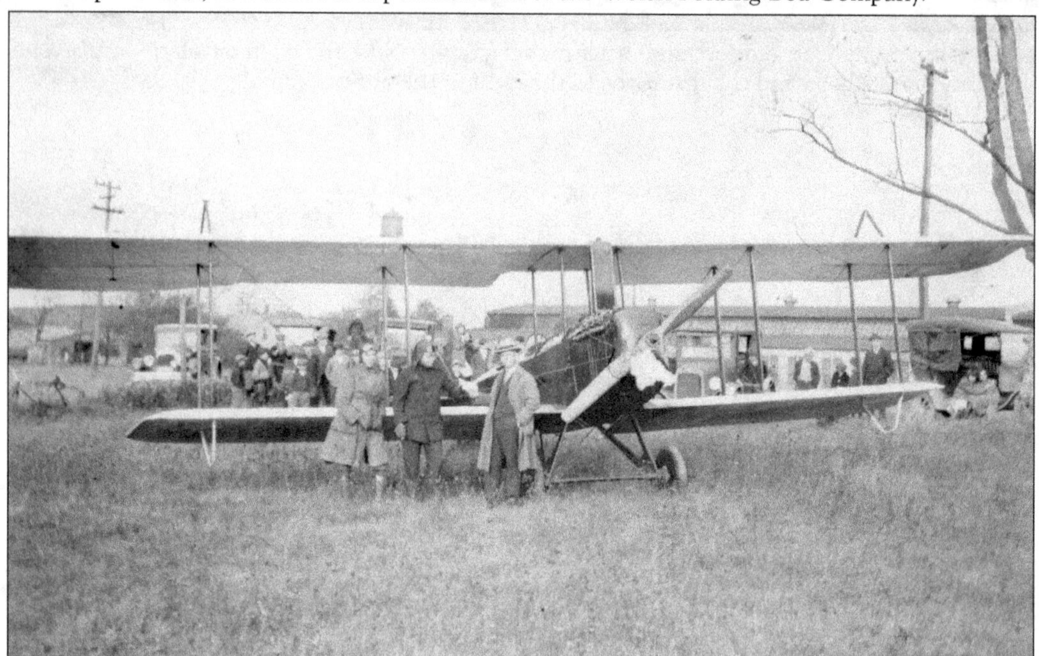

George Bettes (far left) is pictured with the very first plane to land in Sparta in 1919. Originally known as the Sparta Aviation Service, the Paul C. Miller Airport was founded in 1944 by Paul C. Miller and George Bettes, who donated the land. Bettes also served as a mechanic on several flights in the Sparta area.

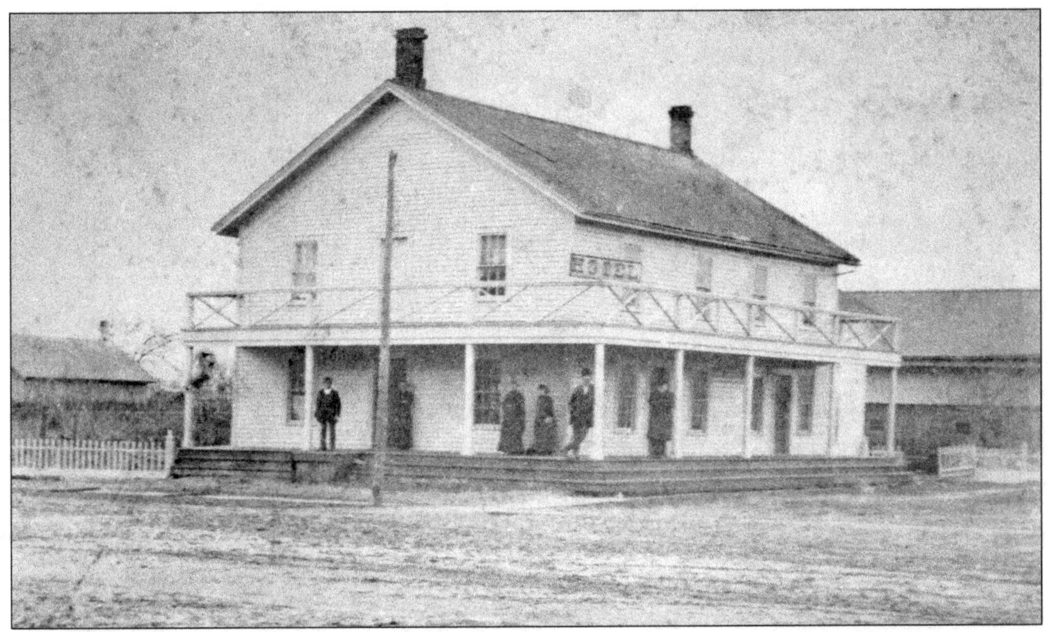

One of the first hotels in Sparta was the Balcom Hotel, located on the northwest corner of Division and Union Streets. Shown in the photograph are, from left to right, John Balcom, ? Balcom, ? Maynerd, ? Myers, Perrion Myers, and Elder Maynard, the pastor of the Sparta Baptist Church. In 1896, Dr. John Gillett bought the hotel and moved his wife, his eight children, and his medical practice into the old hotel.

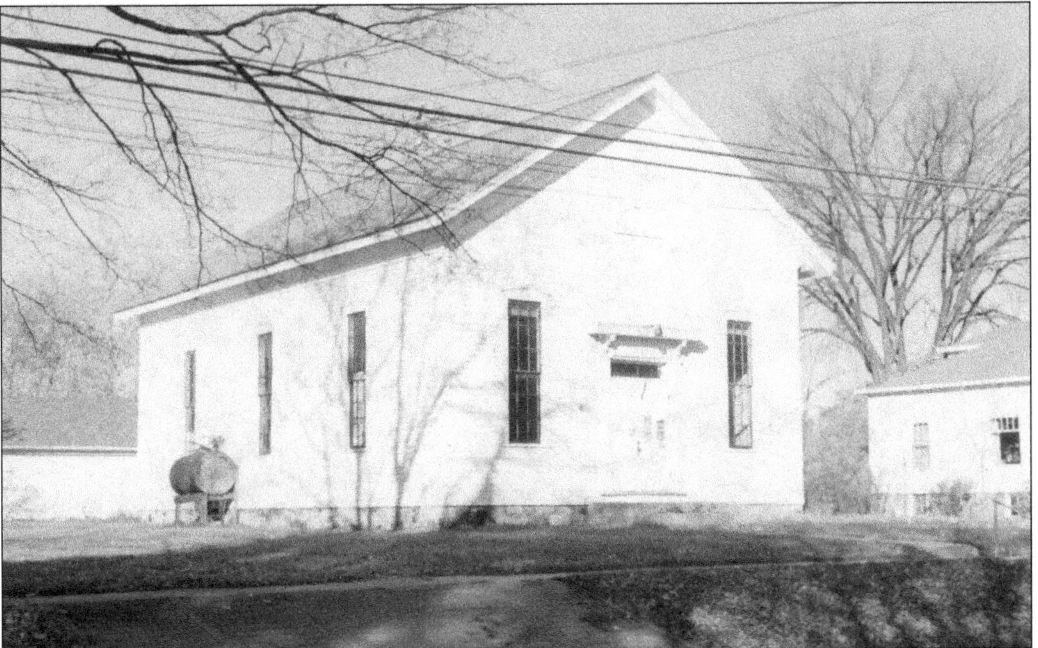

The old town hall is believed to be one of the first buildings to be constructed on North State Street. It was used as a courthouse in early years, and it was where townspeople voted. It was also used for Saturday night dances, and classes met in the old town hall while the new schoolhouse was being built.

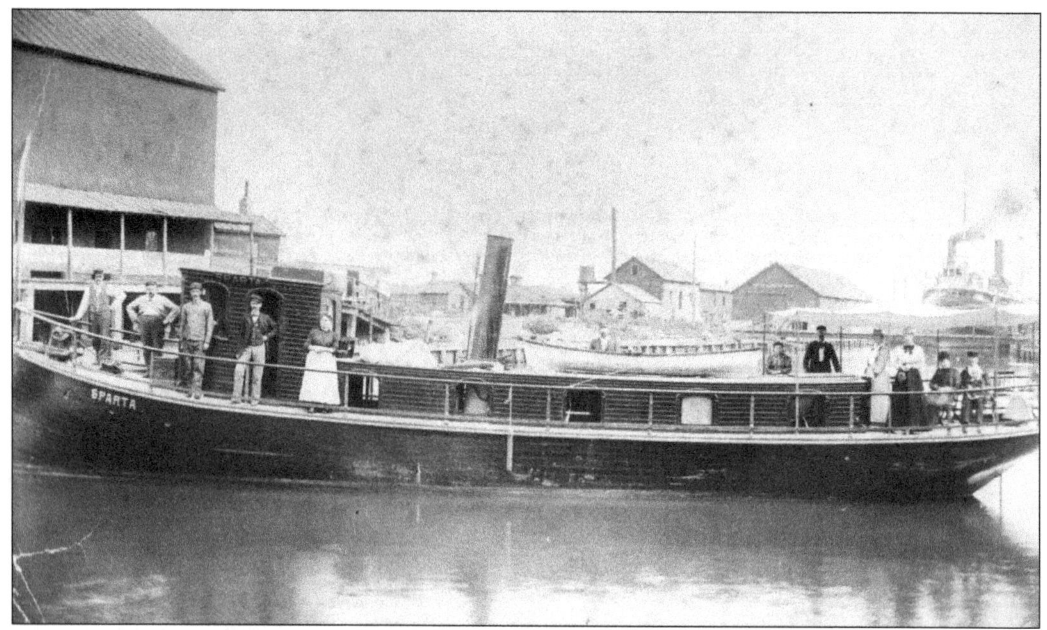

Lyman Welch's steamboat, the *Sparta*, was launched from Muskegon to make a trip to Chicago for the Columbian Exposition. Along the way, the boat nearly sank in a storm. The boat was brought to Camp Lake and was renamed the *Lady of the Lake*, and passengers of this boat were able to take cruises around the lake. The boat was troubled again by a severe fire that sank it in the southeastern corner of the lake.

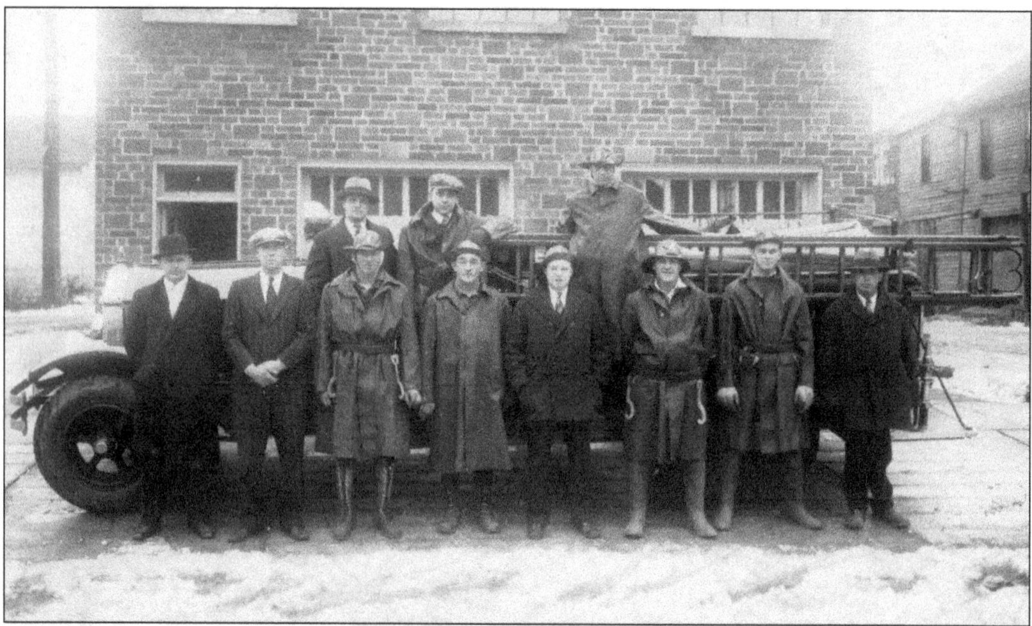

When the Methodist church burned in 1927, the need for a fire department was evident. The only fire truck was destroyed in 1926, when the department caught fire. In 1928, a police station and fire department were built on North Union Street. Some of these firefighters are Willard Amidon, Sherry Ballard, Paul Johnson, Lawrence Johnson, Bob Lundry, Thom Powers, Harvey Stebbins, and Bunch Vandenhout, pictured in front of the new combined building.

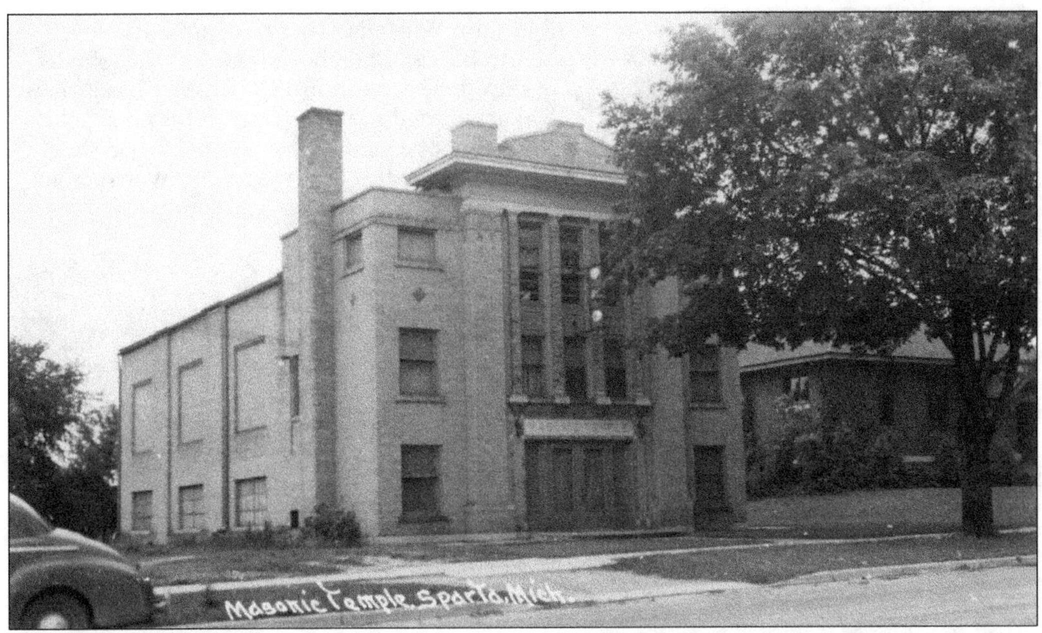

The Fraternal Order of the Masons and the Order of the Eastern Star were housed in this building on North Union Street, near Nash Creek. The Sparta Masons were established on January 26, 1876, and the first Worshipful Master was Amherst B. Cheney. The Order of the Eastern Star began October 9, 1884, and Cordella Bonner was the Worthy Matron.

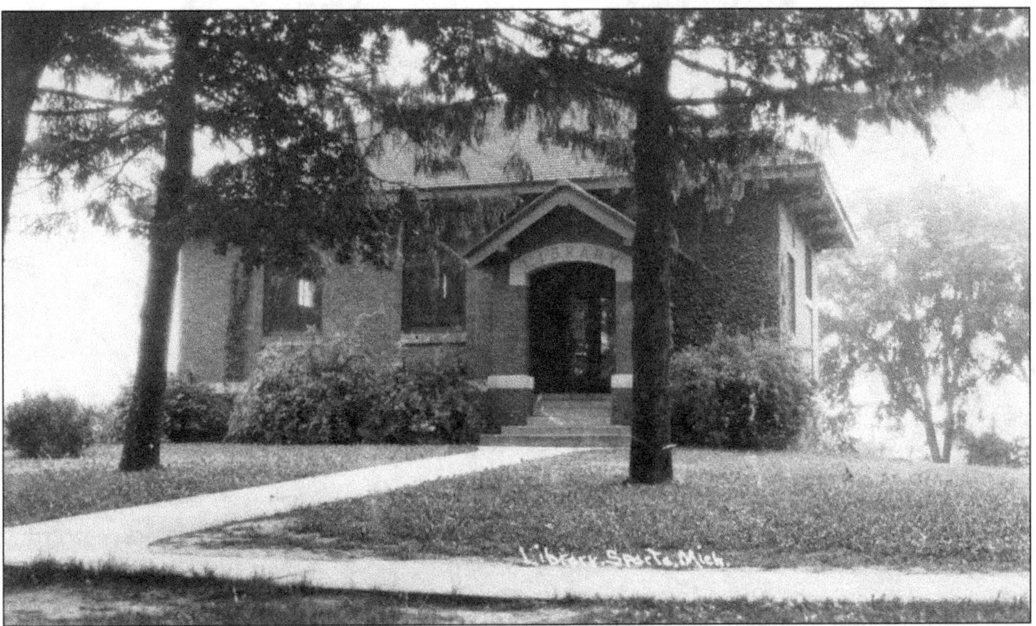

In 1915, members of the village council signed a resolution to accept a $10,000 donation from the Carnegie Corporation to build a library. It was stipulated that the village and township boards would pledge not less than $1,000 per year to maintain the building. Signers of the resolution were Charles J. Rice, township supervisor, and Frank D. Kellogg, township clerk. On December 1, 1917, the new building was dedicated.

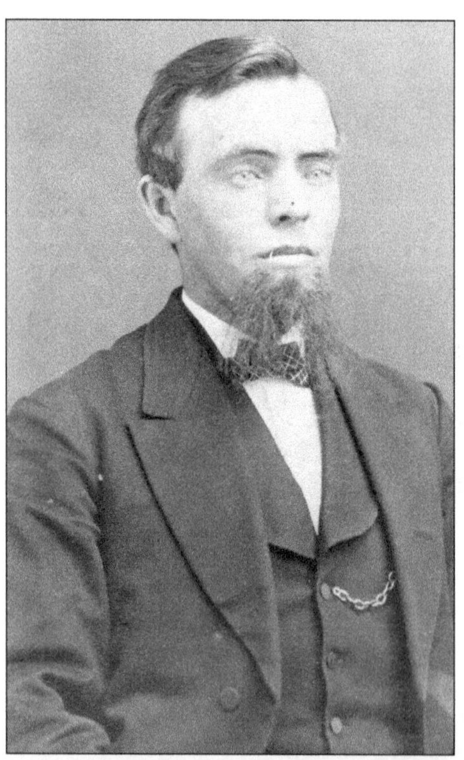

Rev. John W. Hallack was the pastor at the Sparta Baptist Church. Hallack was the founder of the *Sparta Sentinel* in 1876. History has it that Hallack started the newspaper in his home, but this cannot be verified. He also published the *Reunion* newspaper and was a Civil War veteran.

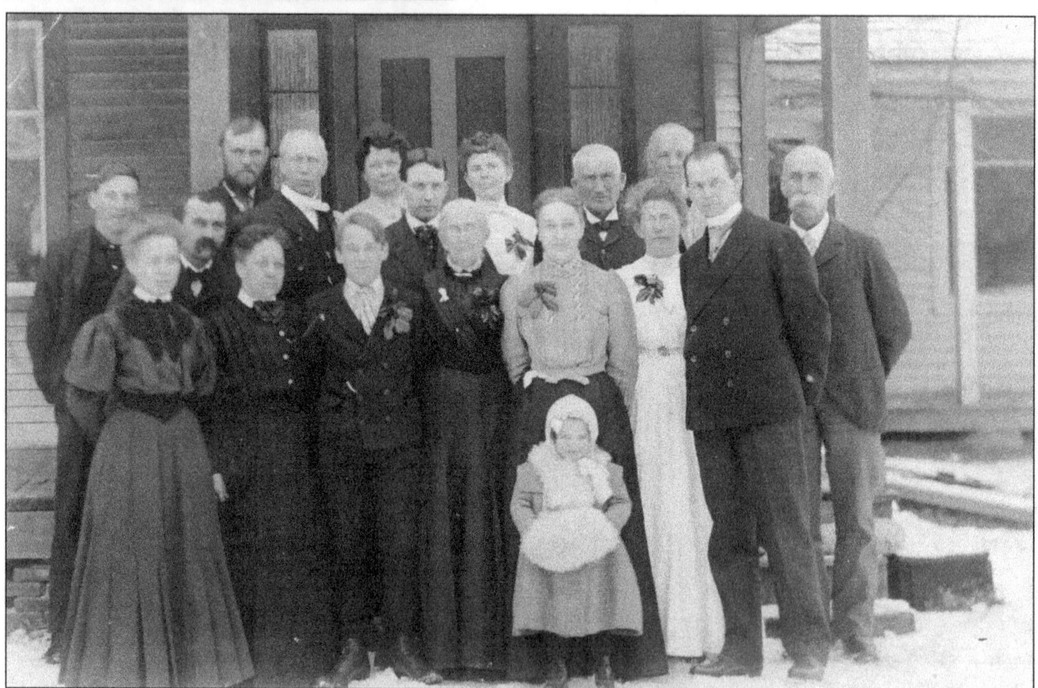

Lewis Purdy was one of the first settlers to arrive in the area in 1844. Although he stayed with his family in Sparta for only a few years, he was considered the first farmer to the area. He established his farm near the area of Eleven Mile Road and Peach Ridge Avenue, where he built a log home. Mrs. Purdy was the first white woman to live in Sparta.

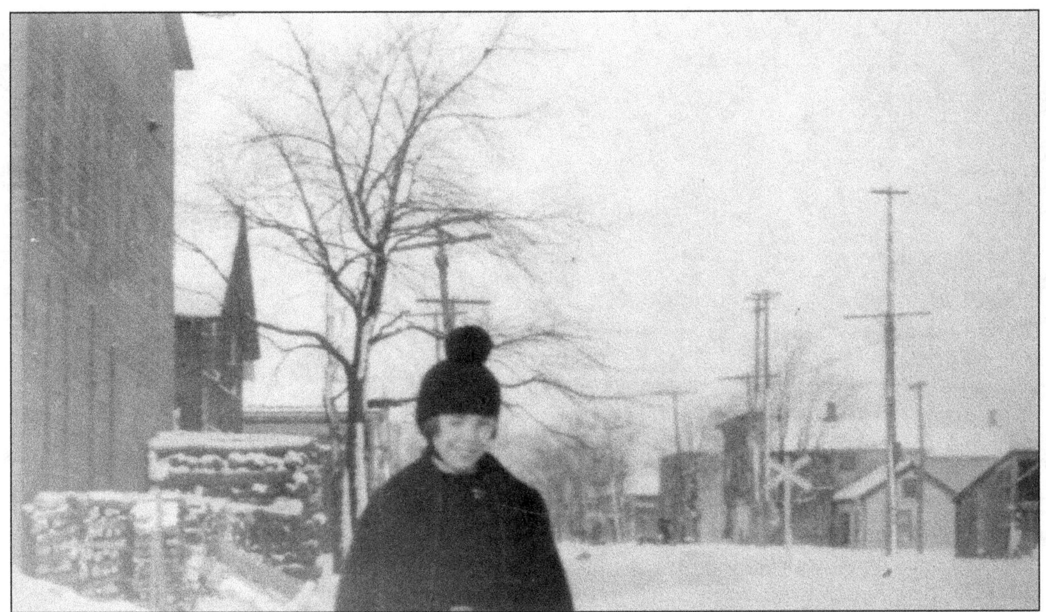

This photograph of Gwen Feerick Welch, born in 1910, was likely taken sometime after 1915. The photograph shows Division Street looking west. South of where Gwen is standing would be Simon's Hill. To her left is the coal shed used for the feed mill, and to the west of that was Welch's home.

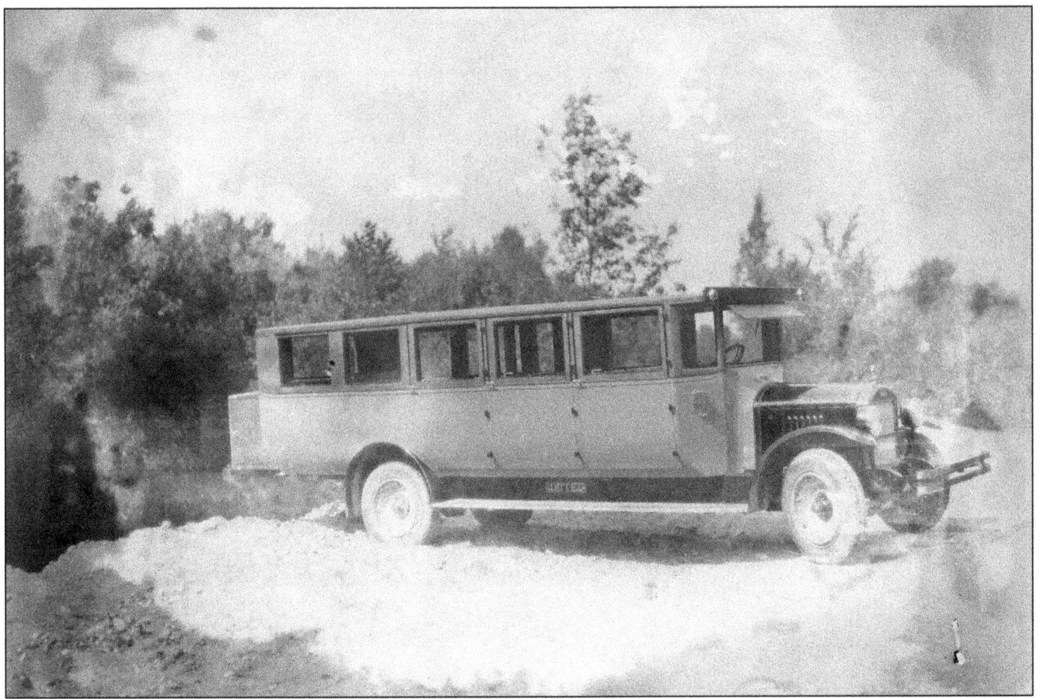

In the early years, when many women did not drive, they would take the bus to Grand Rapids. Passengers were able to catch the bus in the morning on the corner of Division and Union Streets. One could spend the day window shopping, touring the museum, taking in a movie, or having lunch, and return later in the afternoon.

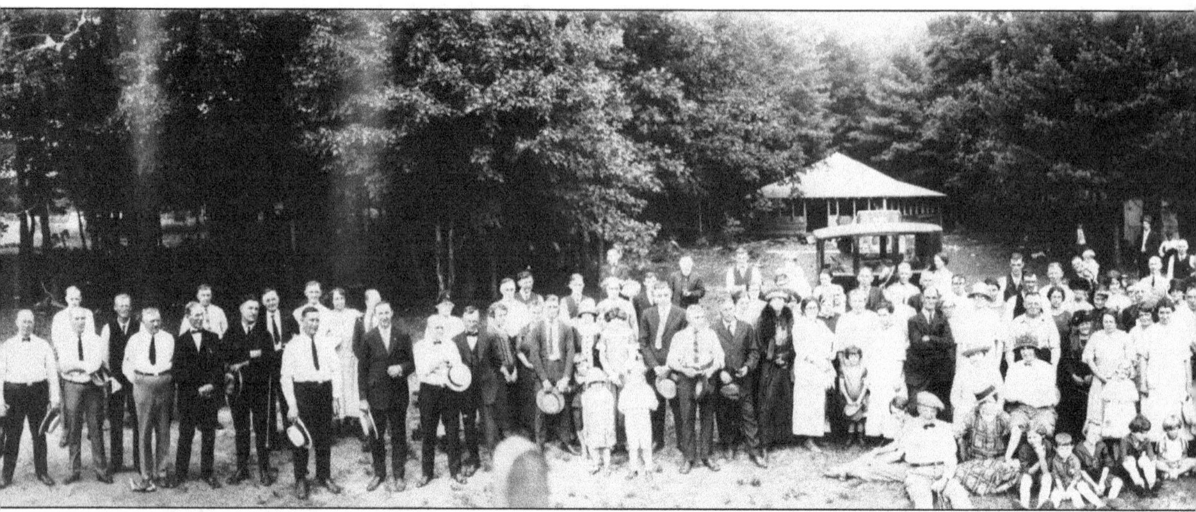

One of the first Sparta settlers' picnics was held at Camp Lake on August 21, 1924. Residents from the area would ride to Camp Lake in hot and crowded train cars on the TS&M Railway. Community picnics were a popular summertime event that brought everyone together for a smorgasbord and a variety of entertainment. There would be music and dancing, games, races,

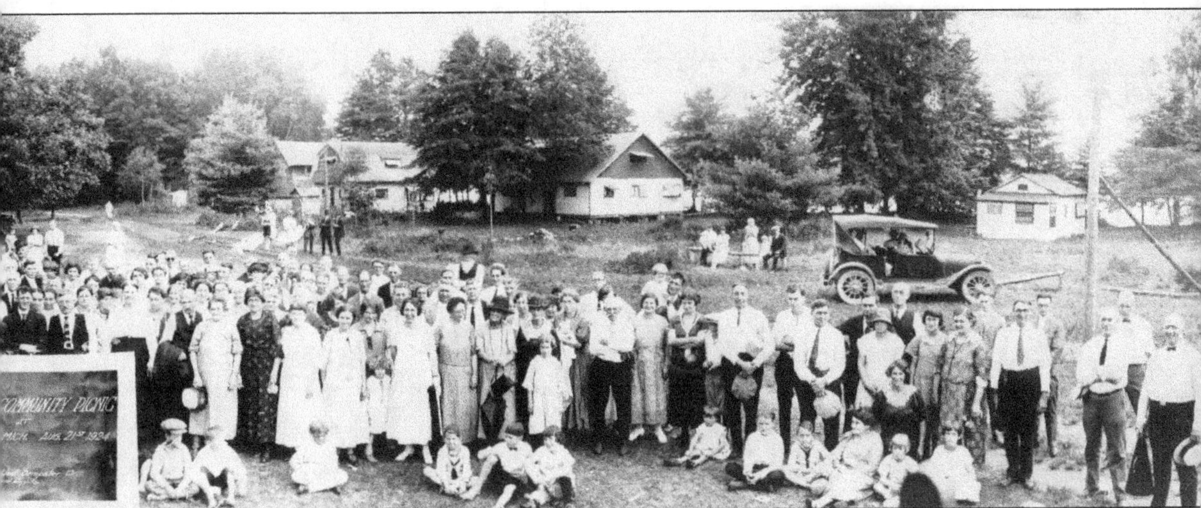

and contests. Often, the picnics were held at Camp Lake and Slocum's landing. One of the attractions at Camp Lake was the steamboat tour of the lake. Visitors were invited to bring their picnic baskets and join the festivities.

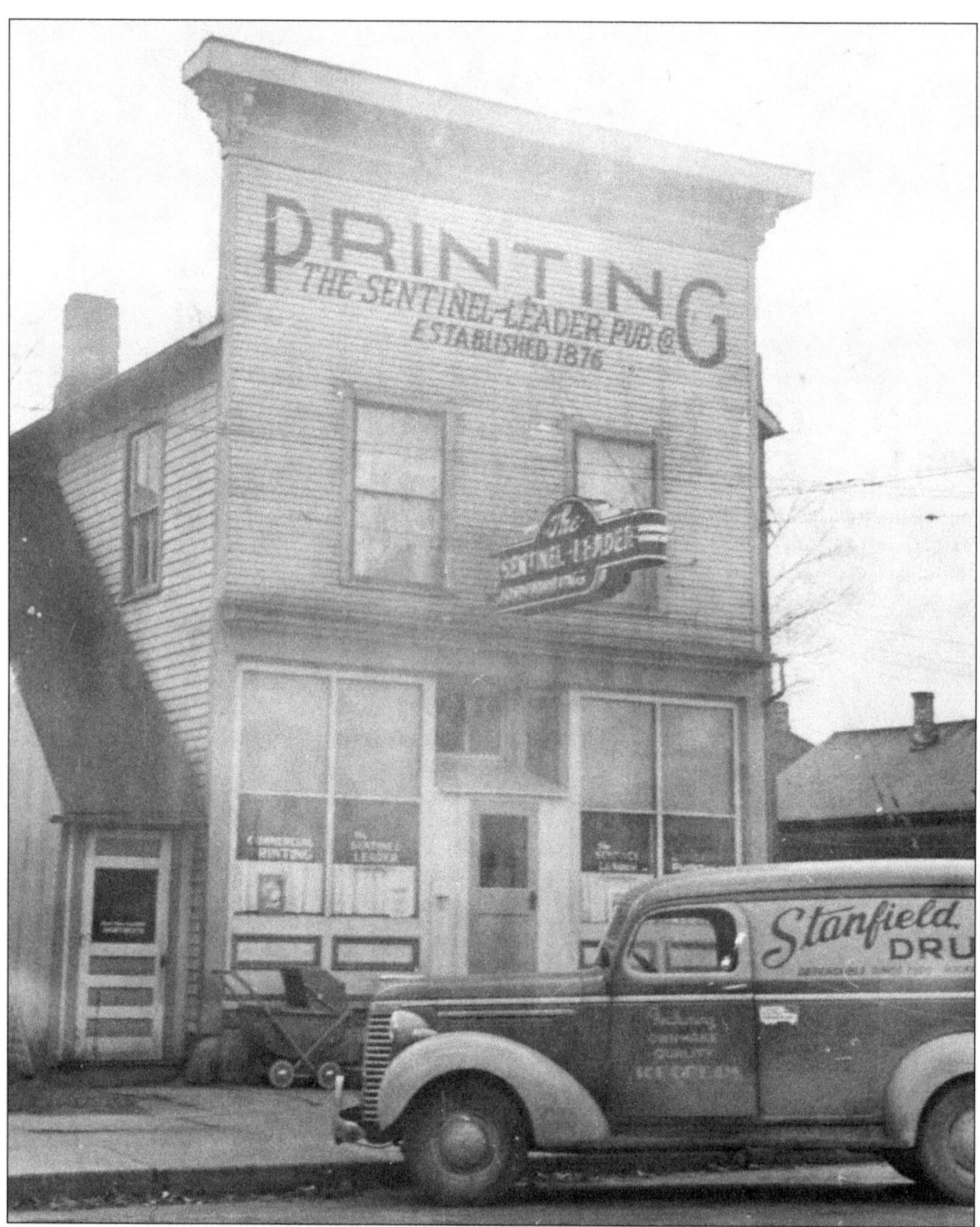

In 1876, the two Sparta newspapers, the *Sentinel* and the *Leader*, merged and became the *Sentinel Leader*. Over the years, the paper had many owners. In 1932, Horace "H. J." Kurtz came to Sparta to help his father-in-law, Frank Holmes, manage the paper. When Holmes died, Kurtz stayed on and continued to run the paper. Kurtz became a great booster for Sparta and was involved in many activities. For a time, he held the position of mayor. During World War II, he served as a regional director of the war bond sales, Red Cross, and community chest fund drives. He also served a term of five years as a director of the Michigan Press Associates, five years as a Kent County jury commissioner, and was a member of the National Editorial Association. Many awards and citations were presented to him during his long career. Kurtz sold the paper in 1961 to Barry Brand.

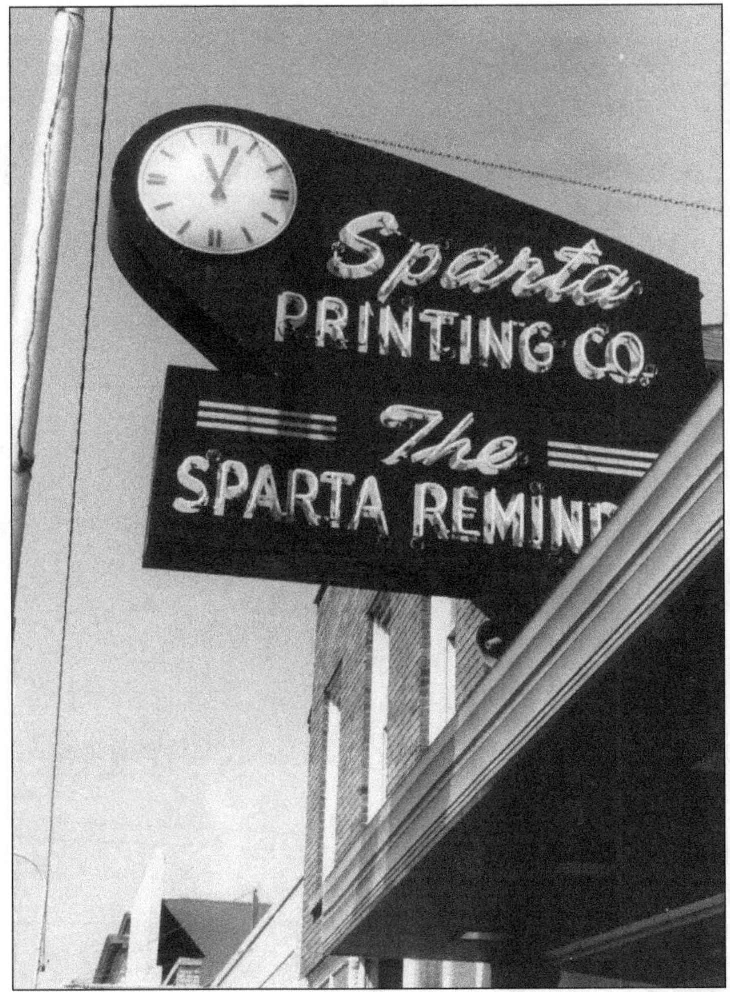

For a time in the 1950s and the 1960s, Sparta again had two newspapers, the *Sentinel Leader* and the *Sparta Reminder*, which was owned by Jack Gerard. For 35 years, Carol Holmes Kurtz, wife of H. J. Kurtz, owner of the *Sentinel Leader*, wrote a weekly column for the paper called "Seeing Life." Here she commented on all of the happenings around Sparta and the world. Carol, like her husband, was very active in the community. She was a member of the Sparta Baptist Church, the Ladies' Literary Club, Sparta Garden Club, Eastern Star, Women's Republican Club, and the Carr Circle of the Methodist Church. Her involvement in these clubs was sometimes the subject of her column.

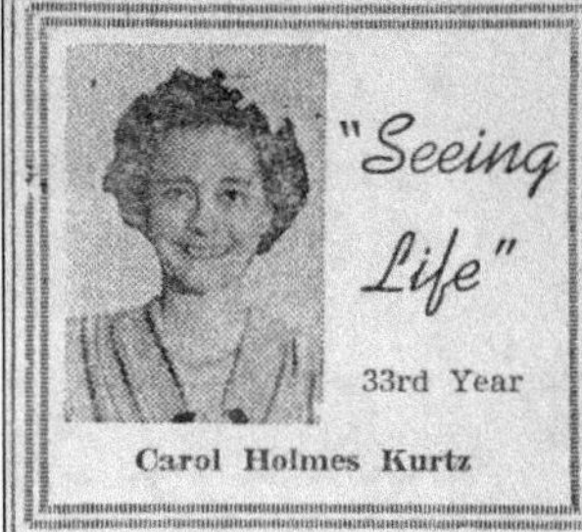

Weather forecast: A cold, cold winter!

* * *

Pleasant receiving a letter from an eight-year old niece saying "Dear Uncle Horace and Aunt Carol, I love you very, very much."

* * *

Friends tell about a well organized family where there are four children. After every meal each child takes his own dishes, rinses them off and stacks them in the dishwasher.

* * *

A friend tells about having a treatment in a doctor's office. Coming out she asked if she should pay then, thinking perhaps they preferred billing her. The cashier snapped, "You didn't think you would get it for nothing, did you?"

* * *

Irene brought us some pale blue eggs, but she said they did not require blue chickens to lay them, neither are they blue inside.

* * *

Resting in a Canadian hotel recently a man stopped and asked for money for coffee. The GM handed him a half pack of cigarettes. In a few moments he returned, saying, "Mister there weren't any cigarettes in the package. It was empty."

* * *

Visited the Kobers, now living on the former Cofer farm. Seems they found a love bird in the garden half frozen. They thawed him out on top of the oven on a towel and put him in to live with their own love bird. Now they have a happy pair.

* * *

We have a new neighbor. A tiny girl, Kay Louise, arrived home from the hospital last week. She is pretty, with brown hair, tiny toe nails and a lovely smile.

* * *

A delicious smorgasbord supper was given by the circles of the Methodist church last week. People loved it and crowded in. We understand the food almost ran out. It was well planned, temptingly displayed with a large variety for selection. Such good cooks!

* * *

Tricks and Treats coming up Friday evening—Halloween!

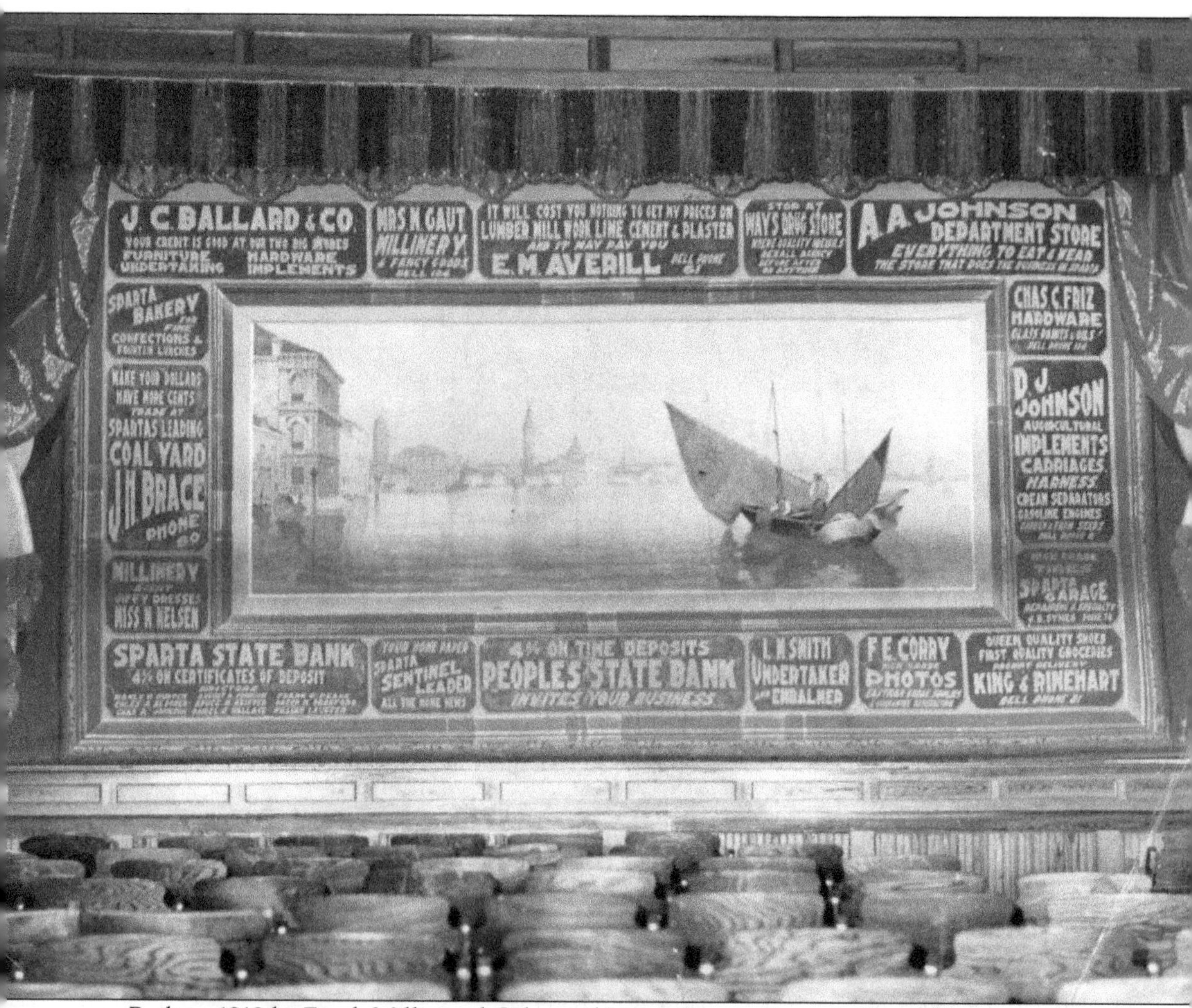

Built in 1912 by Frank Miller and Orley and Myrta Brown, Brown's Opera House stands at 188 East Division Street. When money was needed for a front drop, space on the curtain was sold for advertising, which was purchased by local merchants. Initially, films were shown to audiences of up to 500 to 600 people, but after a fire inspection halted the showings, the opera house was used for plays, dances, and parties.

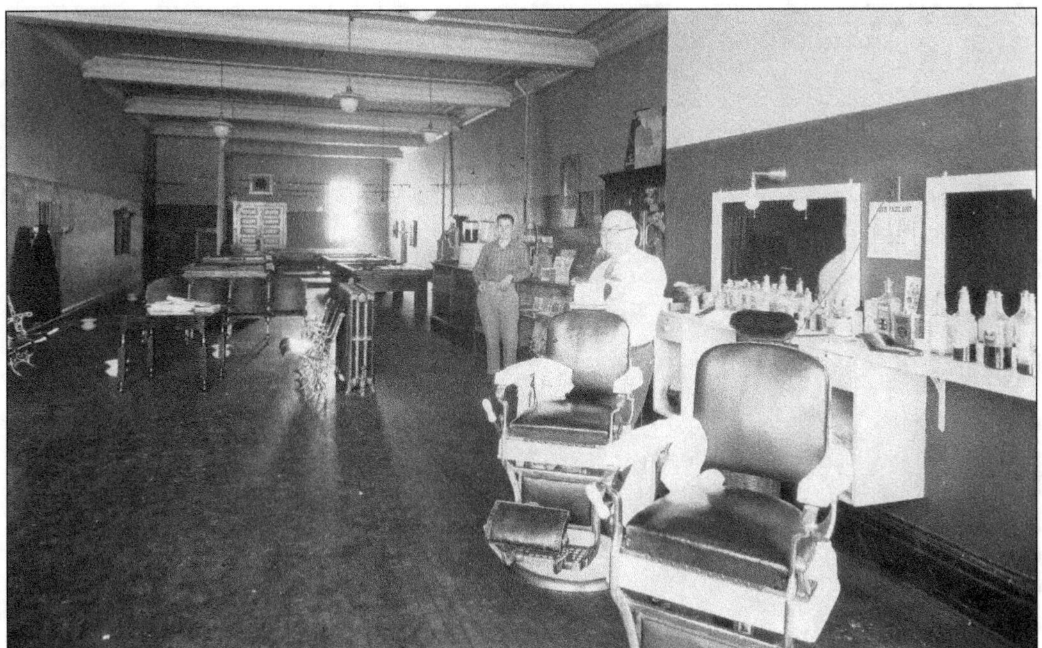

This photograph was taken of the west side of the Brown's Opera House building. In the foreground is Fred Spicer, the operator of the barbershop that was located on the main floor of the building. In the background is Albert M. Hale, who operated the pool hall behind the barbershop. (Courtesy of Albert and Mary Hale.)

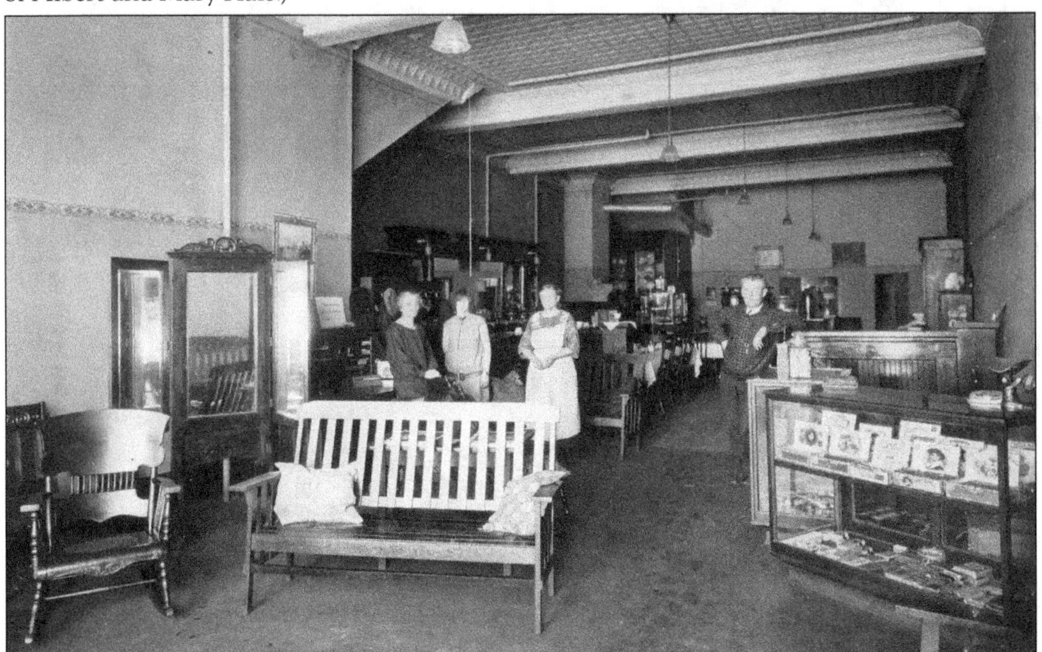

On the east side of the opera house was a restaurant that was operated by Myrta Brown, who is pictured on the left. The others are, from left to right, Mary T. Bisard; ? Briggs, who was the cook; and Orley Brown, who is standing behind the cigar case. Mary would go on to marry Albert M. Hale, the operator of the pool hall. (Courtesy of Albert and Mary Hale.)

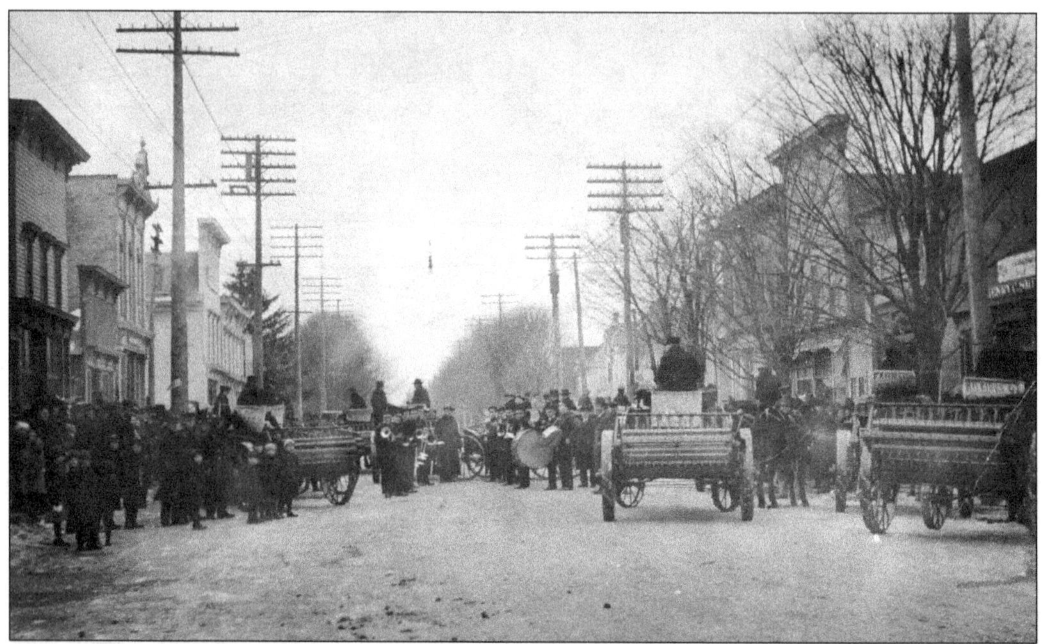

Farmers Days in town provided the opportunity for farming demonstrations and a market to sell and swap machinery. This photograph was taken looking west on East Division Street. It is believed to have been taken around 1912, as there were no cars present. Horse power was relied on to bring the farmers and their equipment to town.

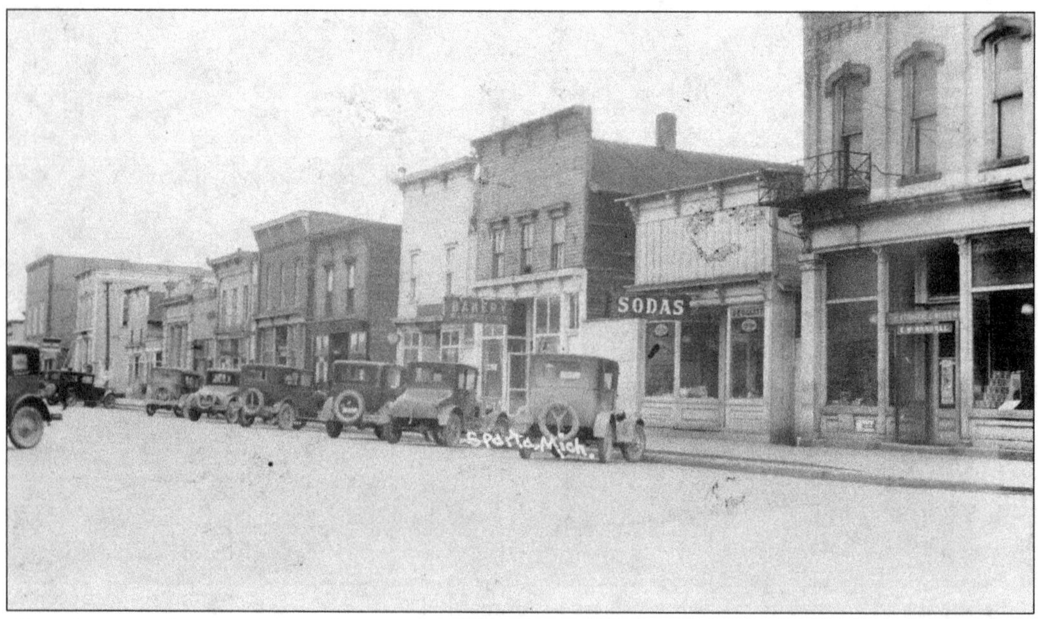

This photograph was taken looking east on Division Street sometime around 1928. Model Ts line the street in front of Cnossen's Bakery and the soda shop. E. W. Randall's grocery store stands on the far right of the picture. Before it was a grocery store, this building was a boot shop.

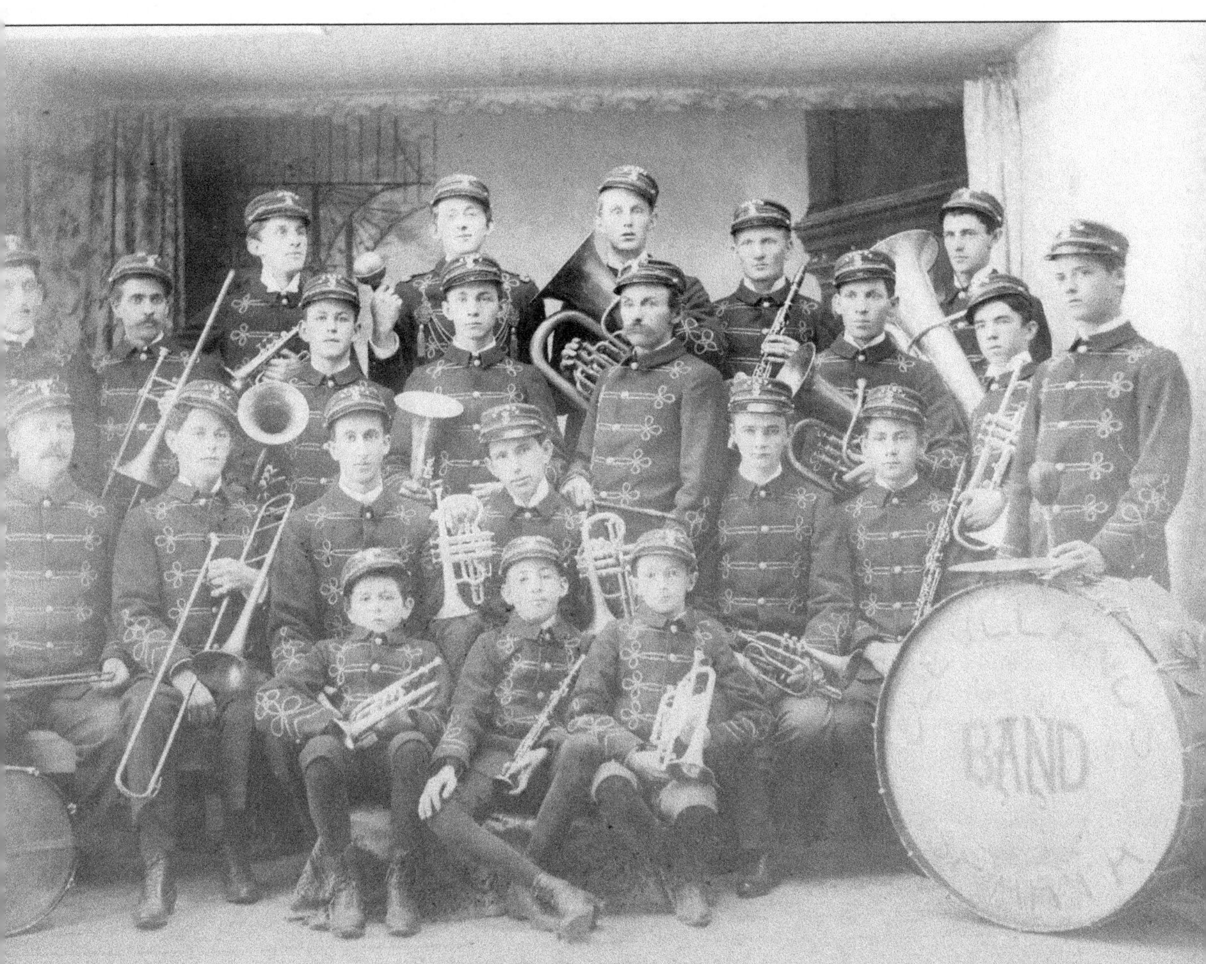

Those pictured are the members of Sparta's first band, the Cleveland Band. They are, from left to right, (first row) ? Kipie, Erastus Smith, and Elsworth Buchanan; (second row) Charles Holmes, Orley Brown, Charles Myers, Charles Ballard, Fred Loop, and Ira VansRiver; (third row) Lou Chilson, unidentified, Noble Gaut, two unidentified, L. M. Cleveland (director), and William Hallack; (fourth row) Arthur Thomsett, Roy VanAntwerp, Edward Beeby, ? Dyberg, and Frank Buchanan.

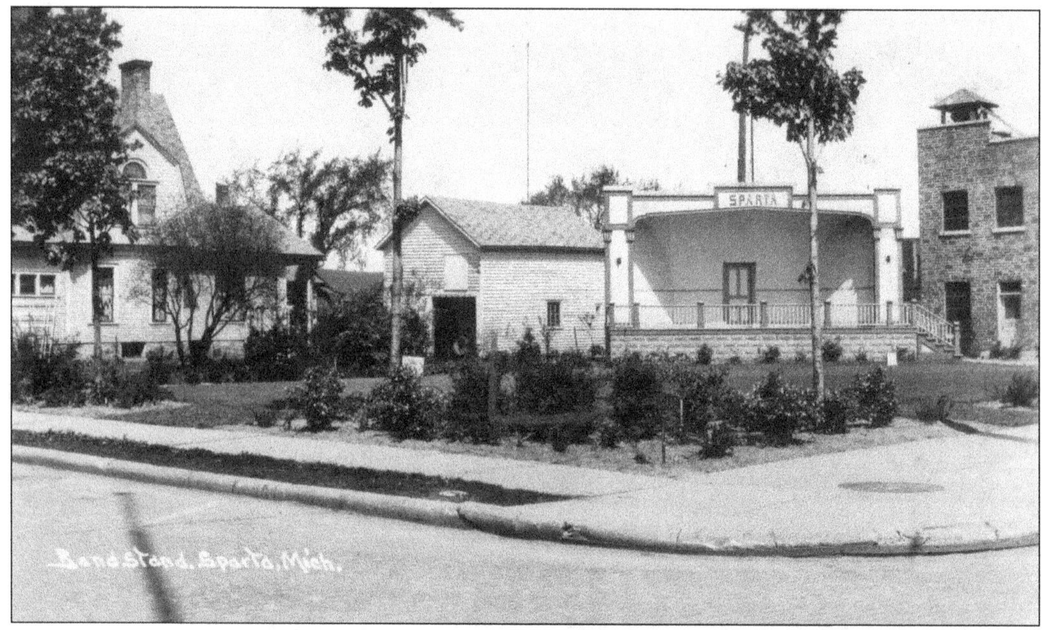

The band shell on the northwest corner of Division and Union Streets was located in a park where many events took place. The beautiful flower gardens surrounding the park were compliments of the members of the local garden club. For many, the most memorable feature of the park was the military honor roll, which listed those local residents who served in the U.S. military.

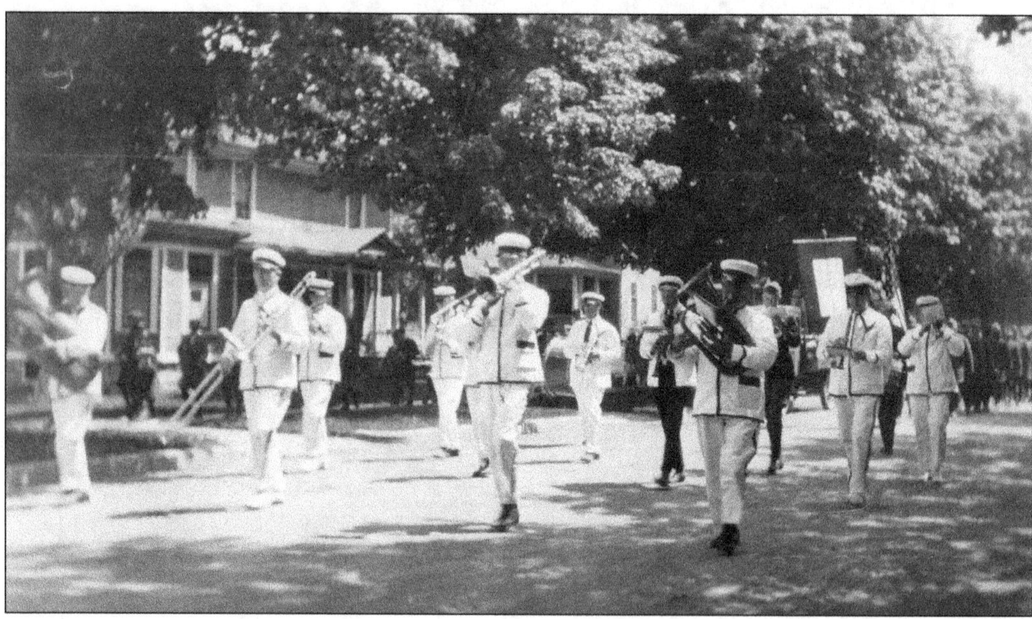

Participating in one of Sparta's many parades is the Sparta Marching Band. Members of the band included Wally Rice, Arthur Johnson, John Bickard, George Baker, Carl Wallace, Clarence Moore, Noble Gaut, Ellis Raymond, Elmer Amidon, Ernie Culp, Charles Amidon, Walter Bright, Bill Cores, Frank Atkinson, and Ira Cattell.

When the land a mile west of Sparta, near the corner of Thirteen Mile Road and M-37, became available, George Bettes purchased it. He was fond of the property, as he had childhood memories of sledding, hunting, and picnicking there. As he developed the land, he built an observation tower at the top of the hill. Visitors were invited to climb the tower and enjoy the 15-mile view of the surrounding area. The tower was taken down in 1978. The recreation grounds became known as "Bettes's Hill" and hosted many picnics for schools, churches, and other organizations. Sometimes the Ham radio operators, Civil Defense, and Weather Bureau used the tower and land as testing grounds for operations. The Michigan Championship Rodeo was held there every Labor Day weekend. Local churches have also used the land for picnics and Easter Sunday sunrise services.

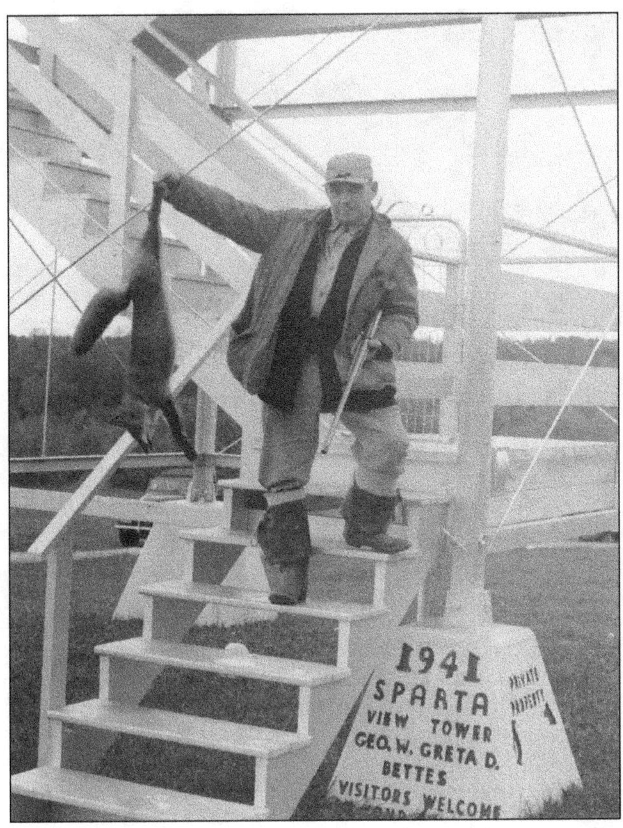

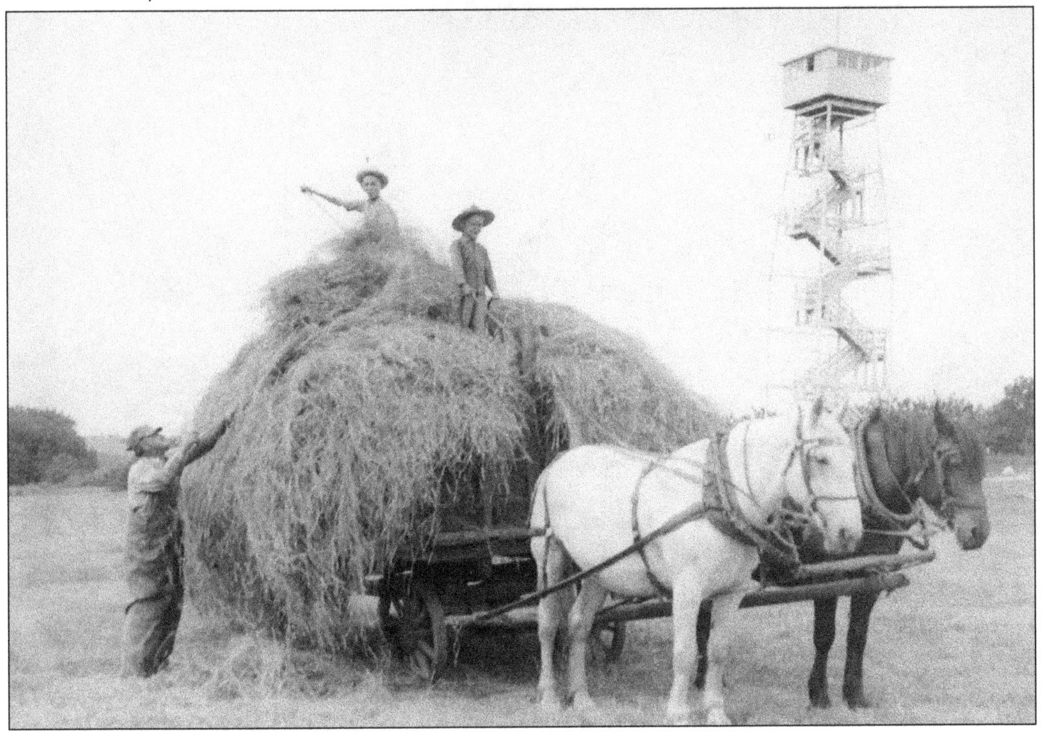

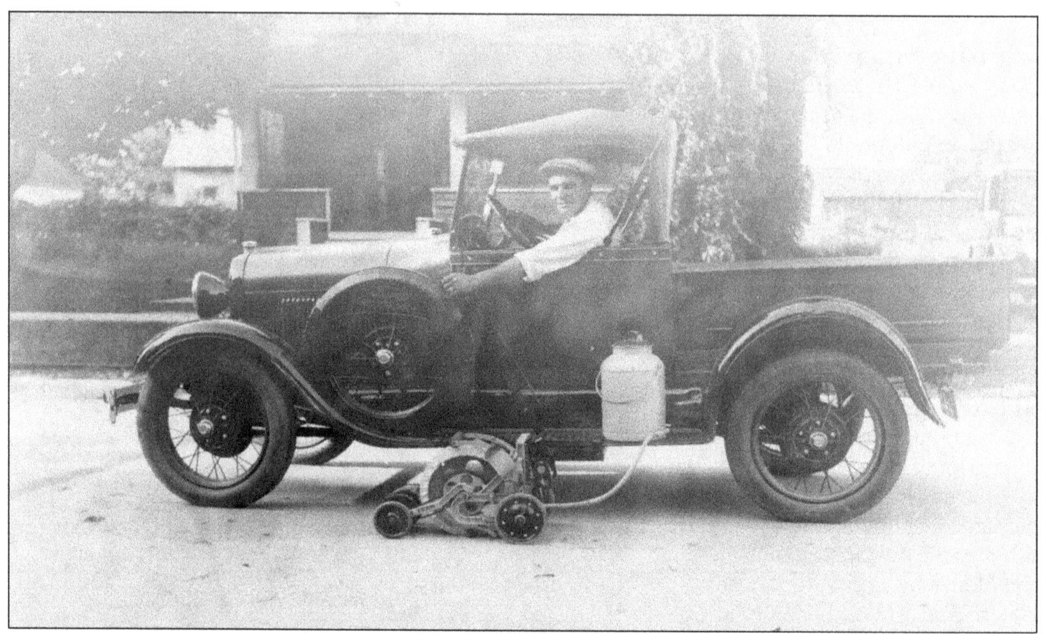

After observing that many of the accident-related deaths occurred as a result of drivers failing to stay on their side of the road, inventor George W. Bettes patented the "road marker." Eventually, Bettes and his machine had marked most of the roads in Kent and Muskegon Counties. The road marker was manufactured by Littleford Brothers of Cincinnati, Ohio, and was used all around the world.

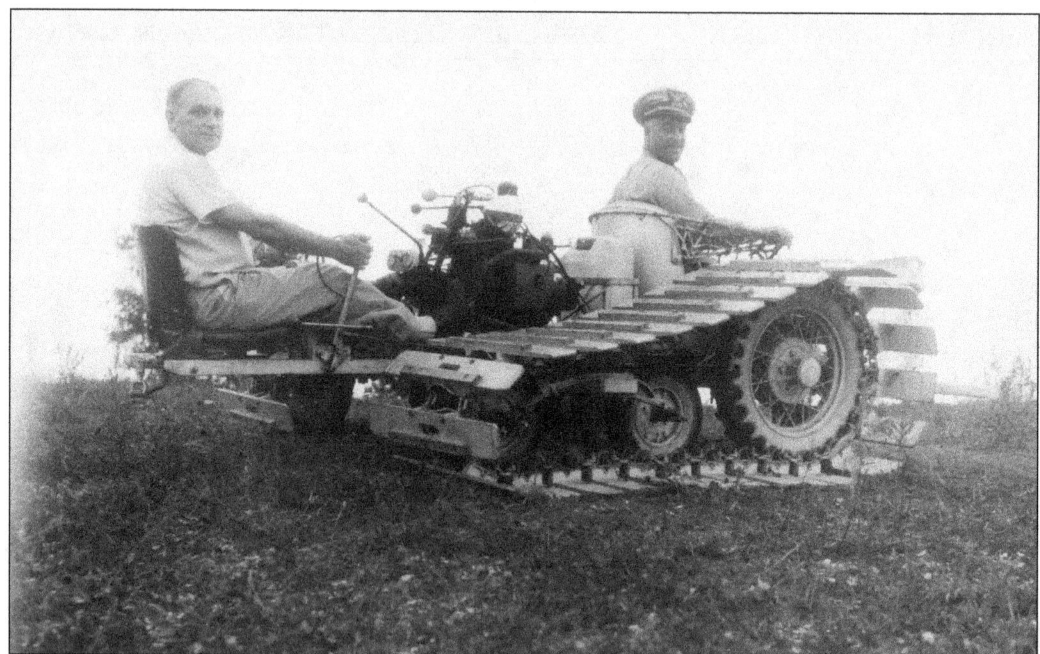

In the late 1930s, George Bettes, lifelong resident and entrepreneur, invented the snow machine for the U.S. Army and traveled to Fort Brady to test and experiment with his invention. Over the years, the machine evolved into a sophisticated machine that could travel over bare ground or snow up to 30 miles per hour.

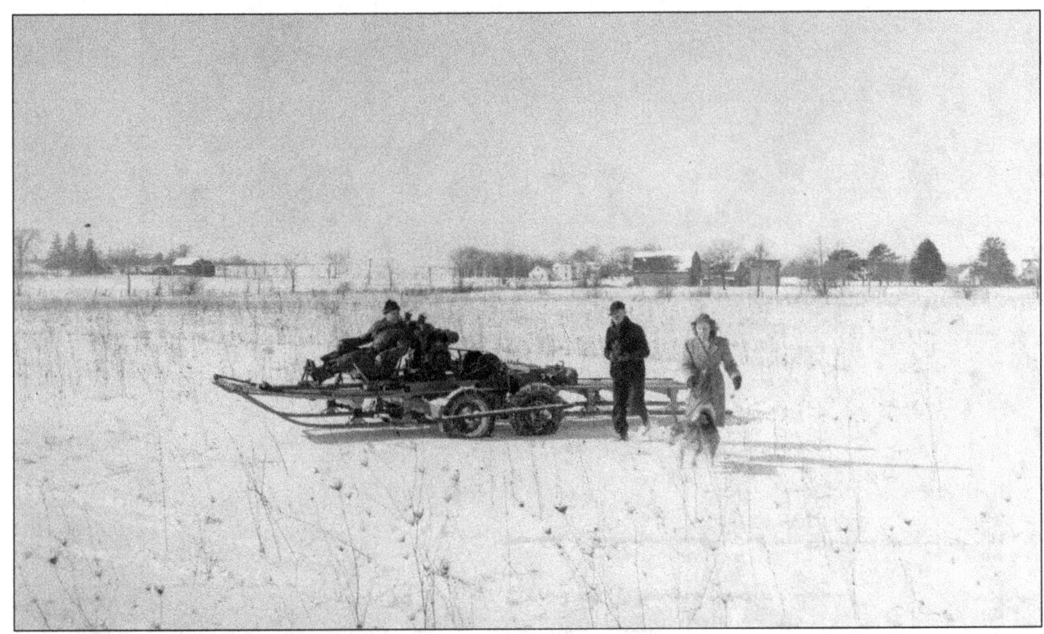

George Bettes was an acquaintance of Lieutenant Commander Bursey, who, in 1955, led an expedition to the "Little America" exploration site on Antarctica with Bettes's donated Polar Sled. The wood used for the sled was harvested from Bettes's Hill, and a local welder fabricated the hardware. On the hill, Bettes also raised Siberian huskies, which he became interested in following his connection with the Antarctic expedition.

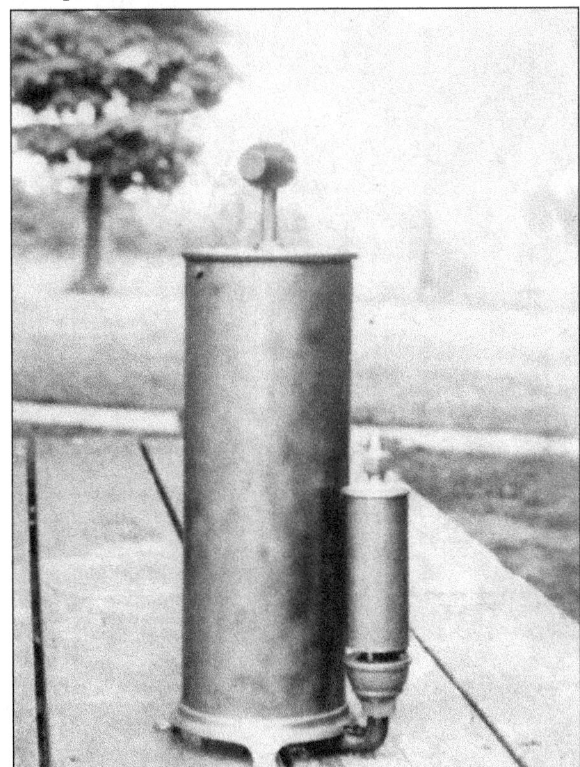

Always an inventor, George Bettes made himself a diving mask for underwater exploration. While searching under water at Camp Lake, he, along with Howard Bettes and Ralph Barnum, discovered the wrecked *Lady of the Lake* steamboat at the bottom of the lake. They were able to recover the ship's whistle that Ralph Barnum preserved.

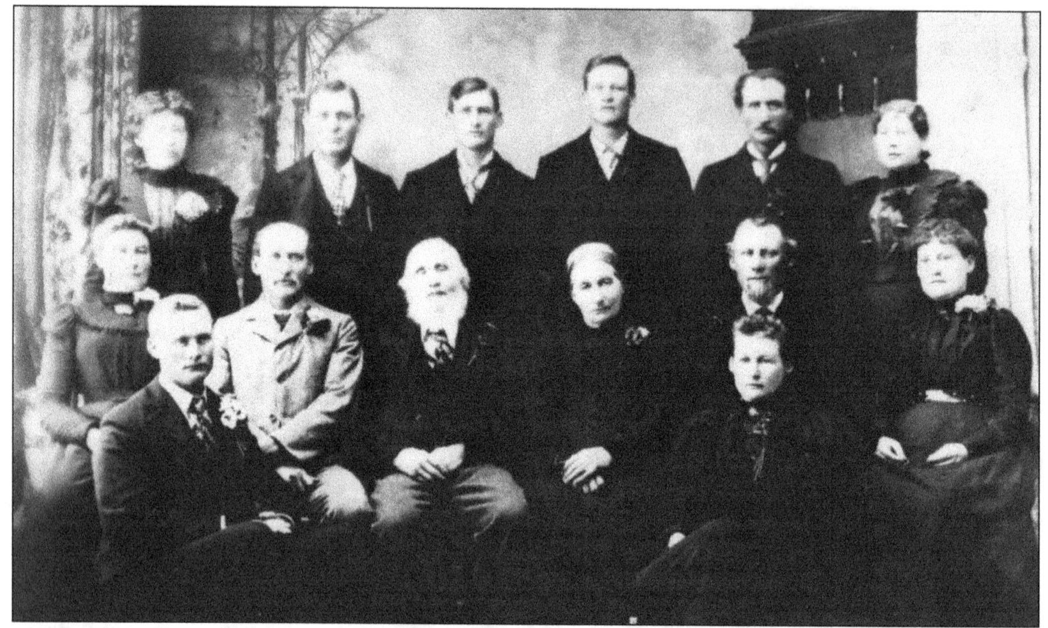

Charles Anderson, third from left, second row, was born in Sweden in 1815, son of John and Marva Bergdahl. His journey to America was an adventure. His ship was attacked by pirates and nearly everyone on board was killed. Charles Bergdahl was reported killed, and Charles Anderson was reported missing. Many attempts were made to correct the error, all in vain, so authorities advised him to take the name Charles Anderson. (Courtesy of Marcia Anderson Fairchild.)

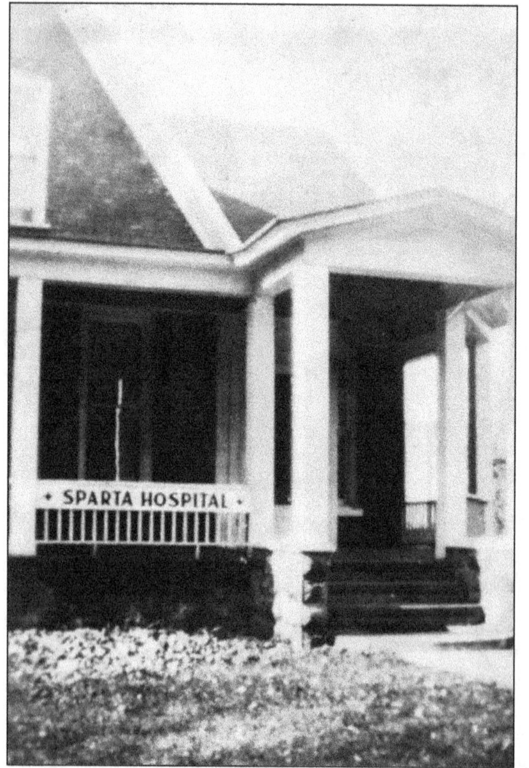

In the early 1930s, Eva Anderson opened a maternity home at 35 South Union Street in Sparta. This location had been a former mortuary and the home of Sherry Ballard. In 1937, Anderson sold this home and opened one at 66 Washington Street. Local doctors were grateful for these maternity homes, and many local babies were born there.

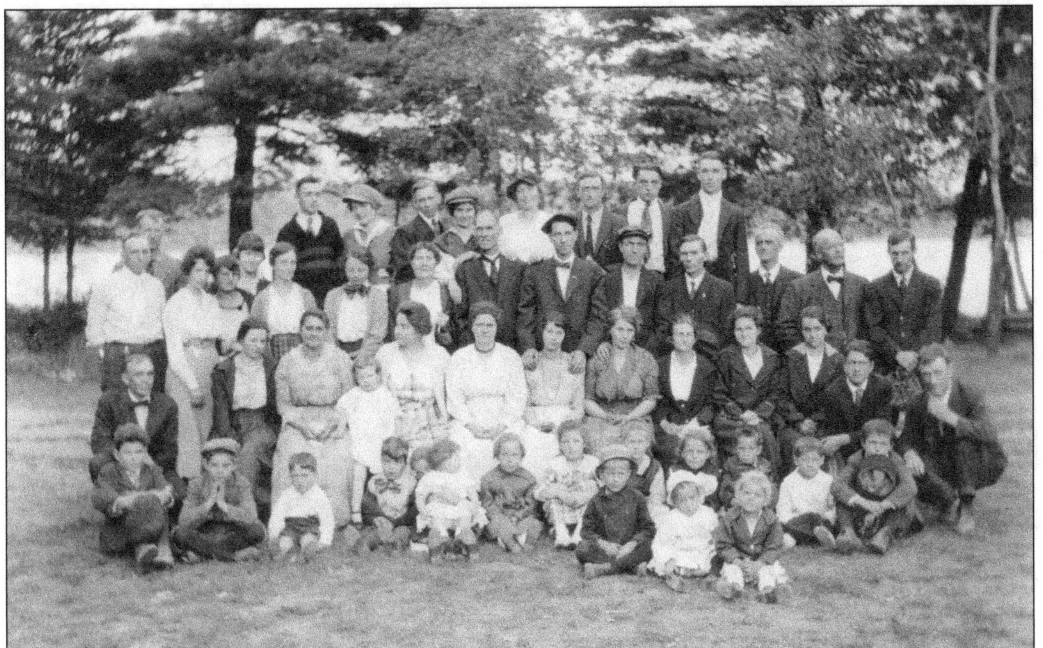

The Carnation company picnic was an annual event held to encourage morale and camaraderie among its valued employees. This photograph was taken lakeside in the 1920s. The employees, their spouses, and children were all included in the festivities. In the third row, far left, are superintendent Arville Ball and his wife.

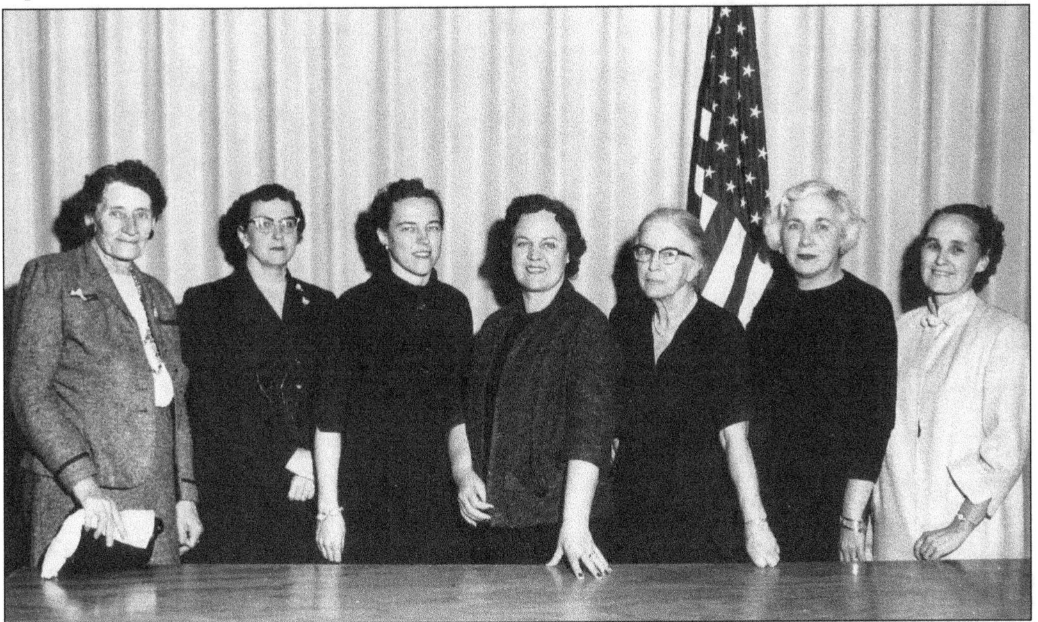

In 1906, the Ladies' Literary Club was formed, and in 1910, members started the first circulating library in the village of Sparta. In 1914, member Cecile Keister proposed the idea of a permanent library as a club project. This began the project of what would become the Carnegie Library. Pictured are, from left to right, Bertha Bloomer, unidentified, Susie Weston, Nellie Burgett, Lou Keller, Norma Slagel, and Donna Baker.

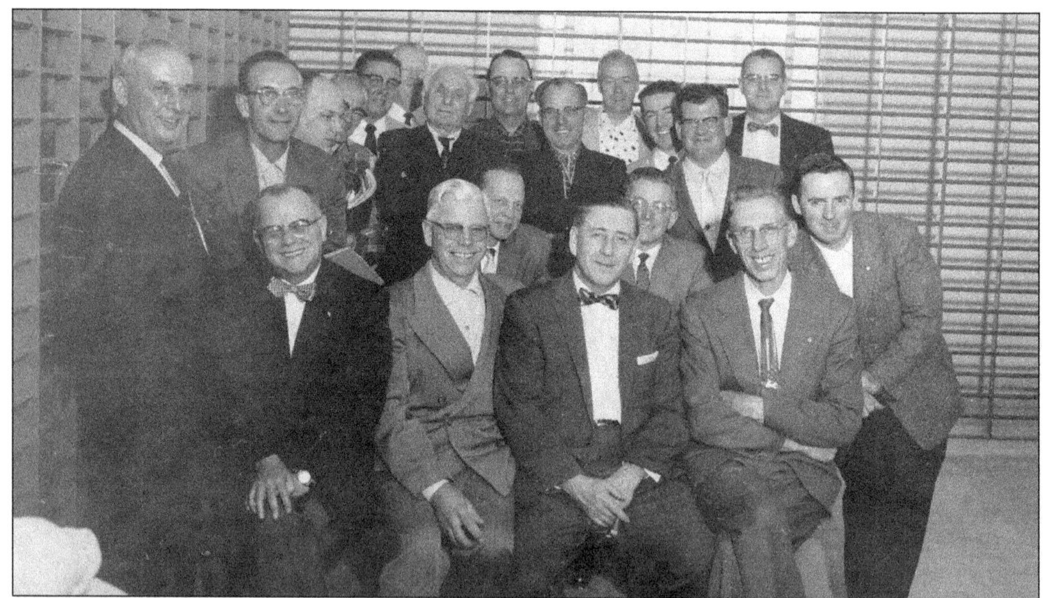

Horace "H. J" Kurtz established the Sparta Rotary Club in 1937. For many years, Sparta has benefited from the club's projects and causes. From left to right are (first row) Joe Brooks, Clifford Dingman, Carl Walstrom, Bernard Hessel, unidentified, Charles Rogers, and Charles Welch; (second row) Charles Warren, Walt Blackmere, Jay Dean, John Feichtenbiner, Jack Davis, unidentified, H. J. Kurtz, Leon Parker, Nan Benham, Roy Titus, Richard Wolf, Ralph Taylor, and Lawrence D'Amour.

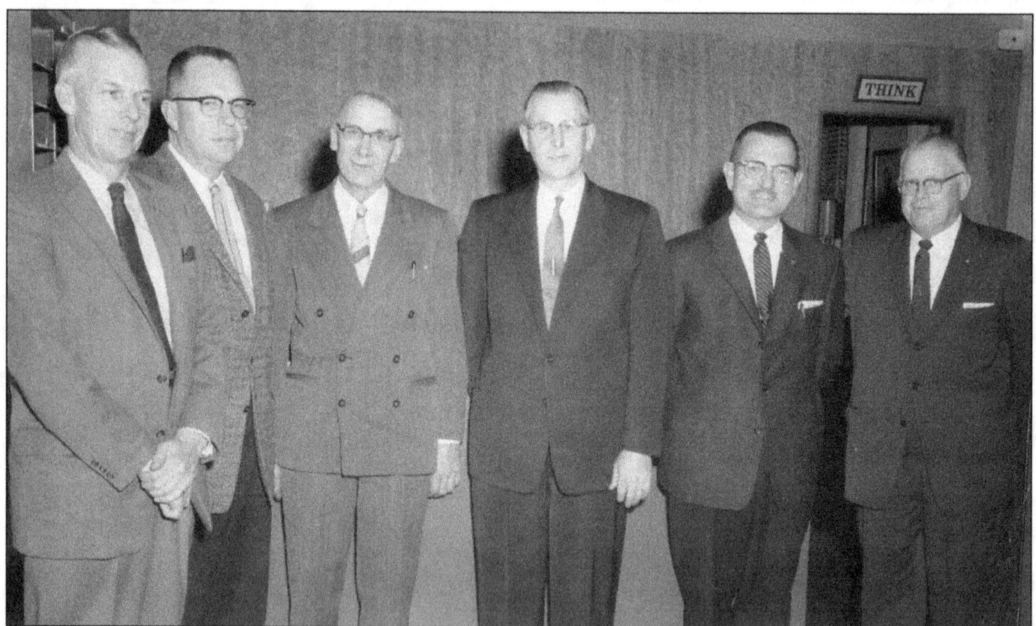

The Sparta Chamber of Commerce began in 1921. Its primary purpose was to promote business in the area and to sponsor many events benefitting the people of Sparta. Members of the chamber are, from left to right, Ed Lane, Sparta Theater; Ivar Johnson, Sparta State Bank; Lynn Bradford, local dairy farmer; Melvin Rogers, Roger's Hardware; Dr. Charles Bromley, local dentist; and Bill DeHart, Sparta Area School District's superintendent.

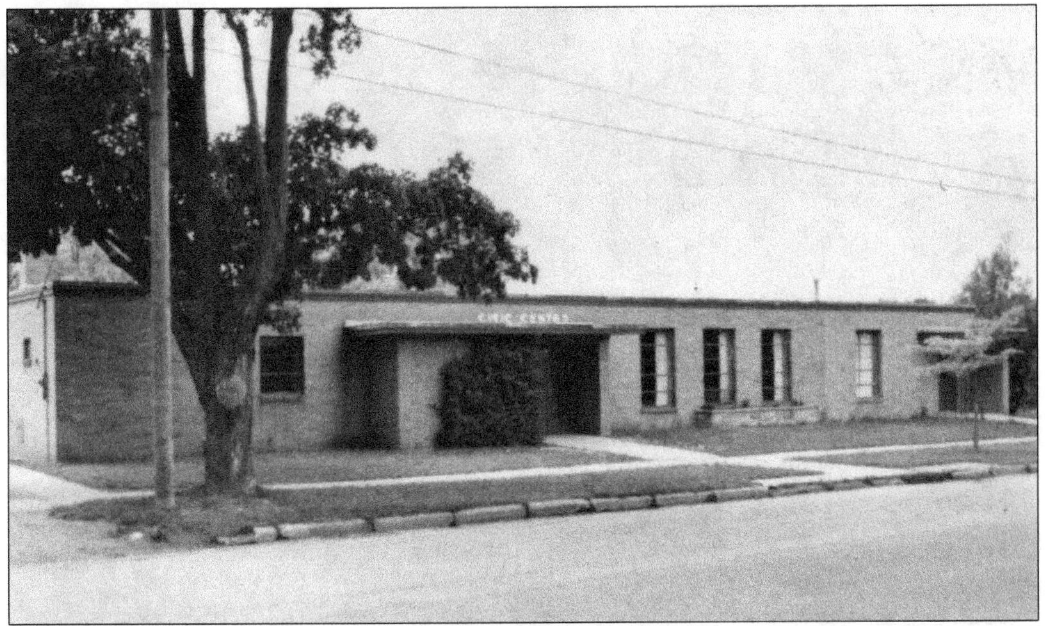

The Sparta Civic Center was constructed in 1956 as a community gathering place. Muskegon Piston Ring donated the original funds for the facility, and more were raised by local organizations. Over the years, the building has been used as a meeting location for many local clubs and Boy and Girl Scout troops, as well as preschool and kindergarten classes, weddings, dinners, fund-raisers, and family events.

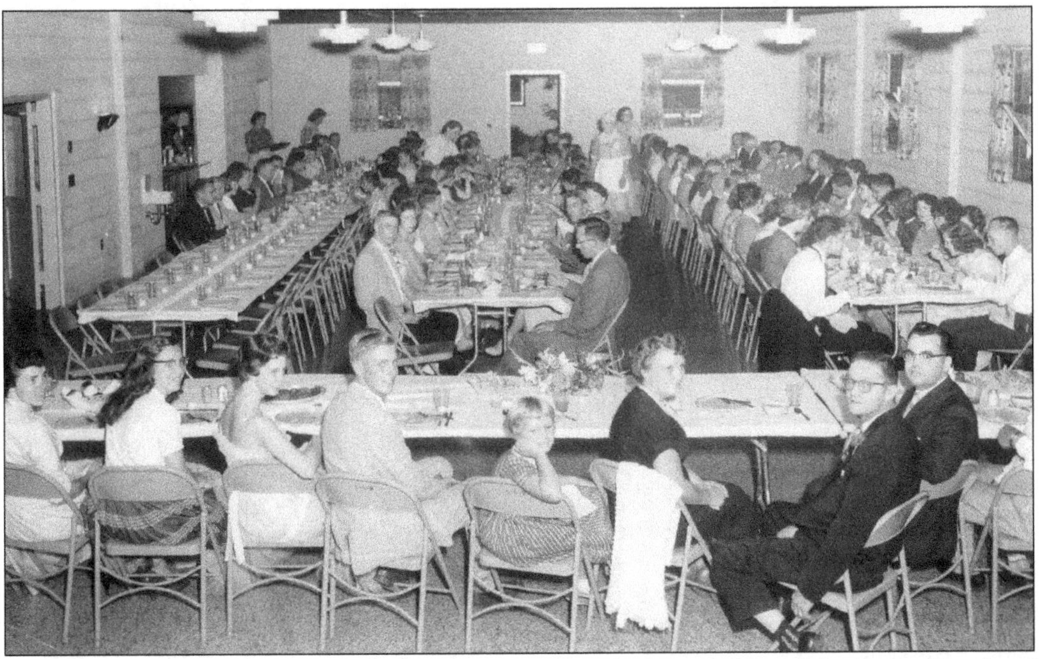

"The terrazzo floor is beautiful and the room is attractively decorated," said the *Sentinel Leader* of the Sparta Civic Center in May 1956. The building has been used over the years by a variety of community groups. Here it is being used for a banquet. For years, the facility was used on Election Day for locals to cast their vote.

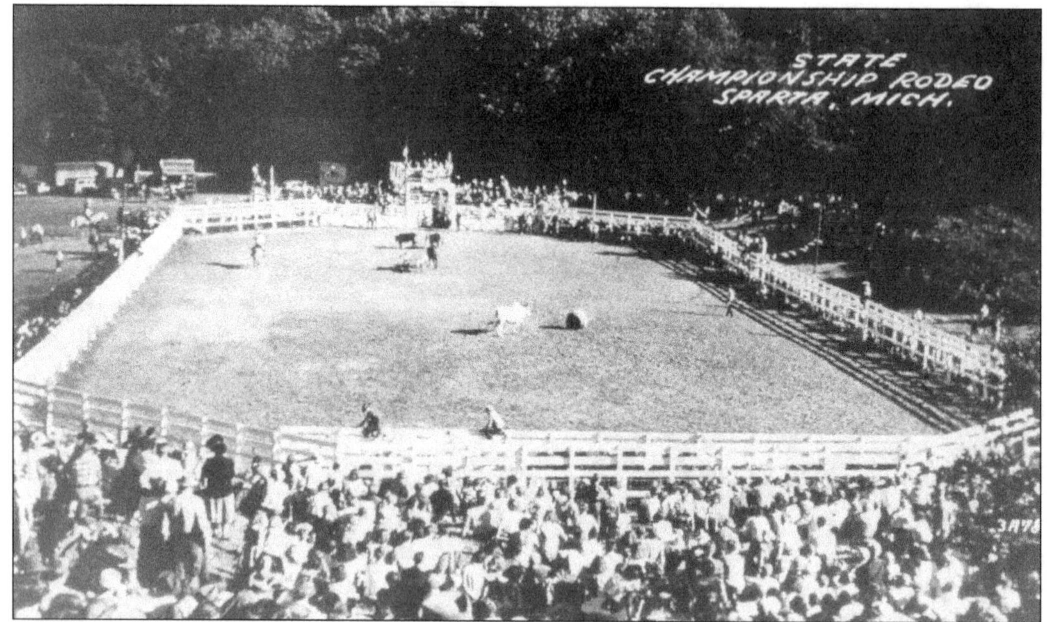

Kenneth R. Klein and Clifford L. VandenHout sponsored the first Sparta Rodeo in 1946 on the land known as Bettes's Hill, later to become the Sparta Rodeo Grounds. The competition took place over Labor Day weekend and grew from a one-day to a weeklong event over the years. Eventually the rodeo became known as the Michigan State Championship Rodeo and drew crowds from across the state.

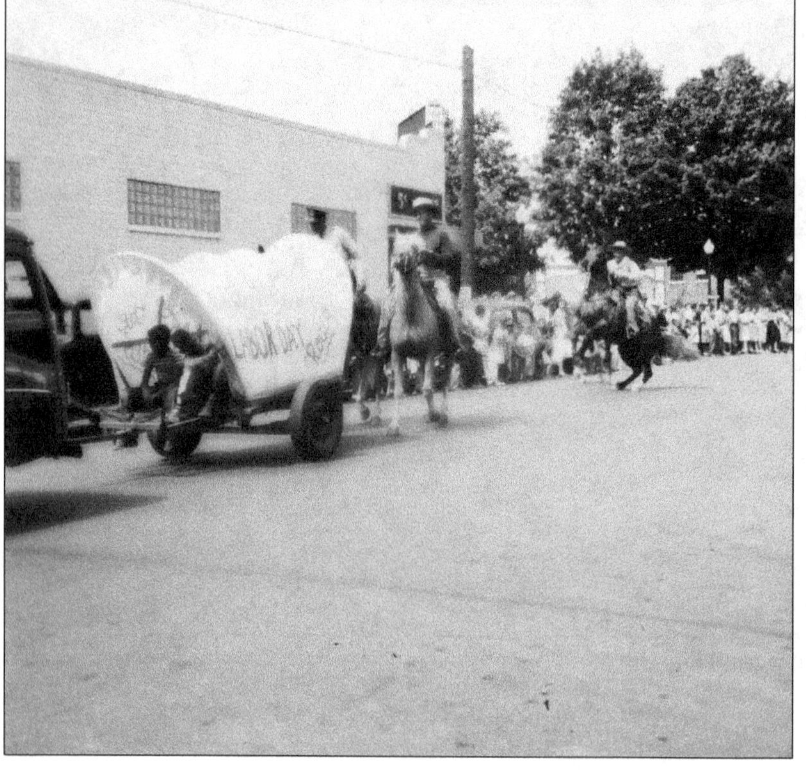

Every year, a Friday afternoon parade would begin the festivities of the Sparta Rodeo. The Labor Day weekend event was held at Bettes's Hill. The rodeo attracted trick riders, clowns, and cowboys from all over the state. A rodeo queen was selected and crowned annually, among other crowd-pleasing events that included bronco riding, speed races, and "wild cow" milking.

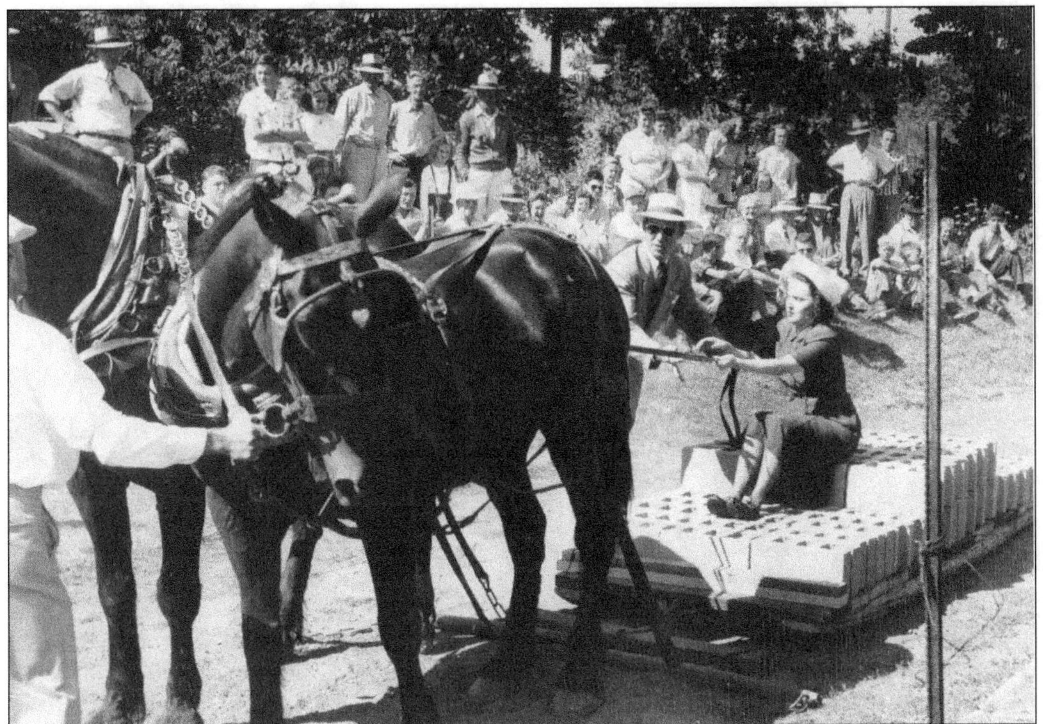

Horse pulls were a popular attraction at the Sparta fair in the late 1940s and early 1950s. The pulls were held at Balyeat Field, near Nash Creek. Phil Schwartz holds his draft horses Bob and Belle, as reporters from the local radio station WLAV, Lenore Little (on the sled) and Glenn LePard (standing beside her, helping with the reins), look on.

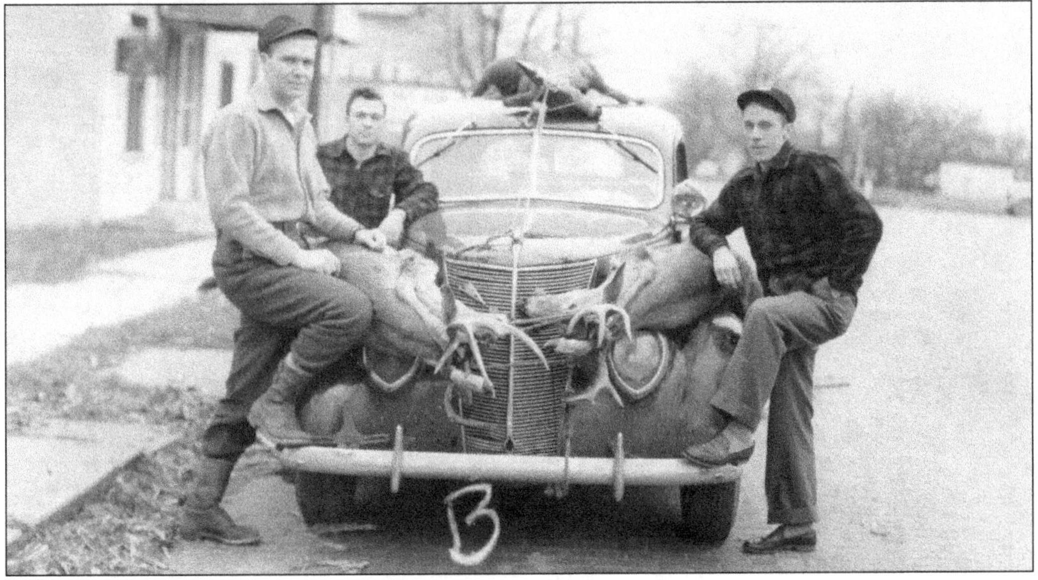

This 1937 Ford belonged to Sydney Blaauw. The deer were shot on a ranch near Houghton, Michigan, in November 1945. The building in the background is the Sparta Tractor and Implement Sales on East Division Street, and beyond that is the Sparta Feed Mill. From left to right are Edward Soderstrom, Robert Engstrom, and Sydney Blaauw.

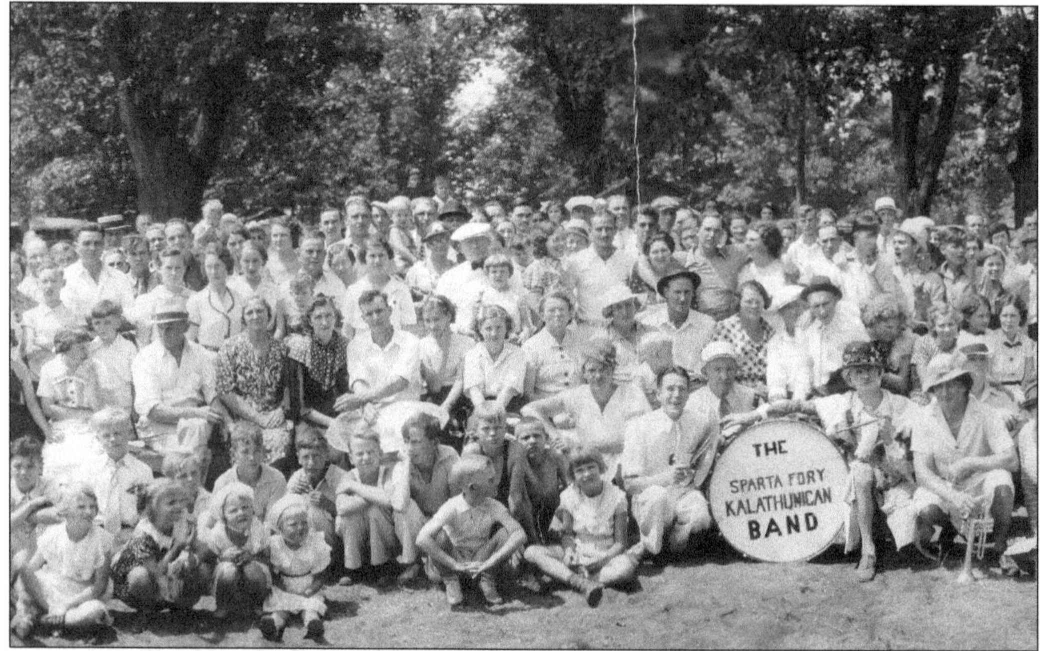

During the years, there were so many people from Sparta who worked for Muskegon Piston Ring, it must have seemed like the whole community attended the company picnic. These gatherings were usually held at Camp Lake, with food occasionally being prepared by local bakery owner Frank Cnossen. Entertainment was provided for the adults and children, alike.

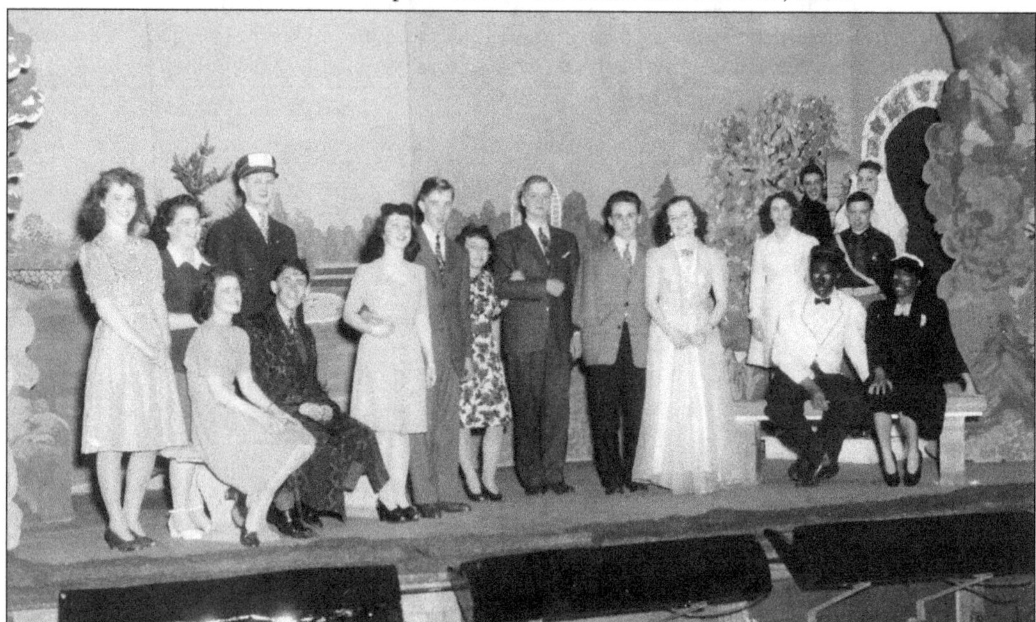

Pictured with art teacher Mary Brevitz, who most likely directed the junior-senior play in 1944, is the cast of *Three Act Comedy* by Katherine Kavanagh. The cast consisted of Iris Axford, Joanne Bettes, Katherine Bull, Allen Cumings, Lionel Fitzner, Ruth Helsel, Phyllis Hussey, Bernard Johnson, Bud LaVine, Esther Lenski, Charles Mills, Wanda Murray, Kenneth Smith, Justin Spangenberg, Glenna Stevens, and Wayne Straight.

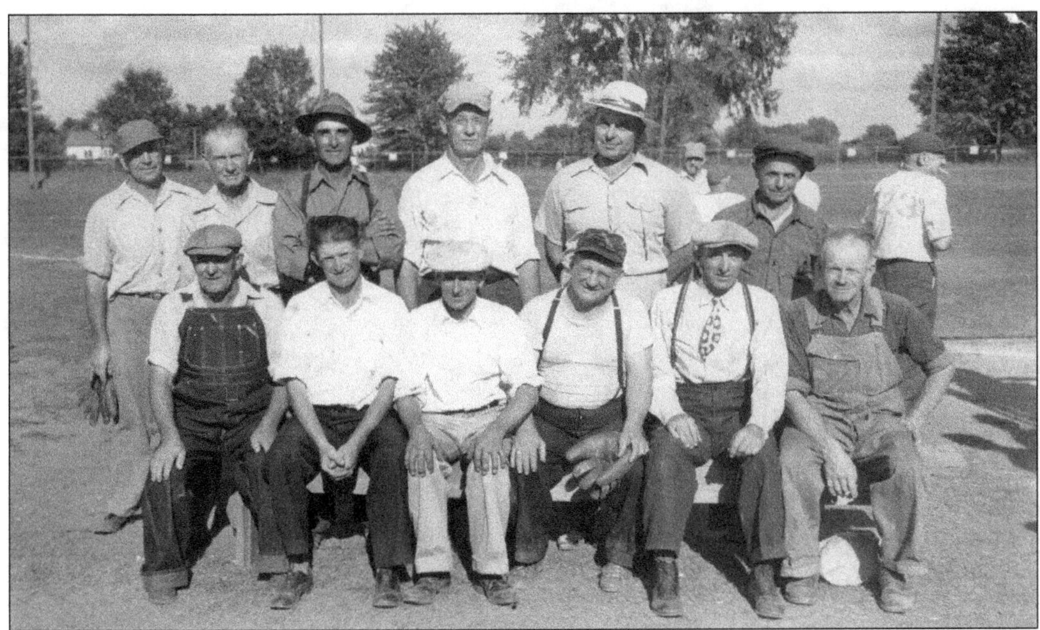

The Sparta Farmers' Days celebration featured an old-timers baseball game in 1948. The game matched up the merchants versus the farmers. The farmers upset the business men by a final score of 19-18. From left to right are (first row) Morrie Raman, "Stub" Colby, O. T. McCready, Hugh Finch, Claude Gillette, and Dr. Frank Bull; (second row) Seth Streeter, A. Barth Carlson, Carl Johnson, Dave Johnson, Elgin Gorby, and Larry Wyse.

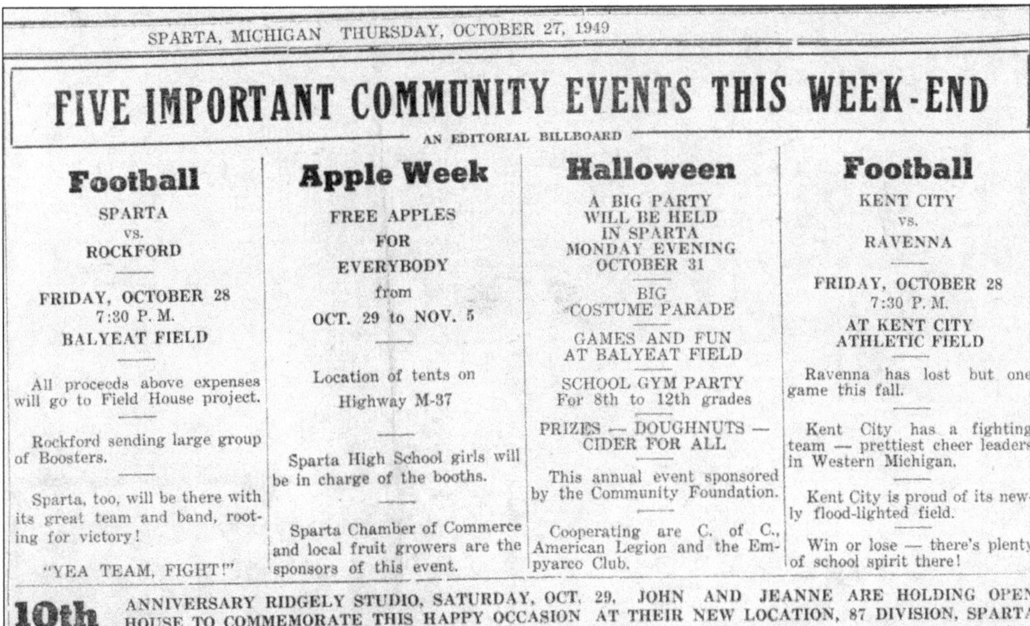

SPARTA, MICHIGAN THURSDAY, OCTOBER 27, 1949

FIVE IMPORTANT COMMUNITY EVENTS THIS WEEK-END

AN EDITORIAL BILLBOARD

Football

SPARTA vs. ROCKFORD

FRIDAY, OCTOBER 28
7:30 P. M.
BALYEAT FIELD

All proceeds above expenses will go to Field House project.

Rockford sending large group of Boosters.

Sparta, too, will be there with its great team and band, rooting for victory!

"YEA TEAM, FIGHT!"

Apple Week

FREE APPLES FOR EVERYBODY
from
OCT. 29 to NOV. 5

Location of tents on Highway M-37

Sparta High School girls will be in charge of the booths.

Sparta Chamber of Commerce and local fruit growers are the sponsors of this event.

Halloween

A BIG PARTY WILL BE HELD IN SPARTA MONDAY EVENING OCTOBER 31

BIG COSTUME PARADE

GAMES AND FUN AT BALYEAT FIELD

SCHOOL GYM PARTY For 8th to 12th grades

PRIZES — DOUGHNUTS — CIDER FOR ALL

This annual event sponsored by the Community Foundation.

Cooperating are C. of C., American Legion and the Empyarco Club.

Football

KENT CITY vs. RAVENNA

FRIDAY, OCTOBER 28
7:30 P. M.
AT KENT CITY ATHLETIC FIELD

Ravenna has lost but one game this fall.

Kent City has a fighting team — prettiest cheer leaders in Western Michigan.

Kent City is proud of its newly flood-lighted field.

Win or lose — there's plenty of school spirit there!

10th ANNIVERSARY RIDGELY STUDIO, SATURDAY, OCT. 29, JOHN AND JEANNE ARE HOLDING OPEN HOUSE TO COMMEMORATE THIS HAPPY OCCASION AT THEIR NEW LOCATION, 87 DIVISION, SPARTA

This is an example of a small-town newspaper being a big-time booster for its community. Events in surrounding communities were also printed in the newspaper. Whether it was an invitation to a Halloween party or a football game, one could be sure there would be some kind of entertainment advertised.

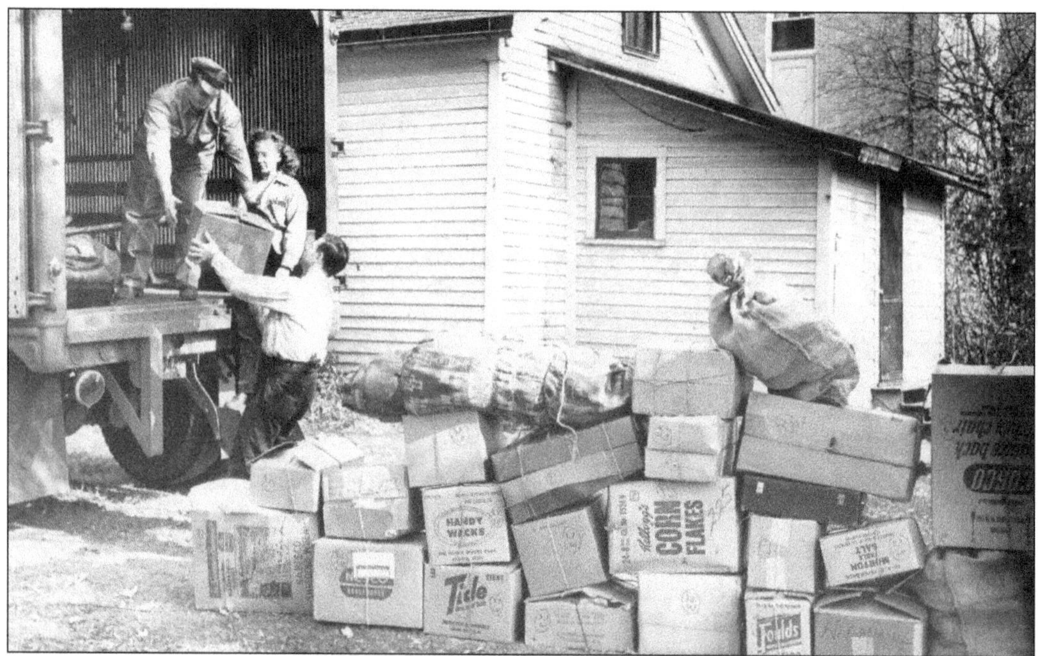

Like many local churches, the Methodist Church often held fund-raisers for local and national causes. The picture above shows a clothing drive called "Klothes for Korea," sponsored by the church. Pictured loading the truck are Harold Beard and his wife, of Church World Service, and Rev. Clarence Hutchens (on the truck), the pastor of the Sparta Methodist Church.

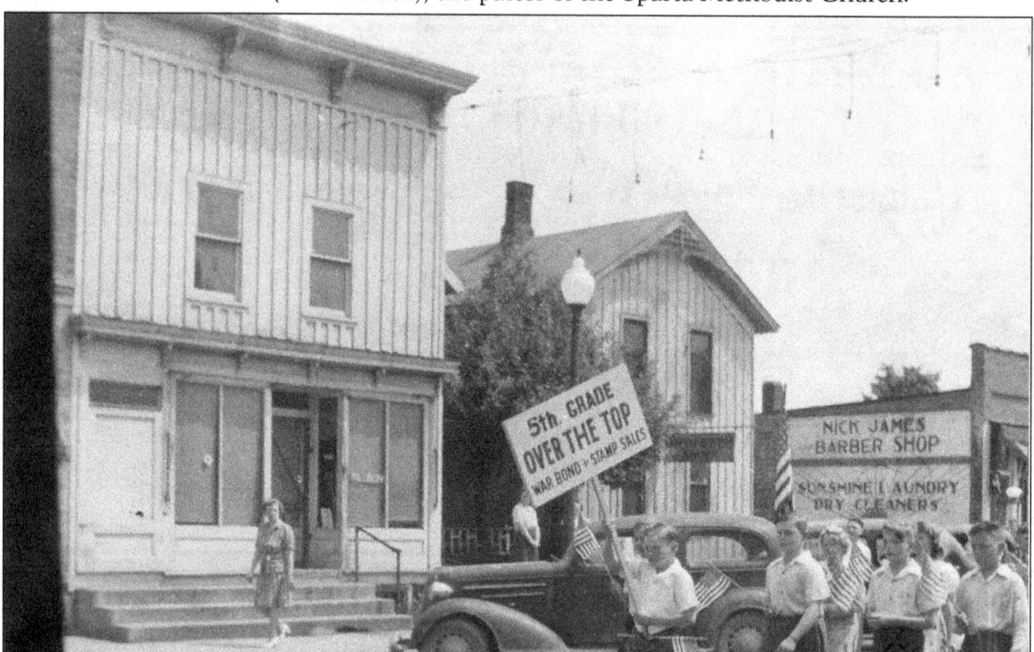

During World War II, communities came together to do whatever they could to help the cause. The photograph above shows fifth-grade students celebrating the success of a fund drive for the sale of war bonds and stamps. These students are marching in a parade, traveling east along East Division Street.

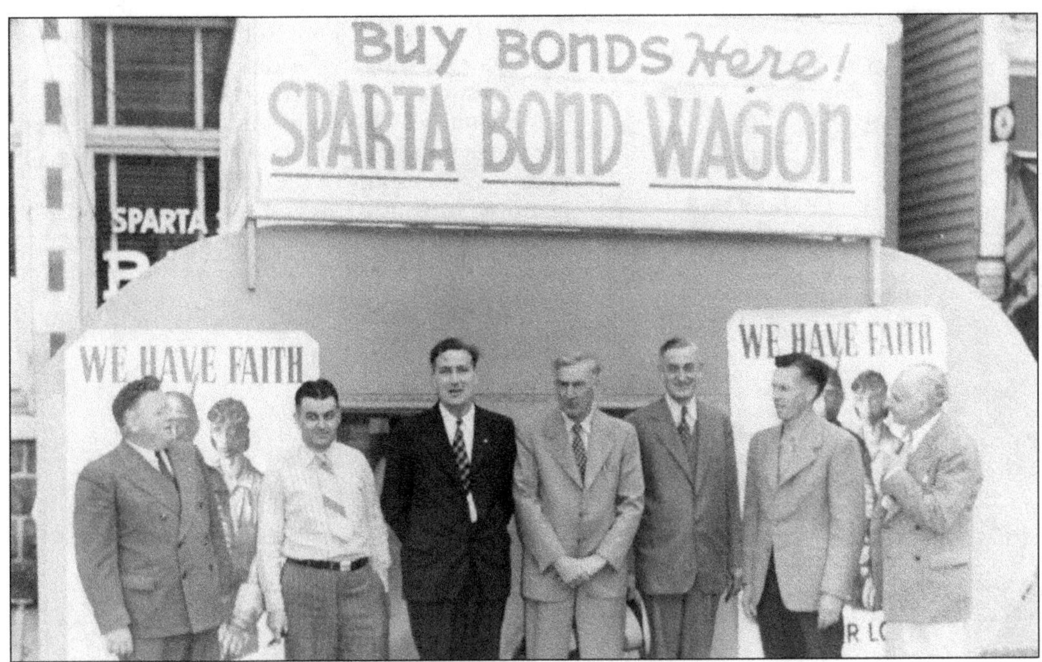

During World War II, Sparta businessmen and educational leaders, shown from left to right, William DeHart, Joe Gass, Roger Williams, Orley E. Balyeat, Arthur L. Brevitz, Ed Lane, and Horace J. Kurtz assembled in front of the Sparta Bond Wagon, which featured art that appealed to the people's desires to get involved and show their patriotism. Bonds were sold to raise funds for the military and to keep inflation at a minimum.

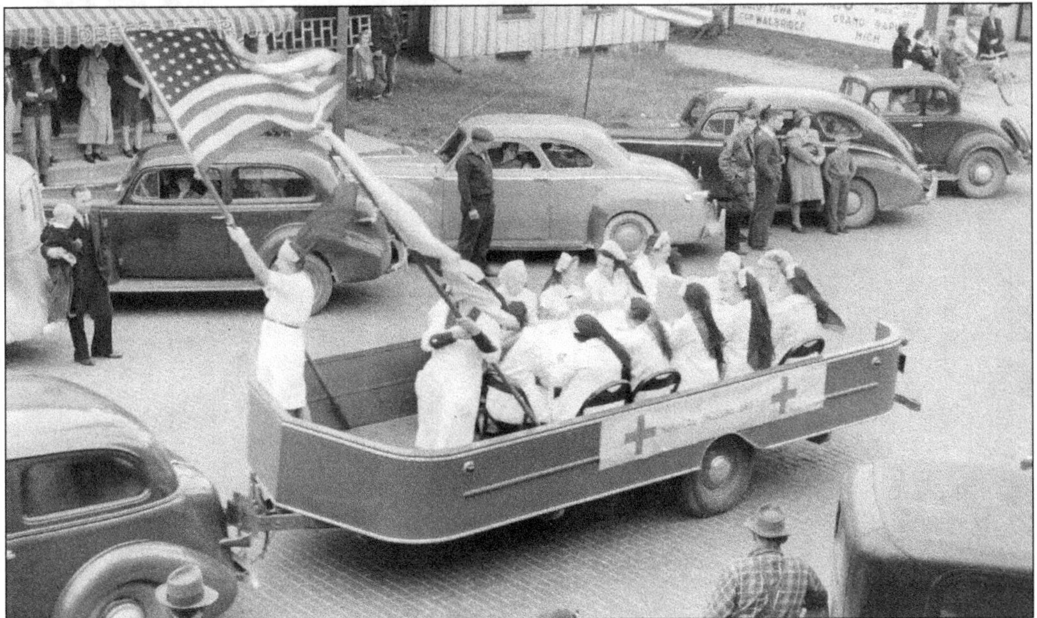

This photograph was taken on the north side of East Division Street around 1942. The local ladies of the Red Cross are demonstrating the rolling of bandages. Normally they would gather in homes or local churches to do their volunteer work. Notice that the main street is still made of brick in this photograph.

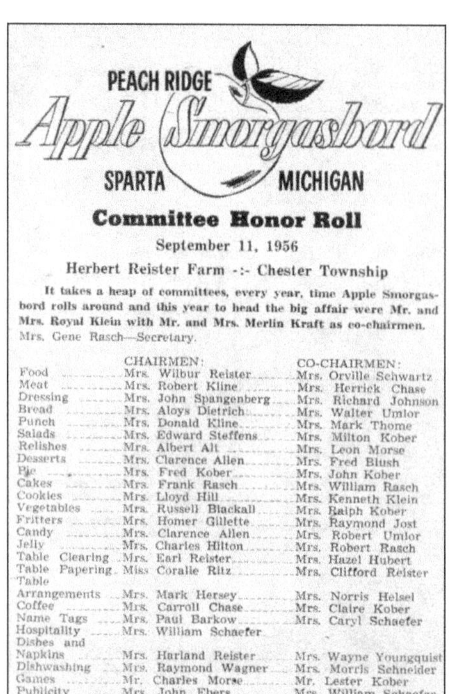

PEACH RIDGE

Apple Smorgasbord

SPARTA MICHIGAN

Committee Honor Roll

September 11, 1956

Herbert Reister Farm -:- Chester Township

It takes a heap of committees, every year, time Apple Smorgasbord rolls around and this year to head the big affair were Mr. and Mrs. Royal Klein with Mr. and Mrs. Merlin Kraft as co-chairmen.
Mrs. Gene Rasch—Secretary.

	CHAIRMEN:	CO-CHAIRMEN:
Food	Mrs. Wilbur Reister	Mrs. Orville Schwartz
Meat	Mrs. Robert Kline	Mrs. Herrick Chase
Dressing	Mrs. John Spangenberg	Mrs. Richard Johnson
Bread	Mrs. Aloys Dietrich	Mrs. Walter Umlor
Punch	Mrs. Donald Kline	Mrs. Mark Thome
Salads	Mrs. Edward Steffens	Mrs. Milton Kober
Relishes	Mrs. Albert Alt	Mrs. Leon Morse
Desserts	Mrs. Clarence Allen	Mrs. Fred Blush
Pie	Mrs. Fred Kober	Mrs. John Kober
Cakes	Mrs. Frank Rasch	Mrs. William Rasch
Cookies	Mrs. Lloyd Hill	Mrs. Kenneth Klein
Vegetables	Mrs. Russell Blackall	Mrs. Ralph Kober
Fritters	Mrs. Homer Gillette	Mrs. Raymond Jost
Candy	Mrs. Clarence Allen	Mrs. Robert Umlor
Jelly	Mrs. Charles Hilton	Mrs. Robert Rasch
Table Clearing	Mrs. Earl Reister	Mrs. Hazel Hubert
Table Papering	Miss Coralie Ritz	Mrs. Clifford Reister
Table Arrangements	Mrs. Mark Hersey	Mrs. Norris Helsel
Coffee	Mrs. Carroll Chase	Mrs. Claire Kober
Name Tags	Mrs. Paul Barkow	Mrs. Caryl Schaefer
Hospitality	Mrs. William Schaefer	
Dishes and Napkins	Mrs. Harland Reister	Mrs. Wayne Youngquist
Dishwashing	Mrs. Raymond Wagner	Mrs. Morris Schneider
Games	Mr. Charles Morse	Mr. Lester Kober
Publicity	Mrs. John Ebers	Mrs. William Schaefer
Gifts	Mrs. Walter Ebers	Mrs. Alice Klenk
Feature	Mrs. George Klenk	Mrs. William Nyblad
Pictorial Feature	Mrs. John Spangenberg	
Wiring	Mr. Caryl Schaefer	
Chairs and Tables	Mr. John Schaefer	

This smorgasbord "Honor Roll" clipping recognizes those participating in the annual Peach Ridge Fruit Growers Association Apple Smorgasbord. The committees' "assignments" included their involvement from set up to clean up, which meant even washing of the dishes. Much planning went into this event, which showcased many delicious apple dishes that were created and prepared by farm wives of "The Ridge."

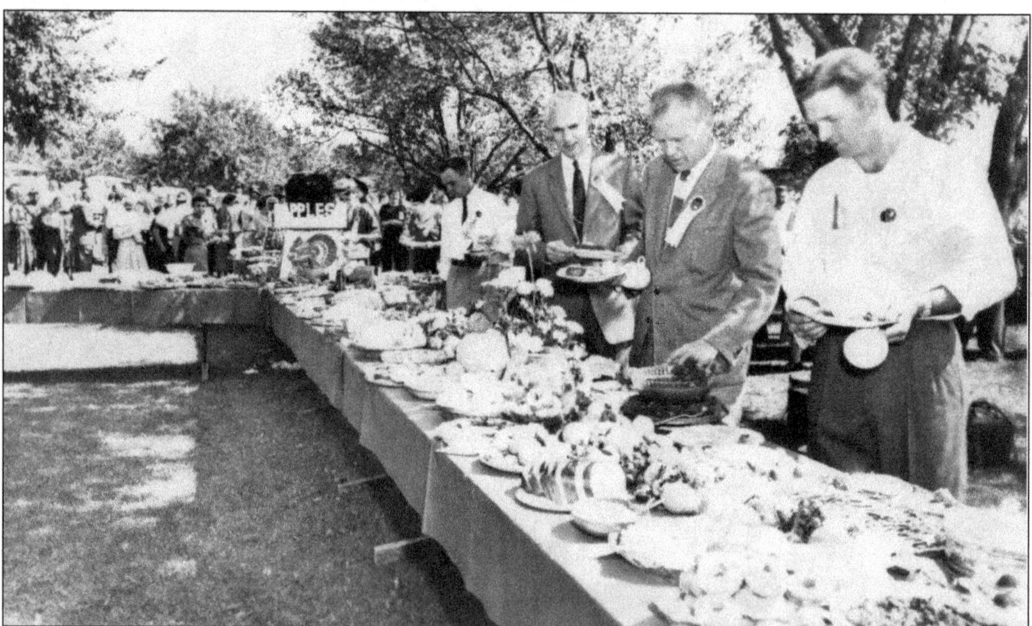

The first apple smorgasbord was held in 1951, when members of the Peach Ridge Fruit Growers Association and their families and guests gathered to sample apple dishes, meet new friends, and visit with old friends. This was an early attempt to market and advertise the apple industry throughout Michigan and the country. Rep. Gerald R. Ford (second from right) and John B. Martin, state Republican committeeman, join the other guests.

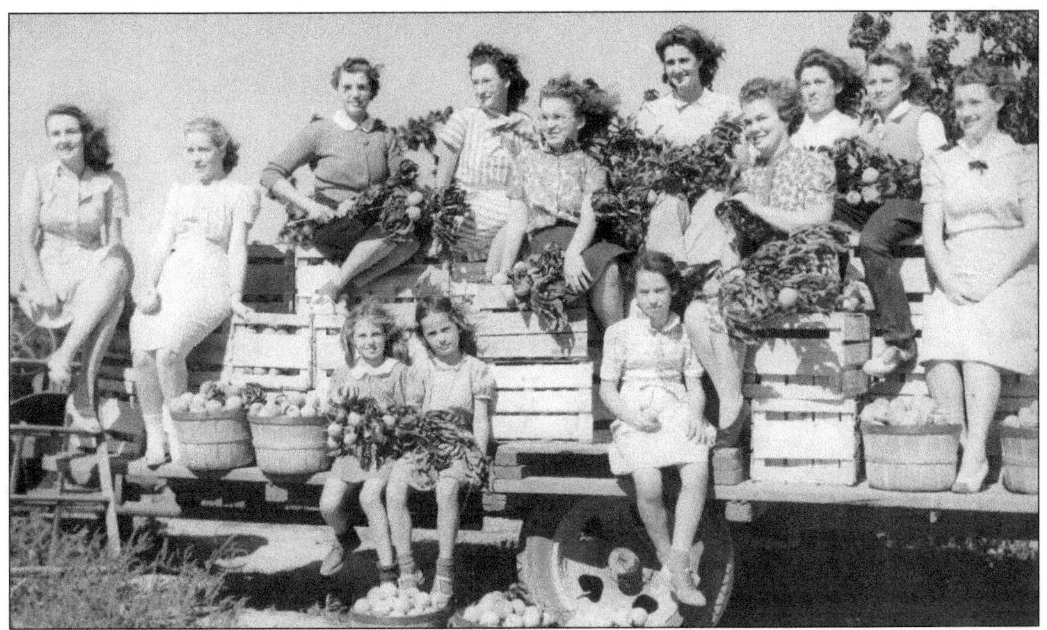

The daughters of leading growers from the Fruit Ridge area show off their peaches in the orchards of Phil Klenk and sons. From left to right are (first row) Norma Fleet, Lois Klenk, and Phyllis Klenk; (second row) Natholee Schneider, Margaret Dunneback, Thelma Dunneback, Dorothy Armock, Frances Dunneback, Agatha Armock, Elizabeth Dunneback, Lucille Finkler, Rosemary Umlor, and Catherine Dunneback.

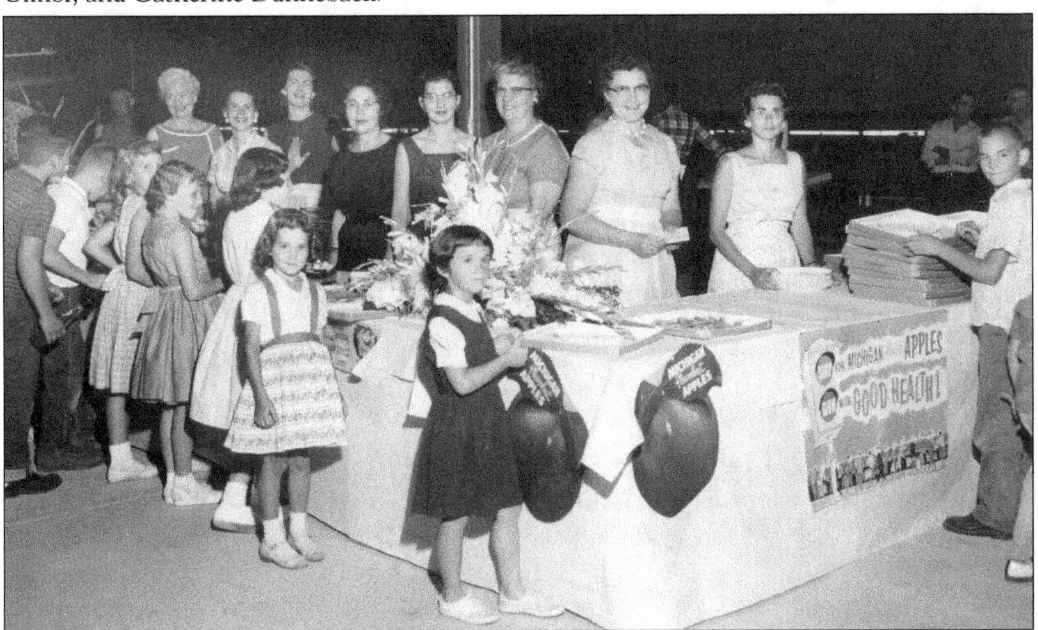

The refreshment stand was a popular stop for these children during the afternoon and evening celebration of the grand opening of Jack Brown Produce, Inc., in August 1960. Serving the children are, from left to right, Mrs. William Schaefer, Mrs. Frank Rasch, Mrs. Ralph Succop, Mrs. Irwin Klenk, Mrs. Arva Dunnette, Mrs. Herrick Chase, Mrs. Herman Rasch, and Mrs. William Rasch, who are all wives of local farmers.

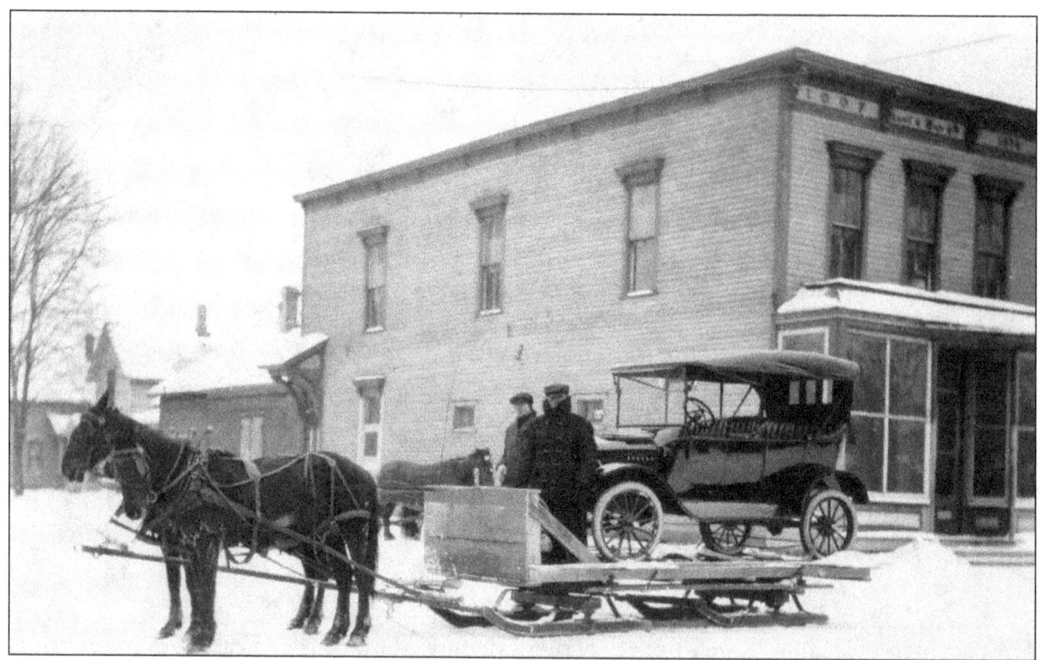

The shiny car being delivered by horse-drawn sleigh was the first Ford automobile sold in Sparta. George Bettes sold the car for $360, through the Kent City agency. They are standing in front of the Odd Fellows Building, located on the southwest corner of East Division and Washington Streets.

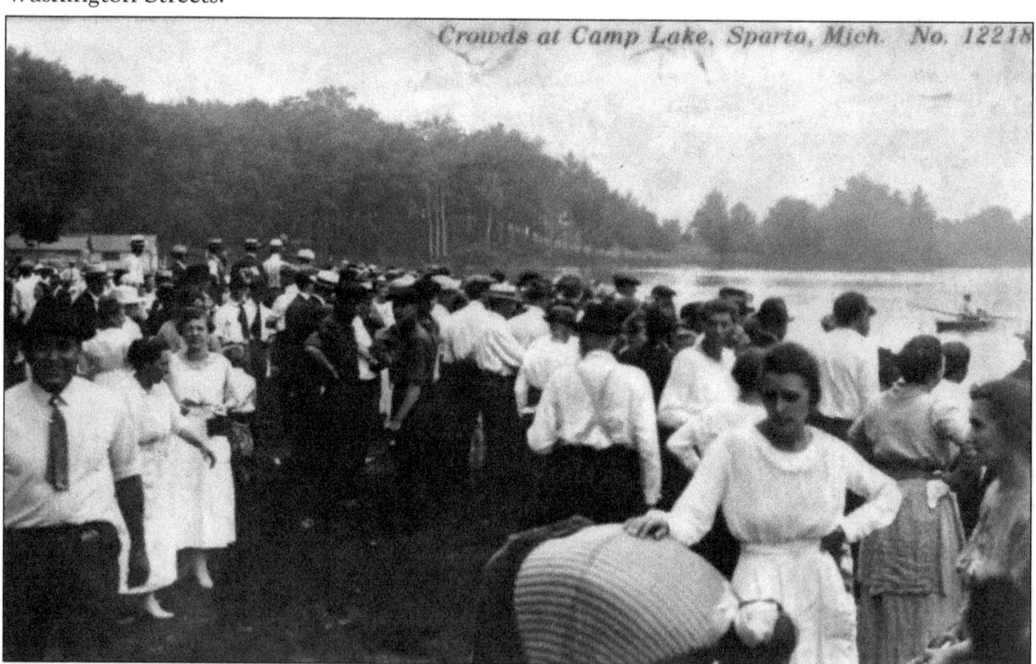

Camp Lake was a popular retreat for the people of Sparta during the hot summer days. After taking the train to the north end of the lake, passengers could board the *Lady of the Lake* steamer, which took them to the south end and Slocum's landing. Here they enjoyed picnics, speeches, contests, and boat races, as pictured above in 1905.

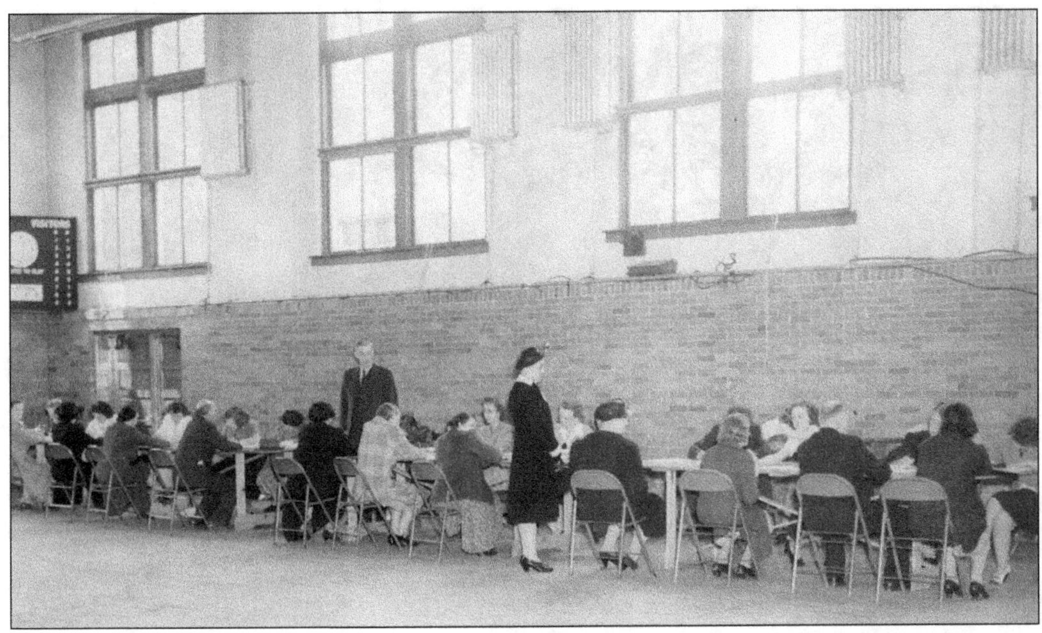

This photograph shows people of Sparta during World War II in the high school gymnasium getting their ration books. During the war, each person was issued a ration book. The stamps in the book were used to buy items that were rationed for the duration of the war. The man standing near the wall is Orley E. Balyeat, registrar of the rationing board and also superintendent of Sparta schools.

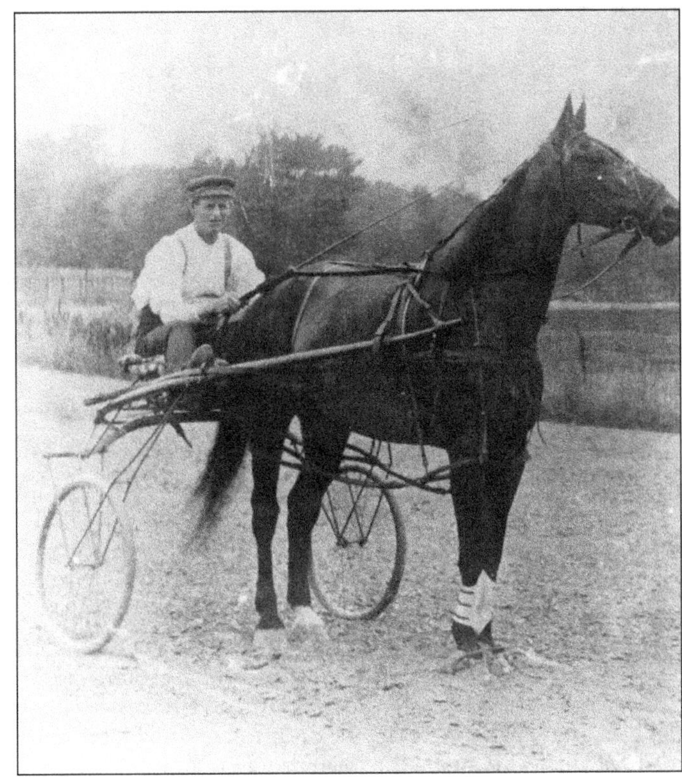

The Sparta Race Track was located south of West Division Street, behind the old Kent County Road Commission building. The harness races featured pacers and trotters. Officials of the track were Van Gordon, Buehl Pease, and Allan Way. Here local barber Frank Kellogg poses with his prize-winning animal.

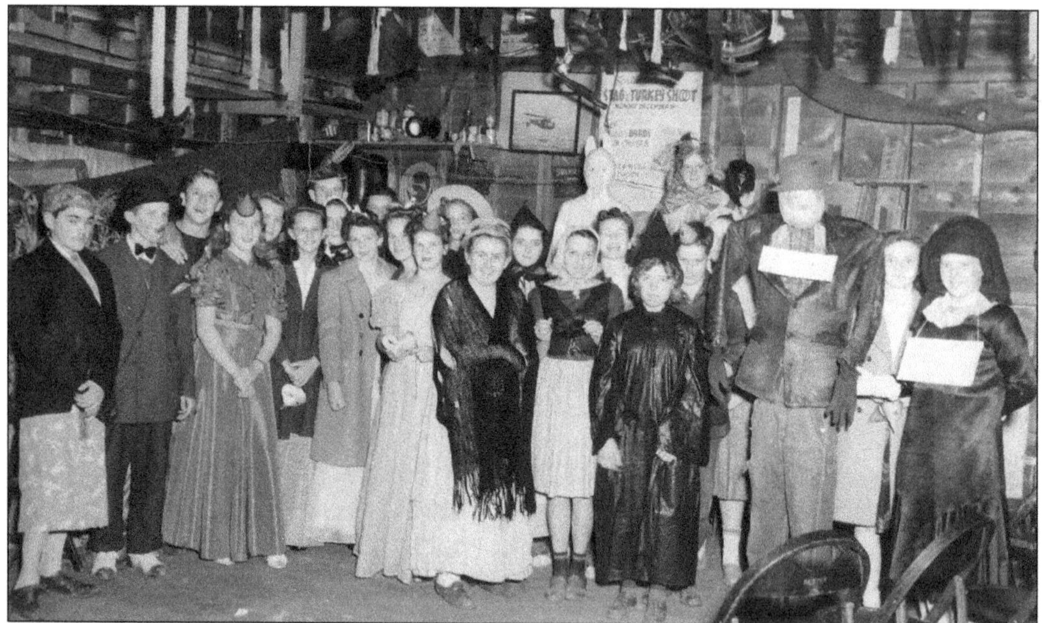

In attendance at the Halloween party in the Bettes garage in 1941 were, from left to right, Bill Young, Jim Badgerow, Harold Miller, Carol Langford, Marcia Beery, Eloise Havens, two unidentified children, Elaine Eynon, two unidentified children, Wanda Murray, unidentified, Mary Lou Heath, unidentified, Margaret Gold, unidentified, Joanne Bettes, unidentified, Bernie Johnson (far back), unidentified, Katherine Bull, and unidentified.

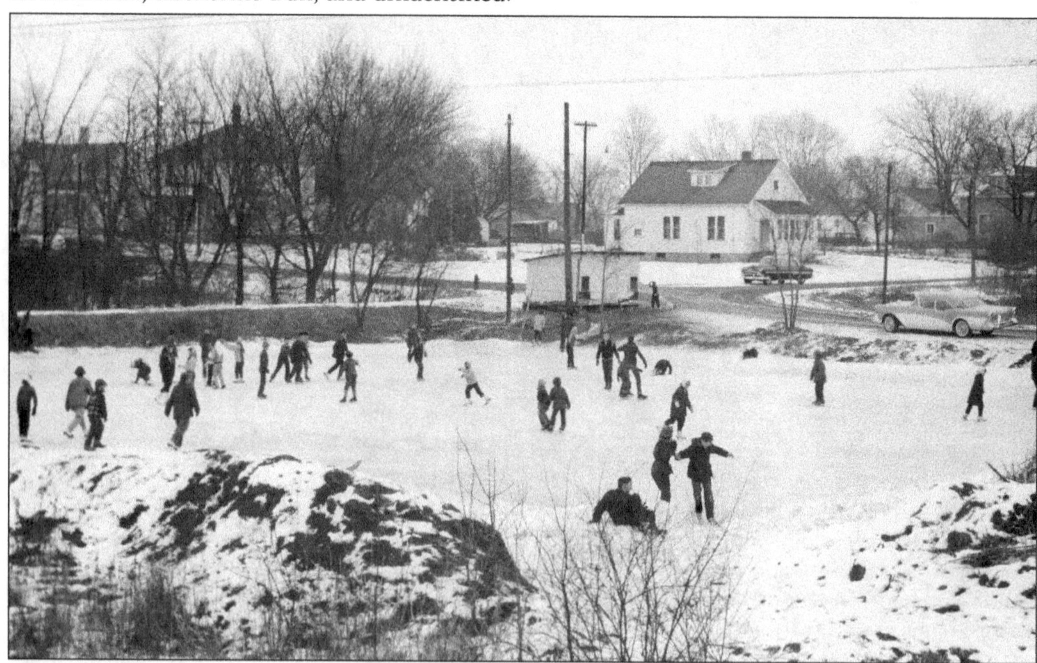

The community ice-skating rink was a popular wintertime attraction within the township. The rink lay in the area north of the feed mill, on the west side of Loomis Street. The white house in the background was the home of Ruth Kent. The bigger house, seen through the trees, was the home of Charles Loomis, the town druggist. This photograph was taken in the 1950s.

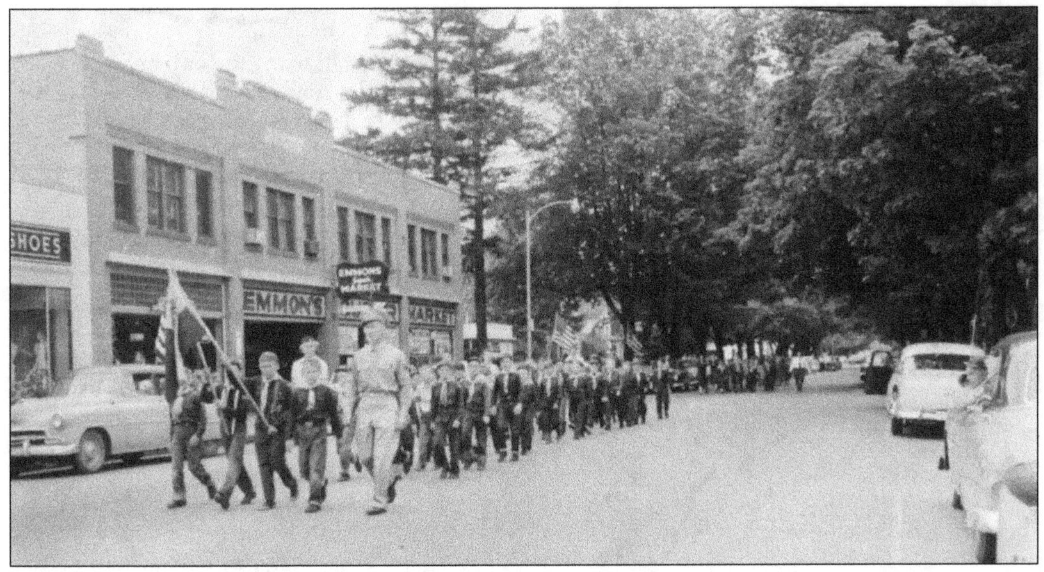

This Memorial Day parade was held on May 30, 1956, and took place on Division Street, heading east into town, past Emmon's Market. The local Boy Scout troop leads the pack, honoring those who fought in the many wars and made the ultimate sacrifice. The people of Sparta have contributed to every war effort from the Civil War to the conflicts of the modern era.

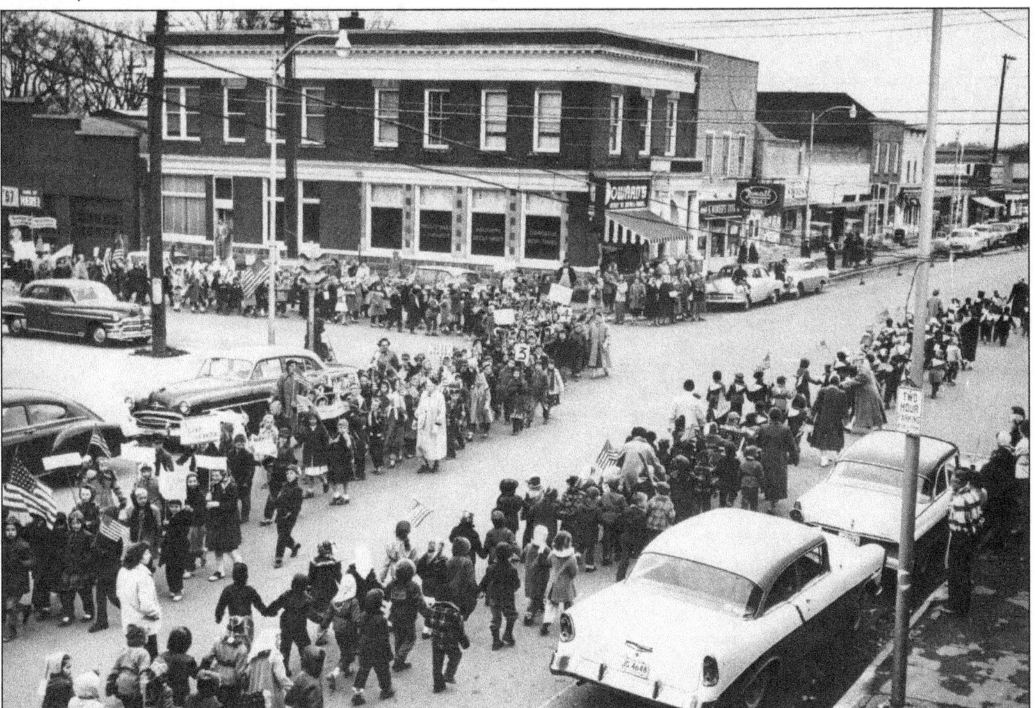

During Education Week in the fall, students would line up with their teacher and class. Classes from every school in the township were represented. Students carried signs identifying their school or proclaiming "arithmetic is fun" or "I like school." This picture was taken in 1957, looking east on Division Street toward Union Street. It was taken from a second-story window—likely from the McGowen Building.

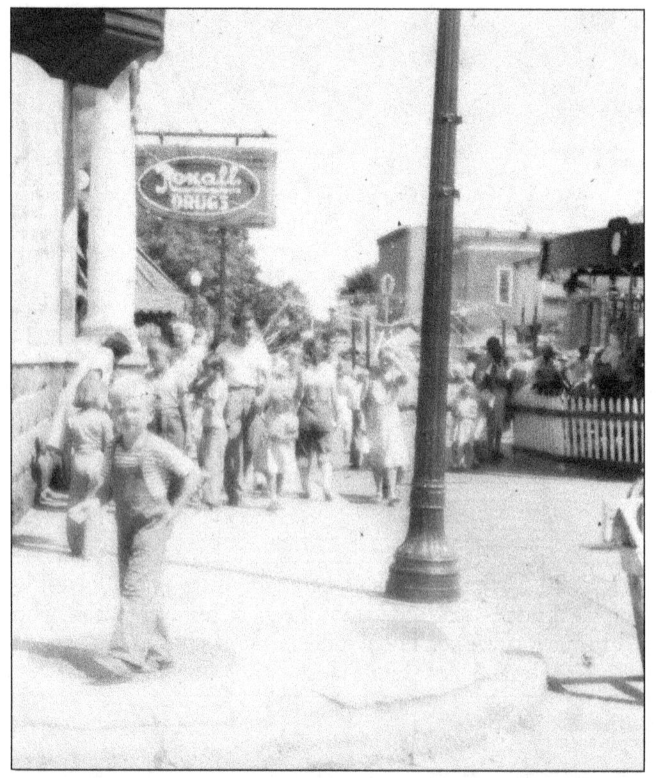

These photographs represent small-town life at its best in the summer of 1947. The war was over, businesses were once again prospering, and the citizens of Sparta looked forward to the annual Farmers' Days. Families would shop the annual sidewalk sales or take in the parade. Events would take place throughout the week, beginning with local children gathering to see the bright lights along the midway. Rides and concessions thrived, especially the stands operated by local groups. In 1947, the softball game played at Balyeat field was one of the best ever at Sparta, according to the *Sentinel Leader*. The display of fireworks signified the end of a very successful week on the part of the sponsors. Special credit was given to general chairman Charles Rogers and cochairman Walt Blackmer.

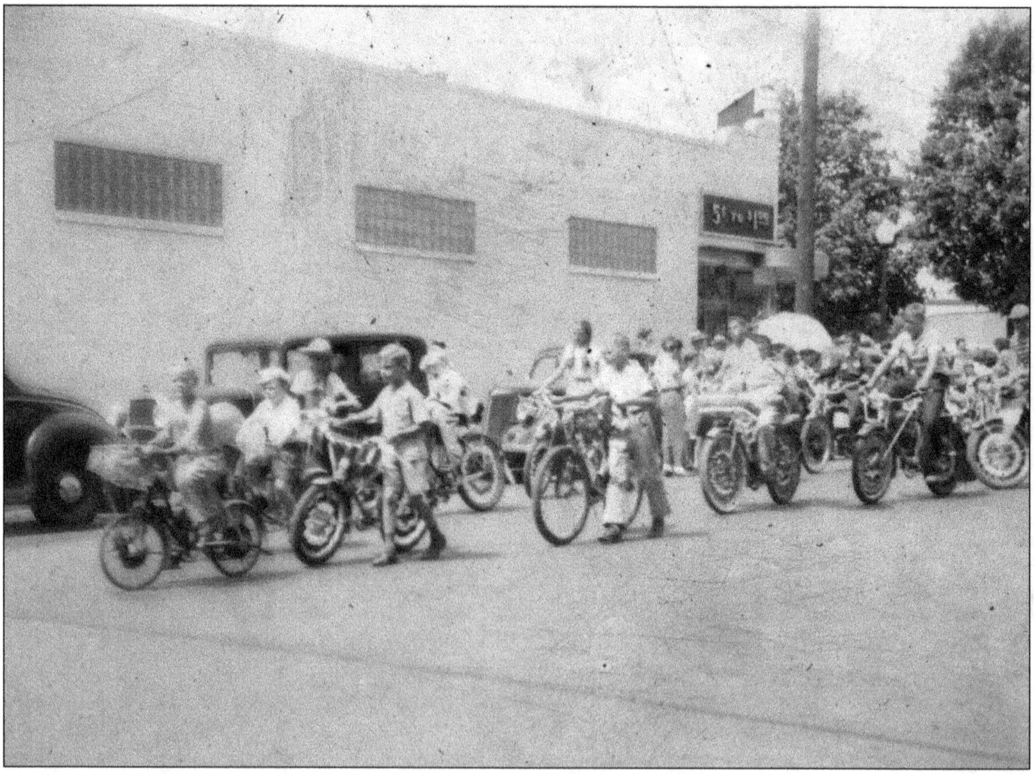

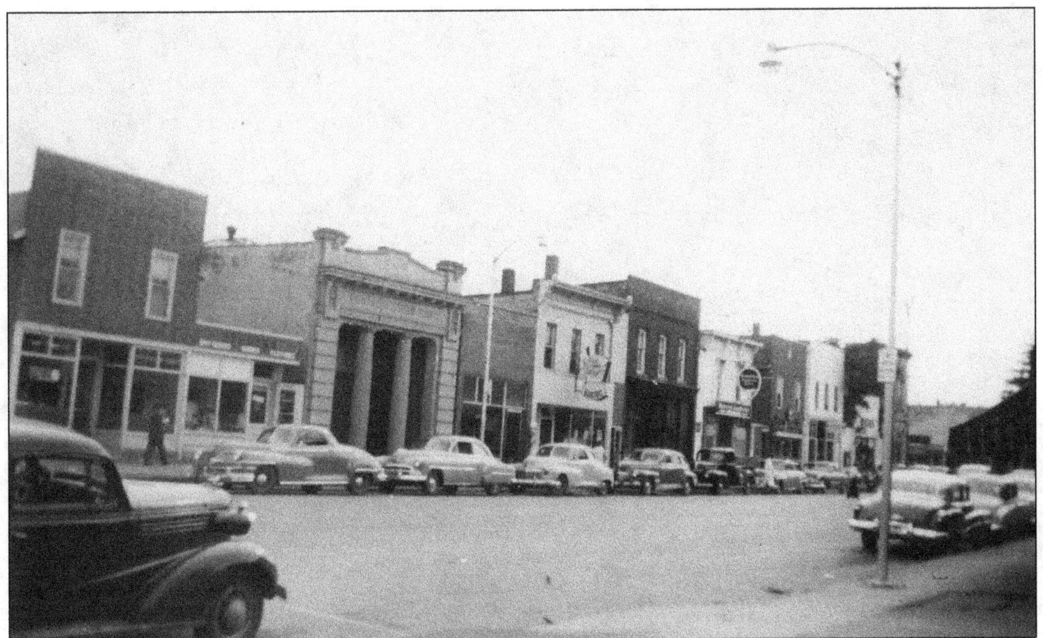

Taken sometime around 1940, this photograph highlights some of the major businesses the people of Sparta relied on for their everyday needs. From left to right are Putnam's store, Sparta State Bank, Pearl Baughn's barbershop, the drugstore, unidentified, Western Auto store, the jewelry store, and Cnossen's Bakery. This photograph was taken on Division Street looking southwest.

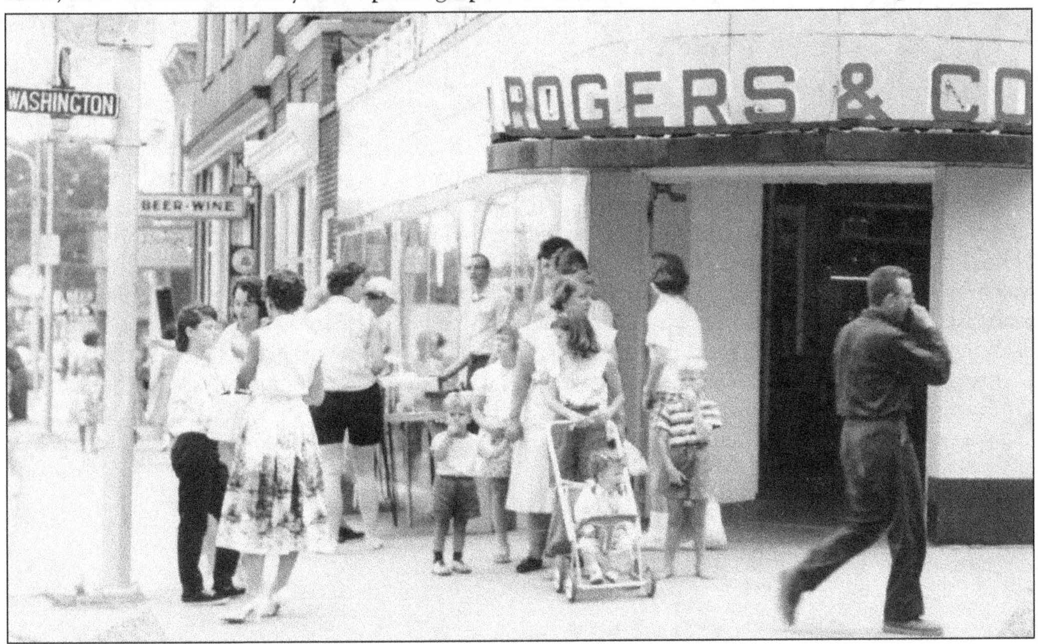

The Rogers and Company Hardware Store used to occupy this building on the southeast corner of East Division and Washington Streets before moving into a newer one across the street, which is where it is still located today. An employee stands at the table in front of the store, probably selling or demonstrating a product. This picture was taken after the new storefront was erected in the 1940s.

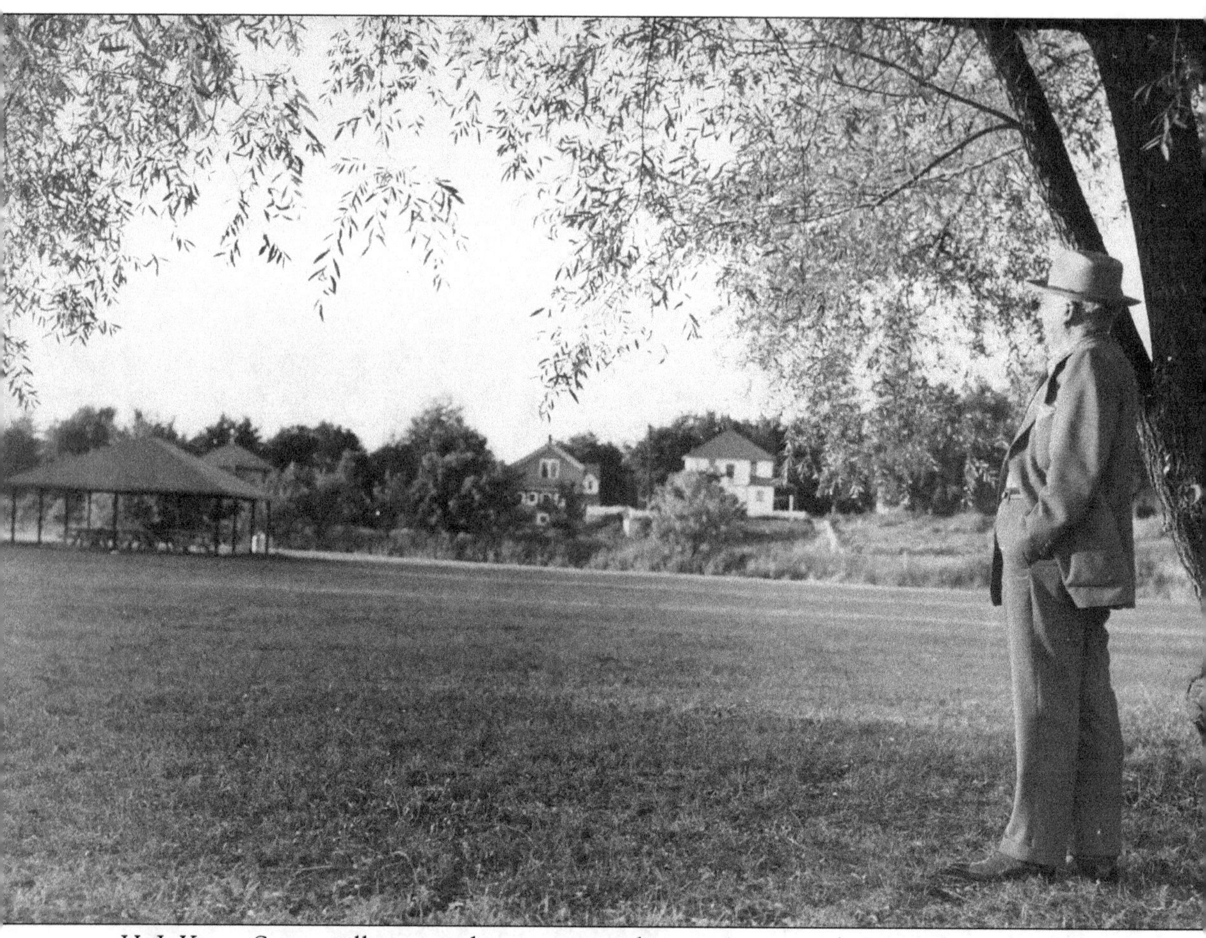

H. J. Kurtz, Sparta village president, inspects the town's new park. It was named in honor of William A. Rogers as a tribute to his service to Sparta. Rogers was active in many community organizations. For more than 25 years, he served as superintendent of the Sparta Baptist Sunday School and was on the village council for 12 years. He also served on the Sparta School Board, was a member of the rotary club, a director of Sparta State Bank, and a general chairman for many Red Cross, war bond, and community chest campaigns. The park, located on the north end of the village, along Nash Creek, included playground equipment, fireplaces, picnic tables, and a shelter. Quoted in an article in the *Sentinel Leader*, when Rogers was named "Man of the Year" in 1952, Kurtz said, "When you think of William A. Rogers, you think of Sparta. When you think of Sparta, you think of William A. Rogers." Rogers was married to the former Lusina Ballard.

About the Sparta Township Historical Commission

Albert B. and Marilyn Hale, Sparta residents, purchased the one-room Myers School House in November 1990, and in December of that year they deeded it to Sparta Township. The Hales then became instrumental in forming the Sparta Township Historical Commission. The first commission consisted of Marilyn Hale, chairman; Vernon Cumings, vice chairman; Bobbie Crawford, secretary; Gail Klein; Lowell Johnson; Albert Hale; and Barbara Erhart. Marijean Cumings and Jim Lyals were associate members. Current members include chairman Martin Pulsifer, Leonard Feerick, Barb Erhart, Vernon Cumings, Jim Tuinstra, Mary Hale, Larry Carter, Jaime Brooks, and JoAnne VanderWerff. All proceeds from the sale of this book are being donated to further the preservation of the history of Sparta Township through the Sparta Township Historical Commission.

Find Your Place in History.

www.arcadiapublishing.com

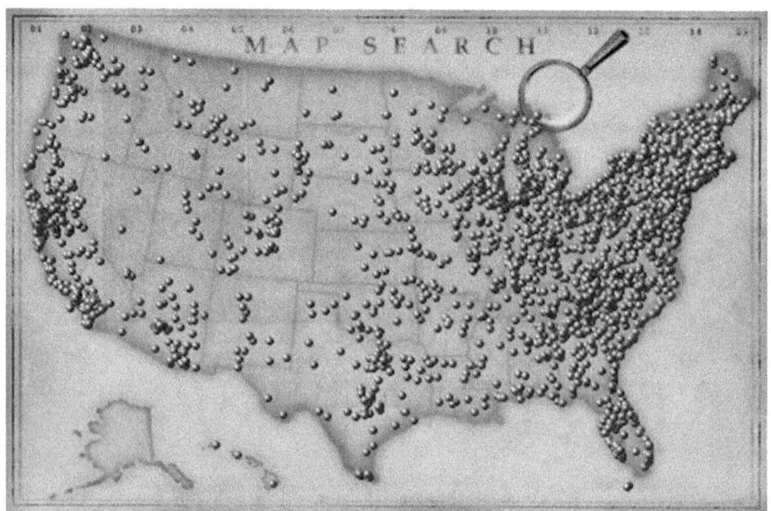

Discover books about the town where you grew up, the cities where your friends and families live, the town where your parents met, or even that retirement spot you've been dreaming about. Our Web site provides history lovers with exclusive deals, advanced notification about new titles, e-mail alerts of author events, and much more.

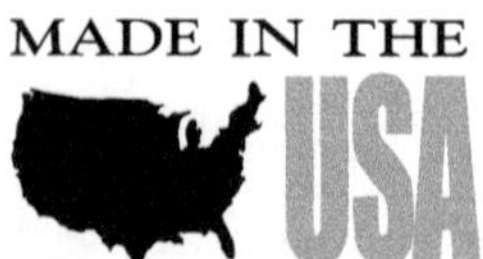

Arcadia Publishing, the leading local history publisher in the United States, is committed to making history accessible and meaningful through publishing books that celebrate and preserve the heritage of America's people and places. Consistent with our mission to preserve history on a local level, this book was printed in South Carolina on American-made paper and manufactured entirely in the United States.

This book carries the accredited Forest Stewardship Council (FSC) label and is printed on 100 percent FSC-certified paper. Products carrying the FSC label are independently certified to assure consumers that they come from forests that are managed to meet the social, economic, and ecological needs of present and future generations.

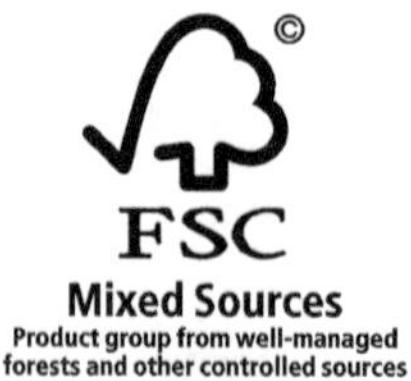

Cert no. SW-COC-001530
www.fsc.org

www.ingramcontent.com/pod-product-compliance
Lightning Source LLC
LaVergne TN
LVHW081556100826
845153LV00004B/395

9781531655396